ACCLAIM FOR *George Cooper's*

LOST LOVE

"*Lost Love* is the true and fascinating story of a great Civil War romance. Smooth and clever in its weaving of the tale, it is scrupulous in attending to the truth."

—Judith Rossner, author of *Looking for Mr. Goodbar*

"Lest anyone think that people didn't have passions a century ago, George Cooper has given us *Lost Love*. What an amazing story! I'm grateful to Mr. Cooper for finding it and presenting it so skillfully, letting the clear-minded and strong-hearted heroine give us so much of the story in her own words."

—Phyllis Rose, author of *Parallel Lives*

"*Lost Love* is an absorbing picture of American history, the law and changes in our social and economic life."   —*Pilot Southern Times*

"[*Lost Love's*] vivid personalities become the basis of a near-operatic, true-life tale ... handled with Victorian delicacy."

—*The New York Times*

"A story of high aspirations, of a failed marriage and a scandalous divorce, and of an 1860's-style murder that might have been dreamed up by William Dean Howells ... evocative and entertaining."   —*Kirkus Reviews*

"Cooper has done a superb job ... a striking social history with the suspense, magnetism, and broad appeal of a novel."   —*Booklist*

"Cooper's account is dramatic, evenhanded and, ultimately, an illuminating portrait of a strong and admirable woman."

—*Publishers Weekly*

George Cooper

LOST LOVE

A graduate of Harvard Law School, George Cooper was a professor of law at Columbia University from 1966 to 1985. He lives with his wife in New York City.

LOST LOVE

LOST LOVE

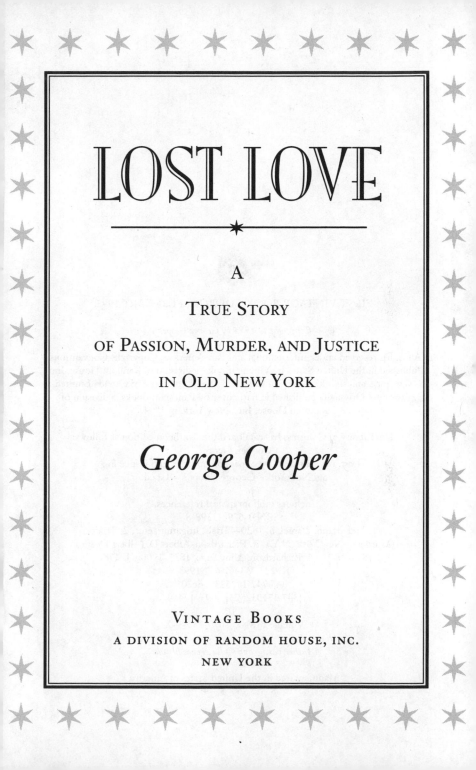

A

TRUE STORY

OF PASSION, MURDER, AND JUSTICE

IN OLD NEW YORK

George Cooper

VINTAGE BOOKS

A DIVISION OF RANDOM HOUSE, INC.

NEW YORK

FIRST VINTAGE BOOK EDITION, FEBRUARY 1995

Copyright © 1994 by George Cooper

All rights reserved under International and Pan-American Copyright Conventions.
Published in the United States by Vintage Books, a division of Random House, Inc.,
New York, and simultaneously in Canada by Random House of Canada Limited,
Toronto. Originally published in hardcover by Pantheon Books, a division of
Random House, Inc., New York, in 1994.

The Library of Congress has cataloged the Pantheon edition as follows:
Cooper, George
Lost love : a true story of passion, murder, and justice in
old New York / George Cooper. – 1st ed.
p.   cm.
Includes bibliographical references.
ISBN 0-679-43398-8
1. McFarland, Daniel, b. 1820—Trials, litigation, etc.   2. Trials
(Murder)—New York (N.Y.)   3. Richardson, Albert D. (Albert Deane),
1833–1869.   4. Richardson, Abby Sage, 1837–1900.   I. Title.
KF223.M34C66   1993
345.747´102523—dc20
[347.471052523]   93–12469
CIP
Vintage ISBN: 0-679-75699-X

Author paragraph © Lawrence Blume

Manufactured in the United States of America
10   9   8   7   6   5   4   3   2   1

To Harry and Hilda

Contents

BOOK THREE: AFTER

ACKNOWLEDGMENTS

This book has been a cooperative endeavor, between me and the sources that enabled the voices of the characters to reach my ears. I am especially indebted to the New-York Historical Society Library and the New York Public Library, to the many manuscript collections acknowledged in the Notes, and to the librarians with whom I worked. Librarians are a special breed—people who genuinely try to be helpful to strangers without expecting anything in return. The least I can do is offer gratitude.

I would also like to thank my wife for her support, her advice, and for so much more than I can say; my agent, Claire Smith, for having confidence in this manuscript; and my editor, Lelia Ruckenstein, for her fine sensibility and her enthusiasm for the book.

Special thanks also go to Louis Brown of Statesville, North Carolina, author of *The Salisbury Prison;* Marshall Ray, great-grandnephew of Albert D. Richardson; and Philip K. Browne, grandson of Junius Henri Browne; who kindly shared their thoughts and sources with me.

Abby Sage and Albert Deane Richardson lived more than a century ago. But from the moment I began researching their story I was struck more by the similarities in our worlds than the differences. Each day, as I read 1869 and 1870 newspaper accounts, I found articles about enduring problems. On the world stage, for example, Haitians were revolting to overthrow a benighted regime, and Irish terrorists were threatening public buildings in London. Here at home there was rising concern about immigrants of color (then Chinese) who worked for low wages and undercut the jobs of Americans.

It was a time of familiar isms, socialism, spiritualism, vegetarianism, and feminism. Women's rights activists, inspired by the grant of freedom and equal opportunity to former slaves, demanded the same for themselves. Traditionalists opposed this reform movement as a threat to the sanctity of the home and society itself. And a story of two people caught up in a love relationship that tested conventional mores suddenly became a *cause*. The media, a profusion of newspapers, latched onto the story and assailed the public with fact, opinion, rumor, and speculation. And when a trial in court followed, the lawyers used the strategy that has not lost any power today: blame the victim.

Albert was a man any man might want to become—celebrated war correspondent, adventurer, civil-rights advocate. Abby was a talented lecturer and writer. I had intended to relate their story in a conventional way, as narrative nonfiction. But as I unearthed the sources of it, I found in books and journals, letters and dispatches, and in court testimony, that they and others had already told it. My task was only to edit and give structure to what was there in the archives..

I have interposed myself where necessary to provide background, but this is primarily a book of voices from the time. All these are genuine, derived from the published and unpublished writings and statements of each character, condensed and edited for narrative clarity, but not otherwise altered.

[x i]

PRINTING HOUSE SQUARE, IN THE 1860s.

AT THE *TRIBUNE* COUNTING ROOM

Dan Frohman thought it was his fault. If he had been more alert, he might have warned Mr. Richardson in time. Albert Richardson, the famous journalist, was his idol. He had given Dan his first job, as an errand boy for $2.50 a week, when Dan was only thirteen, selecting him from three hundred applicants. Dan had no idea why he was picked, but he quickly destroyed all the other applications. When the job was finished, Albert got him a position at the *New York Tribune*, so he could learn about the newspaper business. Tending the mail in the first floor counting room was one of Dan's duties. He saw Albert almost daily, whenever the former *Tribune* correspondent stopped by to check for letters.

It was five o'clock in the evening on November 25, 1869, when Albert dismounted from a horse car and walked across Printing House Square to the office of the *Tribune*. The gas had been lit in the buildings because of the early winter darkness, and lights shone through the windows of the daily newspaper offices that lined Park Row. The *News*, the *Sun*, the *Tribune*, the *Times*, the *World*, the *Express*, and the *Herald* stood almost shoulder-to-shoulder, with the *Post* just behind. Each was a beacon of enlightenment in its own way.

It had been a week since Albert's Thanksgiving rendezvous with Abby in Massachusetts. He was expecting a letter from her, telling when she would be returning to New York, and he wanted its comfort for the night ahead. Abby's divorce had been granted, and she was finally free to become his wife. His plans for starting a new paper in Chicago were well along, and Abby was beginning to share his enthusiasm for a move away from New York and the persistent plague of her disgruntled ex-husband McFarland. Some day perhaps, Chicago, too, would have its Printing House Square and Albert would edit one of its beacons. The 1860s were ending, and the 1870s promised a new life in the West.

But McFarland was there at the *Tribune* office that evening. For almost an hour he had been hanging about, behind the counter near the Spruce Street door. "When McFarland was around, I always warned my benefactor," Dan later recalled, "because McFarland had made threats of vengeance against Mr. Richardson." But Albert had been in earlier that day, and told Dan he would not return, so the boy's guard was down.

Albert walked into the office and passed by the counter where McFarland was lurking. He continued to the mail desk at the far end. Dan had his head down and did not see him immediately. When Albert caught his attention, Dan jumped right to the pigeonholes, completely forgetting about McFarland.

Albert, preoccupied, did not see the shadowy figure either. Not until the assassin rose, drew a pistol, and pointed it across the counter at his target, barely five feet away, did Albert look up. Dan cried out to warn him, but it was too late.

The pistol explosion blew out the nearby gas lights. In the darkened confusion, McFarland leapt over the counter and ran out. "I thought the shot had missed," said Dan, "because Mr. Richardson made no outcry. Instead he turned and walked to the staircase." The office was in bedlam. Dan ran out to the square.

With a shot in his belly, Albert walked up four flights of stairs to the editorial offices. He collapsed on a sofa and calmly asked his sometime assistant Nicholson to obtain medical assistance. Albert's garments were already saturated with blood. Someone stanched the wound with a wet handkerchief while Nicholson sent for Dr. Swan. The doctor came immediately, but could do nothing other than give Albert morphine and order him taken to a bed. Albert's friends helped him walk down to the street, and they carried him in a chair two blocks on Park Row to the Astor House hotel, at Broadway and Vesey. They put him in a room on the second floor.

"I followed along with my heart beating fast and a choked feeling in my throat," Dan continued. "That night and all the other nights, I slept in the passageway before his door. I just wanted to be of service."

• *INTERVIEW WITH PRISONER*

MCFARLAND •

New York Post and *New York Herald*

NOVEMBER 26, 1869

Daniel McFarland sits quietly in the city jail, ominously called the "Tombs," not in a cell but in a large room near the entrance, looking out upon a courtyard. He is a fifty year old man, about five feet six in height and thickly set. He has a despondent look on his face, which is deeply pitted with pock marks that appear more striking from the total absence of whiskers. Neatly dressed in a business suit of dark hue, he is freshly shaved and wears a round top felt hat to meet visitors.

The prisoner has the same story for anyone who asks. He denies any recollection of the events in the *Tribune* counting room on November 25. But, being told what happened, he shows no remorse.

"Albert Richardson robbed me of everything I had dear on earth—wife, children and happiness. I wish you would review the circumstances and do me justice. I lived harmoniously with my wife for many years—absolute happiness—until she formed the acquaintance of this man Richardson. We had differences of opinion, and oftentimes

THE ASSASSINATION IN THE *TRIBUNE* COUNTING ROOM, AS
DEPICTED IN *THE TRIAL OF DANIEL MCFARLAND*.

unpleasant words in regard to her conduct, but these quarrels were condoned and mutual happiness existed between us up to the time she left me. I entreated her not to go. I told her history could not produce the parallel of such heartlessness on a mother's part as that which prompted the step she was about to take. But it was of no avail. She was infatuated with the destroyer of my domestic peace and she left my home with him, taking with her my two children.

"I am still devoted to dear, sweet Abby. She has not been the cause of my tribulations but is the victim, as I am, of that man."

When a visitor remarked to him, "Mr. McFarland, it is

a lamentable affair," he buried his face in his hands and sobbed.

"Yes, it is the ending of my life."

ABBY, FROM AN AFFIDAVIT PUBLISHED IN THE *New York Tribune*, MAY 9, 1870

I think, in all fairness, that my side should be heard. I fully believe that anyone of any degree of pride or delicacy will bear even the vilest slanders in silence rather than drag out to public comment the most sacred details of his inner life, and that only the meanest soul will babble of that which concerns itself most deeply. But during the last six months, and not a little during the last three years, I have been exposed to such a storm of public opinion that all others I ever knew sink into insignificance beside it.

I have been advised to speak out by a good woman, who said, "Do not be afraid to tell your story to the world. Tell it once exactly as you would tell it to your Maker, and then keep silence forever after." That is what I mean to do.

This is Abby's story, but it is also Albert's—of the parallel paths they took from Puritan New England homes, of the fateful circumstances that drew them together and led to the tragic episode at the *Tribune* counting room, and of the events that followed. But most of all, it is the story of their love, and of its time and place.

BOOK ONE

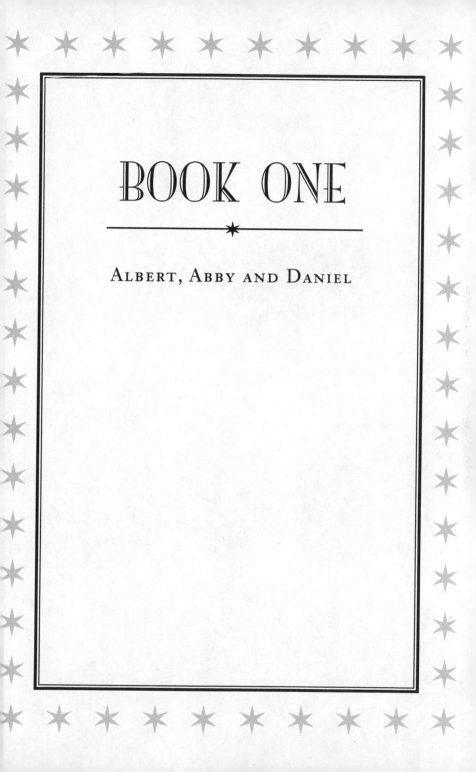

ALBERT, ABBY AND DANIEL

i

Albert Goes West

 Albert Deane Richardson was born in 1833 to a classic American family. His ancestors had been Massachusetts farmers for seven generations, ever since they emigrated from England two hundred years earlier. His parents expected their youngest son would follow the same course. But, though he dutifully did his chores, farming was never for him. America had changed during his parents' lifetimes. It was no longer a modest, fledgling coastal nation but an immense transcontinental empire.

As a boy growing up in the 1840s, Albert's imagination was fired by books about the West, about pioneers opening new territory, about broad plains, spectacular mountains, and surging rivers, all crying out that life is more vast and more dramatic than anyone on his gray little Massachusetts farm could possibly imagine. In 1851, when he was just seventeen, the soonest he could prevail upon his parents to let him go, he struck out, going to Pittsburgh and on to Cincinnati, then the virtual limit of civilization to the New England mind. Within the year, he wrote home with youthful enthusiasm, "I always expected to like Cincinnati, and at present I *do* like it. You inquire if I design taking up permanent residence 'out West.' I *do!*"

He quickly established himself as a reporter in the Queen City and embarked on a career that would carry him to the top of the profession. He moved from the *Sun* to the *Unionist* to the *Columbian*, as he gained in experience and his responsibilities grew. Within a few years, the raw youth who had ventured west had become a self-assured, bearded, and married young man.

Marriage had come on Albert suddenly. Not that he was opposed to the institution. He had grown up the son of a proper, Calvinist New England farmer and he respected the traditional values— honesty, success through hard work, disdain of ostentation, and, not least, a solid family-based home life. But he was not quite ready to embrace the last of these when he met Mary Louise Pease.

Lou was an appealing girl of nineteen, the daughter of the owner of a local book shop. Albert had always gone to such shops in his spare time; he preferred browsing books to quaffing ale. But she gave this place a particular allure. They had much in common, these two young book lovers, and one thing led to another, and another, until, on October 6, 1855, the Reverend Abiel Livermore, new minister of the First Unitarian Church, joined them as man and wife. The ceremony was private. The bride was already five months pregnant.

Although he did not exactly choose the timing of his marriage, Albert never indicated that he regretted it. After the birth of their son, Leander Pease, at the end of February 1856, Albert and Lou moved into a small house on Clinton Street. He pursued his career at the *Columbian* avidly. Its new owner was a merchant-become-publisher named Albert G. Richardson, who took a liking to his namesake and promoted him to associate editor.

In December 1856, the senior Albert offered the junior the managing editorship of the *Columbian*, which had become one of the city's leading newspapers. The young journalist considered the offer carefully. It was, in so many ways, the right thing for a proper man with family responsibilities to do. But he was not ready for it. "I decidedly declined," he wrote his brother Charles. "However ambitious I may be to get on, I did not want to wear my life out, while still so young, by assuming such an Atlas load. Still, I love the business and wasn't made for any other."

What he loved best about journalism was being in the most exciting places, where the most interesting events were happening. In rejecting the offer, Albert committed himself—at least for the time—

ALBERT DEANE RICHARDSON.

to a career path *he* wanted rather than the conservative one his parents might have chosen. Family man or not, he would be a reporter of the frontier. He would follow the colorful course of history and tell readers stuck in ordinary lives, in dreary eastern cities, of the drama beyond their horizons.

Now, four years before the formal outbreak of the Civil War, the place to be was the plains of the Kansas Territory, where a violent conflict raged between those advocating slavery and those who stood for a free state in forthcoming elections. That is where John Brown was riding, and where Border Ruffians from Missouri crossed over to do battle with antislave Free-Soilers packing rifles supplied by abolitionist eastern churches.

To support a trip to Kansas, Albert had worked out a new arrangement with the *Boston Journal*. He would have the unusual right of a personal byline, as A.D.R., and his reports would now be published not only in provincial Cincinnati but in an eastern metropolis. His career had moved to a new level.

This was not to be a flying visit, a casual stroll through the fields. Just getting there was an enterprise. The train ran only as far as Jefferson City, Missouri, where Albert would have to switch to a river steamer going to the developing town of Kansas City. From there, the only transportation west into the territory and beyond would be stagecoach. But "Bleeding Kansas" was where Albert's pen was needed; inconvenient travel only made it more appealing. Once there, Albert planned to settle in and stay awhile. The young reporter had brought his wife and child along.

It was on May 28, 1857, that the twenty-three-year-old journalist and his family boarded the Missouri river side-wheeler. There was no charm to this stream of flowing mud, full of dead tree trunks and confined by banks of collapsing soil. But Albert did not see only turbid waters. His notes were filled with enchanting visions—the silvery gleam of dawn, the blood-red glow of sunset, waters sprinkled with stars in the darkness. He was on his way to a great adventure.

ĭ ĭ

A b b y   G o e s   W e s t

Abby's New England roots were as deep as Albert's. Six generations of Sages, the descendants of Welsh immigrants, had lived in Connecticut and Massachusetts. She was the first born of William and Abigail Sage, in 1837, and was named for her mother, a strong-willed and forthright woman. Lizzie followed in 1840 and Sarah in 1841. The next year the family moved from Massachusetts to Manchester, New Hampshire, where they opened a harness and twine shop. The new Concord Railway line had just reached the town, bringing with it expansion and opportunity. Mr. Sage hoped to capitalize on the growing local economy.

There Abby grew up, the daughter of a modest shopkeeper. The Sage family had added two sons who died young, but a third, William, was born in 1849. Her younger sisters and brother all looked up to Abby. She was always the family leader and was often busy helping her father in the shop or her mother in the house, as befitted an eldest and responsible child.

Manchester had a smart new brick town hall and some cultural activities at the Lyceum, where speakers traveling the New England lecture circuit could appear. But the place was dominated by the Amoskeag Manufacturing Company's massive red-brick textile mills and locomotive works, and the workers who labored in them. It was a coarse factory town.

Abby loved the more refined and romantic atmosphere she found in the world of books, and they became her life. There were few children's books published then. Sometimes she could go and read at the Manchester Athenaeum, the public library. But most of the time she read and reread the only three books in the Sage family library—the Bible, *Pilgrim's Progress,* and *Arabian Nights' Entertainment,* expurgated of course. The Bible for her was not a religious book but a source of stories. She read them over and over, committing each to memory and "investing it with the Oriental landscape and atmosphere borrowed from the *Arabian Nights."*

Once, when she was about ten or eleven, she found some tiny books at the bottom of a trunk in the attic. It was a miniature set of Shakespeare, barely readable even by young eyes. Years later, in her introduction to a book of children's stories, she recalled the pleasure these brought her. "I grieve to say that I did not consult anybody about the propriety of reading these books," she confided to her youthful readers. "Only a little while before, my papa had taken away from me a delightful novel, whose heroine (her name was either Melissa or Amanda, or something of that kind) had just got into the most dangerous part of the book. My father had said it was not a fit story for a small girl to read, and I had shed some bitter tears over my loss, had thought my papa very cruel, and mentally resolved to read the rest of the story as soon as I was grown up. Alas! like many other things we mean to do some time, the resolution never was fulfilled and though the little girl is now a woman, I do not know to this day what became of the forlorn Amanda, or Melissa, whose fortunes I left in such desperate condition.

"Remembering my latest loss, therefore, I concluded that at present no one should share the secret of the Shakespeare books. So I devised many hiding-places for them, and used to read them at night, and in the gray dawn of morning in my little bed, and out of school hours in the broad sunny window-seat in the attic, where I had a secure retreat. I cannot tell you how eagerly I devoured these books. No child of the present age would understand my delight, they have such plenty of new books, such a surfeit of literature. But to me, these two volumes were better than Aladdin's lamp or his ring."

Abby's parents encouraged their bookish daughter to seek broader horizons and sent her to Normal School in New Brighton, New Hampshire, to prepare for a teaching career, one of the best opportunities open to women. On graduation, at age eighteen, she found a job teaching at Webster's Academy in New Haven, Connecticut. It was a long way from New Hampshire. But she hoped that there, in a town more established than Manchester, she might better be able to meet people who shared her interests.

It did not take long. In the spring of 1857, a year and a half after she went to New Haven to teach, Abby met Daniel McFarland. Born to immigrant Irish parents, McFarland had grown up in New York and New Jersey and begun to work at fifteen. After apprenticing as a tailor and harness-maker, he spent several years in the South, at Charleston, working at various trades. At age nineteen he enrolled at Dartmouth College, but remained only a year or two. He withdrew to travel in England, Ireland, and France, where he attended lectures at the Sorbonne. Though he had no formal degree, he became a professor of elocution at Brandywine College in Delaware for a brief time and he managed to become a member of the Bar of Massachusetts. Now, he was living in Madison, Wisconsin.

McFarland was captivated by the shy young woman with blue eyes and rifts of hair of a marvelous tint between gold and brown. She had a tall graceful figure and an exquisitely fair complexion.

Abby was fascinated by McFarland's culture and sophistication. She had never met anyone like him. He shared her love of literature and he could quote endlessly from Shelley and Shakespeare. McFarland could talk with apparent knowledge on almost any subject. Oh, could he talk. He told her of his travels and adventures. He told her he had a flourishing law practice and brilliant political prospects in Madison. He told her of his property holdings worth twenty to thirty thousand dollars. He told her in the most romantic and poetic way of his love for her and swept her off her feet. He was the man of her dreams. It hardly mattered that he was thirty-nine years old, twice her age.

DANIEL McFARLAND.

On December 14, 1857, in Boston, Daniel McFarland and Abby Maria Sage were married by the Reverend Theodore Parker. McFarland had chosen the minister with care. Parker was not just any cleric. A brilliant, erudite graduate of the Harvard Divinity School, the Reverend Parker was renowned for his progressive religious and political positions. When he was denounced as an infidel for sermons denying the special authority of the Bible and of Christ, and excluded from the established church, Parker founded an independent ministry. His fame grew as he preached to an adoring audience from a square-topped desk in Boston's Music Hall, lecturing them on man's duty to right social wrongs. And he practiced what he preached, supporting John Brown and the underground railway and getting himself indicted for attempting to free a captured slave.

Abby had heard Theodore Parker speak at the Manchester Lyceum and admired him. She admired even more her new husband for choosing such an enlightened and progressive minister, and for the way in which McFarland had distanced himself from the conservatism of his immigrant Irish background.

Immediately after the marriage, Abby and Daniel departed for their home in the West. For a young woman then, marriage was the way to a new world, as career was for a young man. Abby was as excited as any young bride could be. It was 1857, and she, too, was on her way.

iii

Albert's Marriage

1857-1860

Life was not easy in Kansas for Albert's wife and baby. Gone were the friends and the pleasures of Cincinnati, and gone most of the time was Albert. He was constantly on the move, his endless curiosity drawing him to everything that might be of interest to his Boston audience. A massacre of Free State settlers by the Marais des Cygnes River, fraudulent land promotions in towns such as New Babylon (complete with a plat showing the main line of the imaginary New Babylon and San Francisco Railroad running through its heart), rowdy sessions of the territorial legislature, and political caucuses, all found their way into his columns. Often he rode through the night on horseback in response to a loose rumor that a rebellion, murder, or other event of journalistic interest had transpired in some distant town, sometimes getting lost in storms and seeking shelter in Indian cabins or simply wandering until daybreak, half-frozen.

At times Lou and the baby would accompany him, and they too had to seek refuge from storms in rude huts. But, for the most part, she tended the hearth while her husband ranged over the territory.

The young couple flirted with the idea of settling in Kansas. Albert, not immune to speculative fever, bought land in the new town of Sumner, and built a house for his family. Sumner was a newly minted river port just north of Leavenworth, the product of a development boom sweeping across eastern Kansas in anticipation of statehood. It was barely a month old, with only a few residences, but its future was promising and lots could be had for one hundred dollars. The Richardson home was a plain, two-room cottonwood cabin, with a door and a couple of windows at one end, but it was a place for the family to test the idea of putting down roots. Albert even ran for the legislature.

But by the spring of 1859, the second anniversary of the Richardson family's move to Kansas, the intensity of the slavery conflict had abated, and rail and telegraph lines had been completed across Missouri, putting the Kansas Territory in direct contact with the East. What had been a trip of immense hardship only a few decades earlier, and an adventuresome steamer and stage journey only two years before, was now a routine business trip.

"The steam engine has annihilated the distance," A.D.R. wrote. "Mr. Brown of Boston steps into a railway carriage on Monday morning. For the next three days he lives at the rate of twenty-five miles an hour. At night he retires to his couch in the sleeping car, almost as luxurious and secluded as his own apartment at home. In the morning he wakes two or three hundred miles further on, to find awaiting him his boots freshly polished by the porter, and convenient bathing and dressing saloons in which to make his toilet. On Thursday morning he breakfasts in Kansas."

If this is what eastern Kansas had become, it was time for an enterprising reporter to move on. A.D.R.'s next destination was clear. The region was thick with stories of old John Gregory's gold strike, on May 6, 1859, near Pikes Peak, in the western part of the territory. There was a grand stampede for the mountains, and Albert joined in.

The newly formed Leavenworth and Pikes Peak Express Company had, in a short few weeks, set up a stage coach route with new Concord coaches, costing eight hundred dollars each, painted bright red and drawn by teams of four Kentucky mules. A hundred coaches and a thousand mules were said to be scattered along the 722 mile route, at stations 10 to 25 miles apart. The coaches traveled in pairs for security. When the maiden pair left Leavenworth on May 25, 1859, Albert was on board, the only passenger.

Two days later, in Manhattan, Kansas, he was joined by another passenger, Horace Greeley. Greeley will live forever in American history as the man who preached, "Go West, young man." But he had not followed his own advice until now, when he embarked on a cross-country tour that put him with Albert on the shiny new coaches of the Leavenworth and Pikes Peak Express. It was an enterprising endeavor for the desk-bound, citified man of forty-eight. Greeley was, by this time, the most famous newspaper editor in America. His *New York Tribune* had a circulation of 300,000 in daily and weekly editions, the equivalent of 2,500,000 today. This readership was attracted not by the usual mass-circulation diet of sensation and gore, but by intelligent, serious coverage of the news. The *Tribune* was easily the most influential paper in the country, and Greeley, at its helm, was a man of great power and prestige. He was, in many ways, a peculiar sort for the role, given to oddities of appearance and behavior. His long white duster coat, bald pate fringed with a wild growth of silvery hair, and wispy white beard made him an easy target of caricature. His ardor and penchant for strong language in promoting causes in the *Tribune*'s pages—ranging from Fouierism to feminism to prohibitionism to abolitionism—made him a common victim of satire. The very idea of a man of his age and stature bouncing along in a stagecoach for Denver aroused curiosity. "Has the newspaper failed, that Greeley has to go dig for gold?" a farmer asked. There could have been no better companion for Albert—a journalistic colleague; an eccentric, older gentleman, newsworthy in his own right; and a father-figure to be honored.

Pressing on at 55 miles a day, with a final day-night run of 130 miles, passing scores of gold-rush immigrants in Pikes Peak or Bust wagons, the road-weary duo made it to Denver City in eleven days. Newspapermen to the core, they did not even pause for lodgings in this incipient town of a few hundred hastily erected, dirt-floored shacks, but rushed directly to the "gold digs" forty miles to the northwest. They studied the situation, interviewed prospectors, and prepared a factual report. Greeley even found time to give a speech exhorting a crowd of one thousand five hundred shaggy-bearded, unkempt miners to live clean lives, without drinking or gambling, so as to make their parents and families proud. That was unlikely to happen in this coarse region, where there were only a bare handful of non-Indian women and no other entertainments. But that was Greeley's quixotic way.

In a few days Albert and his new collaborator had a scoop. They wrote the first reliable, detailed account of the extent of the gold discoveries, which was published immediately in an extra edition of the new *Rocky Mountain News*, and soon reprinted in the East.

After a few weeks' stay, during which Greeley recuperated from injuries (sustained when their stagecoach had overturned on

HORACE GREELEY.

the trip out), the senior editor continued west. Albert remained a bit longer, but soon had to return to his family. Lou had given him another son that past fall, Frederick, who had died within months, and now she was six months pregnant again. He wanted to stay in Denver, but he obviously could not consider relocating his wife to a place even more primitive than Sumner. Instead, he moved her and young Leander to his old family farm in Massachusetts, where they could live with his relatives.

Albert could not linger. He always spoke fondly of his family. There was a bittersweet edge to his adventuring that came from having a loving woman waiting at home. But he knew what he had to do to get material for his dispatches, which, thanks to his new friendship with Horace Greeley, were being printed in the New York *Tribune*, the finest and most influential paper in the nation. He was a reporter of the frontier and he had to be at the brink of civilization.

SANTA FE, NEW MEXICO, OCTOBER 1859
BY A.D.R.

While here I received word that my wife had given me a daughter, Maude, on October 16. I designed returning from Santa Fe by the weekly mail direct to Kansas City, eight hundred and forty miles. But the Kiowa Indians, after blockading the route for a month, had captured the two last eastward coaches, stolen the stock and left thirteen passengers, including two women, killed and scalped by the roadside. My own line of march was cut off. Eastward the Kansas City route might remain closed for months. I could retrace my steps south to El Paso, and return by the Butterfield Line; but with that, familiarity had bred contempt. Northward, toward Pike's Peak, were no carriage roads, but the lonely trail promised novelty and adventure.

At my hotel I shared the supper-table with a stout middle-aged man, with straight brown hair, mild eye and kindly face. He wore a suit of gray, and looked like an Illinois farmer. But I soon learned he was Kit Carson, the mountaineer.

Carson was about to return home to Taos, and at ten the next morning we galloped away together. He was reputed the most daring and reckless of riders. I had not mounted a horse for months and was still weak and reduced in flesh from a bout with typhoid fever a few months earlier. But we flew over the rocks through canyons and across ditches until my blood tingled to the fingertips. Carson's special delight was to dash down steep hills at full gallop. This new experience made me shudder. But he was far heavier than I and his American horse nearly twice as tall as my steed, a little Indian pony. Moreover these ponies rarely stumble, so the odds were largely in my favor. Our road was nearly all hills; and after three or four trials I began to enjoy it and forget the Spanish proverb: "A running horse is an open grave."

The route led over barren plains and among snow-streaked mountains; but passed some rich valley-farms, with speckled ripening corn and plump wheat. Turning our horses out to graze, we lunched upon bread and dried buffalo meat, and smoked our mid-day cigars upon the grassy bank of a clear stream. Starting again we struck the Rio Grande, here an insignificant stream in a narrow valley. At four, P.M., the sun had disappeared; so we halted at a spacious adobe whose swarthy owner received us in great dirt and dignity. We performed our ablutions in the little acequia or irrigating canal; supped on mutton, frijoles and eggs and slept on the floor-mattresses with yellow-haired saints and a pink-faced virgin staring down from the walls.

Breakfasting at daylight before our host was up, we left a quarter-eagle upon his table and started on. We entered a dark cold canyon, its frowning walls crowned with odorous pine and hemlock. The mountain scenery grew so wild that I lingered behind my companion to enjoy it. In a lonely dell I was stopped by two brawny Indians, who imperiously demanded whisky and tobacco, and manifested an unpleasing interest in my saddle-bags. A handful of smoking tobacco failing to satisfy these brigands, I drew my revolver and sternly motioned them away. They instantly obeyed; but had they known how poor a marksman I was they would have laughed in my face. Next I encountered a party of Apaches moving their village, with children and household utensils in baskets suspended from the dragging lodge-poles.

At two, P.M., sore in every joint from the ride of eighty miles, equal to one hundred and twenty upon level roads, I reached Taos, and was soon housed under Carson's roof.

Albert eventually made it home, and spent the winter with his family in Massachusetts, but the West beckoned again in the spring of 1860. He returned with his good friend, Thomas W. Knox. They toured around Kansas and then went back to Denver, this time not in the regular stagecoach but in a covered wagon with a pioneer. There they spent the summer and fall, first as correspondents and then as coeditors of the *Golden City Weekly Mountaineer*.

Albert's reputation in the region grew, and he is credited with proposing the name "Colorado" for the new territory that was authorized in 1861.

For a diversion, Albert struggled up Pikes Peak with four friends—two of them female—and published a three-part series on his mountaineering ordeal. There was no trail, their equipment consisted of little more than thick boots, blankets, and of course revolvers, in case of unwanted visitors. The women wore "bloomer costume, with broad rimmed hats," which, he reported, "is better than full drapery; but for this trip women should don trousers." Nonetheless, the party spent six days on the mountain, undeterred by cold, rain, shredded skirts, vomiting fits, and the loss of their whiskey supply due to defective corking.

When they finally reached their goal, thirteen thousand four hundred feet above sea-level, Albert reported, "The ladies of our party—one a native of Boston, the other of Derry, N.H.—were the first of their sex who ever set foot upon the summit. Each of the ladies had lost eight pounds of flesh. One, whose shoes were cut through by sharp rocks early on the journey, had been walking for three days with portions of her bare foot striking upon stones, gravel and snow."

While Albert's career and exploits continued apace, married life was not exactly as his wife had anticipated it. Lou dearly loved Albert. Her first two years with him, when they lived in Cincinnati, were the happiest she had ever known, and she was so proud to have given him a son for his first born. The years after that were confusing for her. She did not mind so much the hardship, or the absence of friends. But she minded the loneliness when Albert was away. He was home fewer than half the nights during their two years in Sumner, and he traveled from spring to fall after that. She also could not stand the constant worry. He was always in danger while on the road, threatened by Indians, political enemies, and natural disasters, any one of which could have taken his life in a moment.

Sometimes she thought she understood why he was away so much. But other times she did not. In the fall of 1860, his return home from Pikes Peak was delayed for over a month as he devoted himself to caring for the sick widow and children of a stranger who had died from the hardships of that primitive area. He then accompanied the woman on the stagecoach journey east to Leavenworth. "Her oldest child was ill," a friend of the woman recalled, "and she was convalescing and heart-broken in her widowhood, and with a baby of ten weeks in her arms. It was not a gay trio for a man to voluntarily take under his guardianship." But Albert did such things.

Lou did not want to begrudge this poor woman the help she got from Albert. But when she learned of it, she wondered why he was not more anxious to return to his own dear family, whom he had not seen for six months.

When Albert returned home from this latest trip to Colorado, the news that accompanied him did not give Lou any promise of a more comforting future. Albert first heard it on the stage from Denver to Leavenworth, shouted to him by a passing Pony Express rider. "Lincoln elected! New York gives him fifty thousand majority!" Everyone knew what that meant. Now the crisis was impending.

i V

Abby's Marriage

1 8 5 7 – 1 8 6 0

 Abby quickly learned that her marriage was not to be the idyll she had imagined. The couple had only gotten as far as New York on their honeymoon trip west when McFarland explained he had no cash and had to borrow money to get them to Wisconsin. Once in Madison, she found his cash shortage was not a one-time event. McFarland had no law practice of any consequence. He had devoted his time in Wisconsin solely to land speculation. He had accumulated a number of parcels, all mortgaged to the hilt, and his economic future depended on his ability to liquidate this hoard at a favorable price. Otherwise, he had nothing.

ABBY, FROM HER AFFIDAVIT.

After we had been in Madison a few weeks Mr. McFarland informed me that he was going to remove to New-York. He told me that there were large opportunities for trading his lands in New-York City, and that he was going to reside there while he disposed of them for real estate or personal property.

We came to New-York, consequently, in February 1858. I was taken ill on the way with a violent cold and fever, and we were detained in Rochester ten days. On leaving Rochester he had to leave his watch and chain in pawn with the hotel-keeper for our board bill. In New-York City he kept me three or four weeks, and then taking all the jewelry I had to the pawnbroker's, to pay the board bill, he sent me home to my father's in New Hampshire.

I simply tell these things to give some idea of how they must have effected a young girl fresh from a comfortable New-England country home, to whom a pawnbroker's shop was almost an unheard-of institution, and not to convey the idea that it was his poverty which shocked or estranged me.

I went home then in less than three months after marriage. Mr. McFarland gave me no directions where to write him, and for fourteen days I never heard from him. Nearly beside myself from anxiety, I went to New-Haven and from thence telegraphed to a friend of his in New-York for news of him. He appeared in two or three days in answer to the telegram, and took me back with him.

Then, for the first time, I had a vague suspicion that he might be intemperate. But I knew nothing about intemperance. I had never in all my life seen a man drunk, except some accidental drunkard in the street, and I tried to dismiss the suspicion. In a week or two I again went back to my father's, and remained through the Summer of 1858. During this time he came once or twice to visit me, and seemed to be attached to me. But during the short time I had lived with him, I discovered that he was not temperate (although I had not seen him *grossly* intoxicated), and that for some slight or fancied causes he would become sullen and morose, not speaking to me for a day or two.

Abby kept her apprehensions to herself. As her weeks in New Hampshire without McFarland grew into months, she continued to act as though everything was fine, and she tried to keep the marriage working.

Abby to *Daniel*

MANCHESTER, JUNE 18, 1858 •

My Darling Husband,

I received your letter this (Friday) morning and read the few scolding lines you sent me, and after I had read them I thought you were real cross and exacting. Just think of the whole week that elapsed when I was at home that you never touched pen to paper in my behalf, and now, because I neglected to write for four days, you are cross.

Be sure to bring me, when you come, darling, that Life of Shelley and Byron.

Write soon and don't be cross. With much love, your affectionate,

Abby

Her separation from McFarland became more problematic when she learned that she was about to have their first child. She held back for a time from telling him, out of fear of his reaction. But the matter could not be put off forever, and she finally brought it up at the end of the summer. McFarland's response at first was positive. He rented a cottage in Brooklyn, at the corner of Clark and Willow streets, furnished a few rooms, and sent for her. He even arranged for a servant.

ABBY, FROM HER AFFIDAVIT

I did not leave my father's roof in the Fall of 1858 without many misgivings; but I was very young and very cheerful in disposition, and hoped for the best.

Some of the time—perhaps half of the time—Mr. McFarland was good to me, and professed for me the most extravagant and passionate devotion. But he here first began to come home intoxicated. He would also come home sober, bringing with him bottles called "Schiedam Schnapps," containing a quart or so of vile liquor, and would put them by his bedside, and drink sometimes the whole before morning. When I begged him not to do this he said "his brain was on fire," and this made him sleep.

As this was only two or three months before my child was born, and all my senses were nervously acute, and as I was also, as I believe, a woman of refined taste and feeling, his breath and whole body steaming with the vile liquor which he drank during these nights while I lay awake beside him, made him very odious to me, so that before I had been married to him a year my affection for him was very much chilled, I might say nearly destroyed.

Abby's eighteen-year-old sister, Lizzie, came to help her with her first pregnancy, staying for five months. It was an adventure for the two young women to be living together in New York, and they enjoyed each other's company. Abby's mother joined her daughters in Brooklyn to help with the birth and the nursing. The baby, a fine girl they named Jessie, was born just after Christmas, on December 29. After a few months, the women all went back to New Hampshire, leaving McFarland to his business dealings.

This was, despite everything, a happy time for Abby, and she began to repair her feelings toward McFarland in his absence. She wanted very much for Jessie to have a proper father. She knew her husband had wanted a son, his little "Percy Bysshe," but Abby thought Jessie was so wonderful McFarland would surely come to love her.

Abby to *Daniel*

MANCHESTER, APRIL 1859 •

My Dear Husband,

I wrote you as soon as I arrived, telling you of my journey. Jessie is a little cross. Every man she sees she springs toward him. I expect she thinks it may be her papa. Mother sleeps with her, and this morning when Dinky waked up she tried to pull grandma's chin. I expect she thinks it was her father's beard she was going to grasp. We think of papa (baby and I) every night and morning, besides every hour of daylight, and we do miss him so much. I long for the time when you will come here. I don't want to go back to New York before next fall, it is so much healthier here for "Percie."

I long to hear the negotiation is consummated, and that you are the possessor of the property on Fourteenth Street. You will be quite landgrave and we shall feel rich, shall we not?

Good-by, dearest; with lots of kisses and love from Dinky and me. I hope I shall get a letter tomorrow.

> Your own wife,
> *Abby*

Abby to *Daniel*
MANCHESTER, APRIL 1859 •

My Dear Husband,

This morning I drew Jersey down to father's shop to get the letter which I knew I should find there and to give baby an airing. We were both weighed. I was first weighed with Birdie in my arms and we weighed 137½ pounds; afterward, alone, I weighed 121½. I weighed 125 when I was married.

You will be astonished at my baby, and I am astonished that you don't make more mention of her in your letters. Mother asked me if you had not sent baby a kiss, and I said, "No, not a word." If it were Percy should you not send a word?

I hope you will be here soon, dear. I long to see you so much, and I shall be glad when you are at home with me. I know I shall. You must believe me.

> Your loving and devoted wife,
> *Abby*

McFarland was having trouble selling off his lands. He did manage to trade some for New York property. But his best source of income

seemed to come from increasing his mortgages. He presented this to
Abby as business success and she went along. "I could not understand
very well about the Fourteenth street mortgages," she wrote, "but it
is this, is it not? You have already a $4,000 mortgage on each of the
four houses, and are going to change them for a $5,000 one on each,
from another company. Ne c'est pas. I was stupid, but now I understand. I am so glad you are so fortunate. I always feel the most perfect
confidence in your ability to bring about favorable results." At least
they had some cash to pay their bills.

When he had money, McFarland spent it, often on Abby, sending her jewelry (that he would later reclaim for pawning). "Please,"
she pleaded, "don't buy any more jewelry. I don't care very much
for ornaments, you know, and I like other things better. Do you
know what present has been the dearest, next to my watch, you
ever gave me? Guess. It is my volumes of Browning. The pleasure
of them has lasted longest; and my stereoscope, too, has been one
of my greatest delights." But when McFarland offered to buy a
wedding ring, she was enthusiastic. "I can see the glitter of my ring
in imagination, and think how proud I shall be to wear it; proud
because I say, 'My husband gave it to me;' because that will give it
the highest value."

To please McFarland, Abby began taking lessons in German, then
the language of high culture. *"Meineu Liebling,"* she wrote, "I am
extremely interested in German and would like to devote many
hours a day to its study. I hope to accomplish something this summer. Don't you wish it? I feel very stupid. I send you kisses enough
to make up for my stupidity." But mostly the new mother and proud
wife delighted in her baby. "The little gipsy is learning new tricks
every day," she wrote McFarland. "She kept running out her tongue
at me to-day, and then laughing and crowing after she had done so.
Don't you long to see her?"

McFarland never came. And in June everything changed. Little
Jessie died for no apparent reason. Abby wanted very much for her
husband to be there with her, to share her loss. But he was still too
busy to come. She had to bury Jessie alone, in the Sage family burial
place. The bond she had hoped might resuscitate her marriage was
gone, and Abby struggled with her feelings and her conscience.

ABBY, FROM HER AFFIDAVIT

In July I returned again to Mr. McFarland. My heart was sorely bruised by the death of my baby, and I was less able to bear up under the brutality and violence of Mr. McFarland's temper. I will not enter into the details of his treatment of me during these three months; but it was so bad that I went back to my father's in October. When I returned home to New Hampshire, if I had had courage to have told my mother and father of my troubled life, I should probably never have returned to this man. But I could not speak. It was so hard a thing to tell. My ideas of a wife's duty were most conservative. I believed she should suffer almost unto death rather than resist the laws of marriage. I had a conscience sensitive to any appeals against itself, and I tried hard to love my husband and convince myself I was in the wrong.

Back in New Hampshire, removed from McFarland and his daily outbursts, Abby's feelings again softened. She tried to carry on as though her marriage was working, and Daniel responded in kind.

Abby to *Daniel*
MANCHESTER, NOV. 11, 1859 •

My Darling Husband.-

I somewhat expected to receive a letter from you to-day. I wanted to wait till to-night, so that I could tell you what a heroic thing I have done. I have had that tooth extracted. The dentist came to the house and pulled it. At the first touch the top came off, leaving four large roots firm in the jaw, which were each extracted separately. Father held my hands or I could not have borne it. I guess he took as many as twenty-five pulls at it. It was awful. Dear, you wouldn't have had me have it out if you had been here. You could not have seen me so tortured.

When you come home you can sit in our little chamber and

read all by yourself, with no one but me. Don't you want to come? I am yours, tenderly,

Abby

Daniel to *Abby*

NEW YORK, NOV. 20, 1859 •

My Dear Wife -

I enclose you twenty dollars. I should have sent you some money immediately on the arrival of your last letter, but I had none about me and I was not well enough to venture out to collect some from Peter, as it rained very hard on that day. For the last couple of nights on my retiring to bed I wet my night shirt with cold water and went to bed in it and took what answered for a "wet sheet." I have had nothing yet to do me so much good, and I think by a few more repetitions of the process I shall be about well.

I delivered to Kingsley's express yesterday something for you which I think will please you. It represents something not unlike a vision which was mine two years ago this night, when you so innocently, so devotedly and so touchingly promised to give yourself to me, a stranger to you, and to couple your earthly happiness and destiny with mine. I could not think then that there was ever a possibility of being angry with you, much less that I should ever get in a violent passion with you, and under such circumstance be so harsh and unjust to you. I think I would be willing to die tonight if by so doing I could change what has been. Every act towards you excepting that of the most devoted kindness and of a husband's dearest love I repudiate. It is a great consolation to me my soul has never done you wrong. You have always been treated lovingly and kindly there. My darling wife, if you will not treasure up anything against your loving husband he will be satisfied.

Your loving husband,
D. McFarland

Abby to Daniel

M A N C H E S T E R ,   N O V .   2 1 ,   1 8 5 9   •

My Darling Husband:

I received your letter of yesterday to-day. Why is it that I got your letter so soon and you are so long in getting mine? I cannot account for it. I am very particular in marking them, and yet they are so long reaching you. I received the $20 enclosed; I shall give mother six of it for last week, and then I guess I shall order a bonnet. I shall try and get one you would like, and I almost always suit you, don't I?

I feel quite worried about your cold; I have every time you write me, although it is quite common for those obstinate colds to hang on all winter. I wish you would go immediately to Dr. Guernsey. He is a gentleman of intelligence, and certainly has more experience in colds than you have; will you, as a personal favor to me, go and see him; if it gets no better in a week or so you must do one of two things, either go on a little trip to Philadelphia or Virginia, where it is warmer, or else I shall come on and nurse you. This taking a wet sheet by yourself without any one to tuck you up in bed is ruinous. You will tell me exactly how it is next time you write, won't you? I shall feel very anxious if you are not frank with me.

I was so delighted with the beautiful engraving you sent. You know how I do when I am pleased. I have looked at it until I know every figure and have interpreted the meaning of the whole group. I shall hang it in my room and study it over and over. I do love the darling, cunning little baby so much. It looks like my little bird when she was undressed at her bath. I thank you a thousand times for such a beautiful memento of our engagement.

I was very deeply affected by your letter, and all you said about our misunderstandings was very painful to me—not violently painful, but it grieved me to think that, in the midst of so much anxiety you have been suffering that you should have had these things to trouble you too. Believe me, even if I had not known how much I loved you, separation would have taught me. I find all my philosophy tried to the utmost to support the thought of so long an absence from you. You don't know how many lonely hours I spend, how much I worry about you, and how much I regret that I ever was perverse or obstinate. It is impossible, perhaps, that two persons should never do each other wrong. That is the bane of all love and affection— the impossibility of a perfect understanding—but there are always atonements as compensation, and there is nothing that cannot become forgotten, or so well forgiven that it is hardly remembered. Don't distrust my affection, and believe I love you as dearly a thousand times more so than two years ago. Write me particularly, exactly when you receive this.

Good-night my dear husband, I hope you will sleep sweetly. I am yours most tenderly,

Abby

Abby's efforts at maintaining the marriage were reinforced by the fact that she was pregnant again, this time from her few months with McFarland in the summer of 1859. In April 1860, while she remained at her father's house in New Hampshire, the child, her first son, was born.

Now she had McFarland's much desired Percy. But Abby did not rush back to New York with him. She put off her return until the end of the summer, rationalizing that the heat of the city would not be good for the baby. She finally returned in August, having been away almost a year.

Shortly thereafter, the family's always precarious finances collapsed. A creditor from Wisconsin, who was aggrieved in his land dealings with McFarland, brought suit, recovered a judgment, and attached all of the debtor's property that he could find in both Wisconsin and New York. At first, McFarland worked his charm on the lawyers, and dissuaded them from selling the property at auction, saying it would soon be worth far more than he owed and that he would be able to pay his debts shortly. The stall worked only for a short time. The property was sold, but because it was already heavily mortgaged, it did not produce enough to satisfy the judgment. McFarland now owned virtually nothing and remained deeply in debt.

Abby was a pawn in this debtor's struggle, moved around by McFarland as his strategy dictated.

ABBY, FROM HER AFFIDAVIT

While this suit was pending, Mr. McFarland ordered me to pack up my trunks and be ready to leave the city, as he might at any time be arrested and prevented from leaving the State. So again in December 1860, I was sent back to my father's with my baby now eight months old. Mr. McFarland followed me there and he stayed till February when he told me again to get ready and go away with him.

He had at this time $1,200 which came from the sale of a piece of property that he had managed to put out of his hands when judgment was obtained against him. With this he started with myself and Percy for Philadelphia, where he left me saying he was going on to Washington to seek office under Lincoln's incoming administration. In a few months he returned and told me he was going West again, as he was disappointed in his political expectation.

The situation was not pleasant for either of them. Abby still wanted to be a good wife, to make her marriage work. And McFarland wanted to be a good husband to her. He wanted to care for her and, as an older and wiser man, help in her social and intellectual development. He wanted to show her off to his friends. But financial circumstances were conspiring against him, and Abby's presence was not a source of pleasure for him but a frustration, an aching reminder of his failure in life.

Perhaps Wisconsin, where they had first gone after their marriage three years before, would be a place for a new start. As the nation's war began, in the spring of 1861, the McFarland family headed back to Madison.

V

Albert at War

 Albert ran his life as did an army of the era. His travels were his military campaigns, conducted from spring to fall each year. When November or December came, he returned to "winter quarters" with his family. So he spent the winter of 1860–61.

For his campaign in the spring of 1861, a wandering journey in the West was not, as he had foreseen, the route to the most compelling news. There was only one story on anyone's mind as the nation prepared for Lincoln's first inauguration in March—the impending hostilities. South Carolina and Alabama had already seceded, the constitutional convention of the new confederacy had completed its work in Montgomery, and Jefferson Davis had taken his oath of office. No shots had yet been fired—the fateful cannons of Fort Sumter would not roar until April 12—but every man and woman in the country was on edge. Were the Southerners bluffing, merely trying to assure the best possible compromise with an anti-slavery administration? If not, did the North have the will to resist by force? Was war inevitable, or evitable? The public thirsted to know.

And Albert thirsted to tell. With his friend Horace Greeley, he worked out a plan. A.D.R. would go to the South as a secret correspondent of the *Tribune* and send back letters reporting on the attitudes and feelings of the people. This was hazardous work. There were enough ardent secessionists to assure a lynching for any discovered spy of the hated, abolitionist *Tribune*. They contrived a disguise and a system for encoding letters. The code was primitive—for example, phrases between certain innocent marks were reversed in meaning, so Albert could call a man a gentleman and mean he was a scoundrel—but it enabled Albert to write seemingly normal letters that had hidden meaning. Perhaps Greeley would not have asked him to take on such a perilous task, but it was Albert's idea, and the *Tribune* editor, with his commitment to the news, could not resist.

By May 1861, however, Albert was no longer a secret agent, but an overt correspondent, covering a full-fledged war. His first assignment was with the Frémont campaign in Missouri, where he joined his long-time friend, Junius Henri Browne, who was also covering the campaign, for a Cincinnati paper.

Junius and Albert had met in 1852, when both were working as young reporters. They were the same age, then eighteen, and immediately took to each other. As Junius related it, "We met at Niagara, where we had been sent to report on a meeting of the Democratic party. Albert was then connected with the *Cincinnati Daily Sun*, a newspaper since deceased, and I with the *Cincinnati Commercial*, for which I wrote sesquipedalian fustian, under the impression that it was eloquence.

"We were stopping at the International Hotel, when the house was crowded to suffocation. I shared a room with a large faction of the Democratic party and being a privileged guest, I was given a table for a couch. Awaking from the only sleep I had succeeded in securing—it was long after sunrise then—I saw on the floor below me a blonde, pleasant-faced youth who greeted me genially.

" 'We've taken our bed and "board" together; how do you like it, old fellow? Is it as good as Dante?' he asked, referring to a copy of the *Divina commedia* which I had brought with me as a refuge from myself on the journey.

" 'Nearly as good as his *Inferno*,' was my reply, 'but as a general thing I should prefer that to this.'

"This peculiar introduction led to a long talk about various things; to our breakfasting and dining together, 'doing' the cataract in company, and returning in the same train to Cincinnati. Before the end of the first day of our acquaintance we felt as if we had known each other for years. Each had the other's antecedents, experiences, and idiosyncrasies as soon as they could be conveniently related."

JUNIUS HENRI BROWNE.

Along with Albert and Junius, there were five or six other correspondents and artists—the latter being the equivalent of photographers in this time when newspapers could print etchings but not photographs—who gathered in Jefferson City with General Frémont's forces. Junius christened the troupe The Bohemian Brigade, for its "nomadic, careless, half-literary, half-vagabondish life." During their ample leisure while waiting for the action to begin, they amused themselves "smoking pipes, playing whist, and discussing Poetry, Metaphysics, Art, and Opera, Women, the World, the War and its future, and various themes on which we then could merely speculate."

Though the profession of war correspondent had just come of age in the Crimean War a few years earlier, every major newspaper now had its representatives traveling with the armies. They paid their own way, of course, but lived and ate as regular officers, sharing the same messes and camping in the same fields. Unlike the officers, however, they were not subject to military discipline. This did not sit well with many commanders, and relations between the correspondents and their subjects were not always cordial.

General Sherman, for one, considered them little better than spies. He and other commanders expelled correspondents from their camps on various occasions. The reporters sometimes contributed to their own plight. Even Junius admitted they were "a little too prone, perhaps, to recklessness of conduct and statement, and unduly sensitive about their own dignity and the importance of the Press. They believed implicitly in the aphorism: *Cedant arma togae*—Let civilian authority be paramount—and did not always understand that the customs of Peace are incompatible with the exigencies of War. Yet, in the main, they performed their duty conscientiously, and deserved more kindly of the Army, Navy, and the general public, than they received."

Albert was among the most conscientious, and among the most vigorous in defending the rights of the press. He believed deeply in the value of his role.

Albert to *Sidney Howard Gay,*

Managing Editor, *New York Tribune*

CAIRO, ILL., JUNE 4, 1862 •

My Dear Sir:

We were all disappointed that General Halleck's expulsion of correspondents should not have been made the occasion of the Press taking <u>some</u> step to assert its dignity & its rights. Until it is clearly settled that an accredited Journalist, in the legitimate exercise of his calling, has just as much <u>right</u> in the army as the Commander himself, & is there on just as legitimate a mission, he <u>will</u> be considered by a large majority of Regular Army officers as an "unauthorized hanger on," & treated accordingly.

If the journalistic profession does not defend its own rights, can we expect any one else to do it for us? And this is so eminently a People's War, that if you deny the People the right—not the privilege—of a medium of information between them, & their sons & brothers & husbands in the army, what may you not deny them? It really seems to me a very grave matter, & a very dangerous precedent. Is it not a mistaken sensitiveness to refrain from taking a stand, lest the People should suppose it dictated merely by self-interest? Could not that be made unmistakably clear?

> Faithfully yours
> *Richardson*

Though he embraced his colleagues and his calling, Albert was different from other war correspondents. Most of them were bachelors and, to use Junius's description, "enthusiastic members of the anti-matrimonial school of philosophy." Albert was an exception. Not only was he married and loyal to his wife, he actually respected women.

Jefferson City, Missouri, October 6, 1861
by a.d.r.

Mrs. Frémont, the General's wife is in camp. She possesses that "excellent thing in woman," a voice, like Annie Laurie's, low and sweet—more rich, more musical, and better modulated, than that of any *tragedienne* upon the stage. To a broad, comprehensive intellect she adds those quick intuitions which leap to result, anticipating explanations, and those proclivities for episode, incident, and bits of personal analyzing, which make a woman's talk so charming.

How much rarer this grace of familiar speech than any other accomplishment whatever! In a lifetime one meets not more than four or five great conversationalists. Jessie Benton Frémont is among the felicitous few, if not queen of them all.

When the same General Halleck who could not tolerate the press also ordered that fugitive slaves be excluded from camp because they might be spies, Albert condemned the "inhumanity" of the order. It "outrages moral sense, and its falsehood common sense," he argued. "The negroes are uniformly friends to our soldiers. After diligent inquiry from every leading officer of my acquaintance, I could not learn of a single instance of treachery. To the cruelty of turning the slave away, Halleck has added the dishonesty of slandering him."

Albert remained in the field steadily through 1861 and into 1862, with only one brief visit home. His second son, Albert Deane, Jr., was born on January 26, 1862, while he was covering the maiden expedition of the new Union iron-clad gunboats. They were heading up the Tennessee River toward the heart of the Confederacy, accompanied by land forces under the command of one General Ulysses S. Grant, then unknown and untested.

Grant's capture of Fort Henry and Fort Donelson a few days later, in the first great Union victory of the war, were the beginnings of his reputation in a nation that was desperately seeking a worthy field commander. He and Albert became friends of a sort. Successful generals like reporters. They shared many meals, and Grant made

Albert privy to his strategy, tipping him off to wait for the Donelson attack rather than rush back to New York. Albert would later write Grant's biography.

So far the young reporter's luck was holding; he was in the right place at the right time, and he had the sense and the ability to capitalize on it. But it was a struggle. Conditions in the field were dreadful, transport was poor, and communication with editors depended on mails made unreliable by war-time conditions. The telegraph was an alternative, but it was expensive and correspondents could use it only for the most urgent dispatches, and then only if the lines were not down. Albert desperately wanted to be the finest correspondent in the West, to be at every important battle and to make the *Tribune's* coverage preeminent. He got testy when he failed, particularly when the arch-rival *Herald* did a better job.

Albert even tendered his resignation at one point, fed up with the struggle, and longing to get back home for some rest and quiet. "For myself," he wrote to his managing editor, Sidney Howard Gay, "I hate this gathering of news. It keeps a man's nerves all strung up so that it misfits him for the habit of mind requisite to writing well; but I of course will do my best at the news gathering as long as the times render it necessary. I long for the period, though, where I can escape from these fierce exactements into simple, quiet descriptive writing."

Gay refused to accept the resignation. Instead, Albert was promoted to head the *Tribune's* corps of correspondents in the western region, and, on his recommendation, Junius Henri Browne was hired to supplement that team. Junius's comradeship was crucial to Albert. When his colleague took ill, Albert, the dedicated reporter, deftly rearranged his priorities. He rushed from Cairo, Illinois, to St. Louis, where he found Junius delirious with "typhoid fever, which seems partially settling upon the brain."

"I must devote the next few days to him," Albert wrote Gay. "Browne has been extremely sick—down in the valley of the Shadow of Death. He is slowly but surely convalescing. I think within 3 weeks he will be able to take the field again. I read your inquiry 'Where is Browne?' to him & he said that he must make the reply of Goethe's grandmother, who in her last hours received an invitation to a party & replied with her compliments she would be most happy to be present, but was just then very busily engaged in dying."

Junius eventually recovered, but had to be sent home to recuperate. With his friend gone, Albert's spirit flagged, and he felt the pain of separation from his family even more acutely. It was now September 1862. He beseeched Gay, "Can I spend two or three weeks with my family near Boston, or have them meet me in Northern Ohio, as soon as there seems to be no special need of my remaining here?"

But Gay could not spare Albert for a visit home just now. Instead he moved him east to the center of the action. General Lee, following his victory in the Second Battle of Bull Run, on August 29—30, 1862, had shifted his forces across the Potomac into Maryland. The South thus carried the war into Northern territory for the first time and threatened a move onward to Pennsylvania. Unless they could be stopped, recognition of the Confederacy by Great Britain seemed likely, and a collapse of Northern will could soon follow.

The showdown between Lee's forces and the Army of the Potomac led by McClellan came at the Battle of Antietam. Albert was there, in the midst of the action with shot and shell exploding around him, for what has been called "the bloodiest day of the Civil War." He filed a moving report, telling not only of the glory of the charges, but also of the fields strewn with mutilated bodies the day after. Albert was a reporter who quoted Carlyle, "In a revolution we are all savages still; civilization has only sharpened our claws."

The Union victory was a turning point in the war, emboldening Lincoln, five days later, to announce the Emancipation Proclamation. Henceforth the battle would be not only for union, but against slavery.

Antietam was also to be the high point of Albert's war-reporting efforts. Though it was a Northern victory, McClellan failed to pursue the retreating Confederates and lost an opportunity to deliver the *coup de grace* to Lee's armies. The Federals pushed forward into Northern Virginia, but then the war settled into an often desultory holding action for both sides. It was as trying for the correspondents as it was for the troops.

Albert to *Sidney Howard Gay*

SHARPSBURG, MD., SUNDAY NIGHT,
10 1/2 O'CLOCK, SEPT. 21, 1862 •

My dear Mr. Gay:

Pardon me for reminding you that in my application to come East I asked for a season <u>at home.</u> I desire to spend fully 3 weeks there to recoup. I have only been there 4 days since last Nov. Will it not be well for me to go before the Fall & early Winter campaign finally opens?

> Faithfully yours
> *Richardson*

Albert to *Sidney Howard Gay*

HARPER'S FERRY, OCT. 31, 1862 •

My dear Mr. Gay:

I forward to you—Mr. Thompson. You may perhaps make him useful in some other field: for heaven's sake don't send him back to this one. He has been bringing us all into trouble & The Tribune into disrepute ever since Antietam. He means well enough; but he has no delicacy, discrimination or sense. He raised a breeze in the mess where I stop (Sedgwick's) by stealing oats after I had instructed him, two or three times, to feed his horse elsewhere. When the President was here, he got himself & another reporter ordered back to the rear of the cavalcade by blundering about, making a noise, & disturbing the party. He raised a fight needlessly & got whipped in an Irish regiment where he was selling papers.

His last exploit was to take dispatches to Balt.—where he was sent specially as our messenger—for The <u>Times</u> & <u>World</u> correspondents, & agree to bring them copies of their newspapers daily on his return—thus letting them know what I had repeatedly told him to keep a strict secret—how we send our dispatches & also getting their letters through as promptly as ours.

Will you please send me <u>at once,</u> in his place, some quiet, faithful, prompt man, with sense enough to hold his tongue, to act as messenger, & make himself useful as we may direct? The work is not hard; I don't care whether he can write or not, as we need one man for messenger the most of the time. It ought not to require a high-priced man. <u>Please get from Thompson, our pass over the Balt. & Ohio Road</u> for the new man & have him report at once to Kenney, <u>at Wenner's Store, Berlin</u> on the Railroad, 6 miles east of Harper's Ferry. You will see the need of haste; until he comes, whenever we need a messenger, we must hire one & pay his fare to & from Balt.

> Faithfully yours
> *Richardson*

Thanksgiving came and went and Albert was still seeking a leave from Gay. "I find I grow fearfully hackneyed & stupid—the effect of a year's writing with only 4 days at home, last February. I am not, as you know, any newcomer to the life of a wandering correspondent. But even an old rover gets <u>very</u> homesick. Three weeks at home, without care, would freshen me into a new man. I shall take it whenever I can go & leave <u>The Tribune</u> strongly and safely represented here—but not till then."

Albert finally got home in early December. Lou hoped that he would be able to stay through Christmas, and Albert wanted it even more. Leander, now six, was his pride. He hardly knew Maude, age three, and ten-month-old Albert, having been away almost constantly since their infancy. But the family barely had time to talk. Albert could stay only five days, because Gay needed him back in the field.

He returned to Virginia for the winter, but when spring came the *Tribune* dispatched him west again, to renew supervision of all its Western correspondents, including Junius, who was on his way down the Mississippi to cover Grant's siege of the Vicksburg fortress. This was now the primary action of the war. Union forces had taken New Orleans in the South and river ports including Memphis in the North. Only Vicksburg prevented them from controlling the Mississippi and slicing the Confederacy in two. There was no doubt in Albert's mind where duty directed him.

On the 3rd of May, 1863, he joined Junius at Milliken's Bend on the Mississippi. This was twenty-five miles above Vicksburg, but the fortress prevented further passage. Grant's forces were fifty-five miles below the city, and the fighting had already begun. The journalists knew they must get to Grant with the least possible delay. A crucial battle might occur momentarily, and they had not come all this way to miss it.

The journey could be achieved overland in three days stealing through Confederate lines. But the *Tribune* correspondents were offered an opportunity to join a river expedition about to run the Vicksburg batteries. It would get them to Grant's headquarters in only eight hours. The expedition consisted of two large barges loaded with hay and provisions, driven by a small tug, the *Sturges,* lashed between them. It was recklessly fitted out. There were no life boats or other means of escape in the event of sinking, and hay was lying loosely about where sparks from a bursting shell could easily ignite it. There was not even a bucket to extinguish fire. The whole thing, Junius observed, "was poorly planned and miserably managed in every particular, except for obituary readers." Worst of all, while other battery-running expeditions had gone down on dark nights, this night was as bright as could be. The moon was full and would be in the zenith just about the time they got within range of the hostile guns. Yet, as Junius tells it, their's "was indeed a merry party."

"A reasoning man with a love of adventure," he explained, "at first feels alarmed at being under fire; and his impulse is to run away; and if he has no motive to stand, he probably does run. But at each additional exposure he grows less timid, and after hearing canister and grape about his ears a dozen times, begins to think he is not destined to be hurt.

"He still feels rather uneasy, perhaps; but the danger acquires a sort of fascination; and, though he does not wish to be hit, he likes to have narrow escapes, and so voluntarily places himself in a position where he can incur more risk.

"So the mental process goes on, until the nerves by degrees become the subjects of the Will; and he only fears who has not the will to be brave."

Perhaps they should have been less brave. But that was not the way of the Bohemian. They were joined by Richard Colburn, of the *New York World,* and off they floated to what Junius called "the music of the grand gunpowder orchestra which the 'gentlemen from the Confederate States' were playing for our reception."

VICKSBURG, MISSISSIPPI, MAY 3, 1863
BY A.D.R.

Inclination joined with duty in impelling us to accompany the expedition. We wanted to learn how one would feel looking into the craters of those volcanoes as they poured forth sheets of flame and volleys of shells. For two or three hours, we glided silently along the glassy waters between banks festooned with heavy, drooping foliage. It was a scene of quiet unsurpassing beauty.

At one o'clock in the morning, on the Mississippi shore, a rocket shot up and pierced the sky, signaling the Rebels of our approach. Ten minutes later, we saw the flash and heard the boom of their first gun. We were soon under heavy fire. The range of the batteries covered the river for nearly seven miles. At some points we passed within two hundred yards of ten-inch guns, with point-blank range upon us.

I ascertained to my fullest satisfaction, as we lay among the hay-bales, slowly gliding past them, how it felt to look into the mouth of a cannon. How the great sheets of flame leaped up and spread out from the mouths of guns! How the shells came screaming and shrieking through the air! How they rattled and crashed, penetrating the sides of the barges, or exploding on board in great fountains of fire! The moment hardly awakened serene meditations or sentimental memories; but every time I glanced at that picture, Tennyson's lines rang in my ears:-

> *Cannon to the right of them,*
> *Cannon to the left of them,*
> *Cannon in front of them*
> *Volleyed and thundered;*
> *Stormed at by shot and shell,*
> *Boldly they rode and well,*
> *Into the jaws of death,*
> *Into the mouth of hell.*

Each time, after being struck, we listened for the reassuring puff! puff! of our little engine; and hearing it, said: "Thus far, at least, we are all right!"

Now we were below the town, having run five miles of batteries. Ten minutes more meant safety. But then a terrific report, like the explosion of some vast magazine, left us breathless, and seemed to shake the earth to its very center. It was accompanied by a shriek

RUNNING THE REBEL BATTERIES AT VICKSBURG.

which I shall never forget, though it seemed to occupy less than a quarter of the time consumed by one tick of the watch. It was the death-cry wrung from our captain, killed as he stood at the wheel. For his heedlessness in fitting out the expedition, his life was the penalty.

We listened, but the friendly voice from the tug was hushed. We were disabled, and drifting helplessly in front of the enemy's guns!

VI

Abby at War

1861–1864

McFarland was desperate for a means to support himself and his family. Despite his law credentials, he had no legal practice or desire to build one. For him the only options worth considering were business schemes or real estate speculations that might enable him to wheel and deal his way to a fortune, or political patronage positions. Having failed with both in the East, he was now trying his luck again in the West.

The family moved into a small house and took up housekeeping. They lived there for a year and two months, which Abby called "the happiest time of my life" with McFarland. "I was so thoroughly weary of the terrible vagabondish life I had always lived with this man," she recalled, "that under almost any condition a home I could call *mine* seemed delightful to me."

But there was no easy solution to their financial problems. McFarland got no support from his supposed friends when he went looking for a government job and he did no other work. His only source of funds was sales of a few pieces of property that he had managed to conceal from his creditors. As time drew on McFarland began to grow more and more morose and ill-tempered. He finally admitted to Abby he was running out of money and had no way of getting any more.

But then McFarland came up with a scheme. Abby had attracted some attention with her "readings." She would entertain the guests at private parties with selections from the stories and poems she loved so well. She read with a fine and dramatic voice and embellished the presentation with knowledgeable comments on the author and his or her work. She even gave a public performance for the benefit of a soldiers' hospital, which was very well received. McFarland, the former professor of elocution, now saw how he could use *his* talent.

ABBY, FROM HER AFFIDAVIT

Mr. McFarland proposed that he should take me to New-York and have me fitted for the stage in the profession of an actress. He also announced that he should himself adopt the profession of an actor in case my success became assured. He began training me in the reading of stage parts.

In June 1862, he sold all our furniture in Madison and brought me East. As soon as we were settled, Mr. McFarland began drilling me for the stage, which I may say, was the first and only instruction of any kind whatsoever he ever gave me; and he also sent me to take lessons of Mr. and Mrs. Geo. Vandenhoff, at a cost of more than $100. I also began to give readings in private homes for a small fee, and paid our board with my own earnings.

Mr. McFarland was unspeakably cruel to me this Fall and Winter of 1862 and 1863. He took all the little stock of jewels I possessed—my rings, brooches, watch and chain (which had by this time been so frequently pawned and repawned that I did not care for them), and sold them all. He would lock himself into the room with me, and give way to such terrible furies that only the extremest pride and self-control prevented me from making my misery known. He brought home what he professed was prussic acid, and threatened to take it and to force me to take it. He would snatch my scissors from my work-basket, and, tearing open his breast, he would brandish them about, swearing he would "let out his heart's blood" before me. He told me (then a shrinking girl of twenty-four) that he kept loaded pistols, with which he would at any moment shoot me.

One morning during this winter, after Mr. McFarland had been out nearly all night in a drunken orgy and had risen from bed in one of his worst tempers, I approached him as he stood by the mirror finishing his toilet and began to say something soothing to prevent the outburst of ill temper which I feared was soon coming. He turned around and struck me a blow across my face which made me reel backward. Although he had often pinched and bit me in some of his fits of drunkenness, he had never before struck me so cruel and cold-blooded a blow. I felt as I shall never forget. I think an American woman does not easily forgive a blow like that. At all events, I remember I said to him without raising my voice, "I shall never be able to forgive you such an outrage."

From that time I took an entirely different course with him when in one of these furies. I had shed a great many tears under his cruelty, had tried to reason with him, had tried entreaties and persuasions. After this, whenever he was in one of his paroxysms—as he himself called them—I never moved or spoke, but, keeping perfectly self-controlled as far as I could, I sat quiet, always keeping my eye on him because I always fancied as long as I looked steadily at him he would not do me any mortal violence. And I believe now as I believed then, that my life has been saved by this silence and self-control. Sometimes he said, "Your d——d silence irritates me more than if you talked," but I was sure my course was the best.

In these furies he would often seize and break anything which was at hand—lamps, glasses, mirrors, and sometimes the heavier furniture of the room. Often he would rise from bed in these incontrollable attacks of passion tearing away all the bedclothing, tearing in shreds his own night clothing, throwing anything he could find which was breakable crashing about the unlighted room, till it seemed to me as if there could be no Pandemonium worse than that in which I lived.

And all this he would do without explanation or even a pretext for complaint against me, and when I knew no more what excited his frenzy than a babe unborn. Sometimes he would keep up this conduct and this abuse for hours, and would then burst into tears, beg my pardon, say I was the best woman who ever lived, and then go to sleep exhausted. I never told him after this winter that I could

forgive or could love him, although he sometimes implored me to do
so, because I could not say so with truth. Generally I told him I pitied
him, which was true.

At the time he struck me this severe blow in 1862, I told Mrs. John
F. Cleveland, the sister of Horace Greeley. I had met her through
friends and she had been very kind to me in my dramatic readings.
I did not tell her all, nor the worst, but I told her how he had struck
me, principally because I was engaged to read at the house of some
friends of hers an evening or two after, and I feared she would notice
the mark on my face. She was the only person to whom I ever spoke
of Mr. McFarland (otherwise than in a manner becoming for a wife
to speak of a husband) till the Winter of 1867. And I devoted all my
woman's skill and tact in hiding his conduct from casual observers at
our boarding-houses or elsewhere. One time Mr. McFarland came
home so bruised and bleeding from some street broil—a not uncom-
mon occurrence on his part—that I had to keep him in his room for
more than a week, carrying his meals to him myself, that his disgrace
might not be seen and commented on by the household where we
boarded.

In the Spring of 1863, I went to see Horace Greeley in company
with Mrs. Cleveland, and also to see several other persons, to get
influence for Mr. McFarland. In doing so I acted under Mr. McFarland's orders, and against my own feelings, which always revolted at
the idea of seeking office for him, though he never scrupled to use
my efforts. Through these efforts, Mr. McFarland got appointed to
a position in the office of one of the Provost-Marshals under the
Enrollment Act.

McFarland's appointment to the enrollment office was indeed the
result of political intervention. This was a time when, even more
than now, connections and loyalties were more important than abilities in gaining appointments. Greeley and Samuel Sinclair, the publisher of the *Tribune,* both made appeals on McFarland's behalf to the
then speaker of the house, Schuyler Colfax. Abby had been instrumental in winning the favor of Greeley. She had also helped with

Sinclair, whose wife Charlotte was Abby's friend and benefactor. But Abby herself had an even larger role in influencing Colfax.

"I had met Mr. McFarland and his wife in the Winter of 1862–1863," Speaker Colfax explained. "It was at a party at Mrs. Pond's in New-York. I remember it well because I had fallen into a conversation with two ladies regarding the Southern rebellion and the prospects of its suppression. They insisted that the insurgents would not be overcome. I contended that they would be. This was a time, you may recall, when Northern spirits were low and all of us loyal to President Lincoln were struggling against this pessimistic attitude. I was then serving as a Representative in Washington, and had just been elected Speaker. The conversation became so pointed as to be embarrassing to me, especially as the argument was with ladies. Mrs. McFarland stood nearby listening to the discussion, and soon participated in it very warmly on the same side as I was arguing. In a few moments, her intervention enabled me to retire from this debate, to my relief.

"I recalled this when, a few months later, Mr. McFarland was proposed as a candidate for the position of Provost-Marshal to administer the new military draft. I understood that McFarland was a Republican and earnestly on the side of the Government, as well as being financially needy, so I discussed the matter personally with Secretary of War Stanton several times. But he decided that, as the Republican Senators from New-York had proposed other candidates, he could not appoint McFarland. However, Stanton said there was much less competition for the position of Commissionership of Enrollment in New York, at a salary not much lower, and I consented to take that position for him. McFarland came to Washington and thanked me personally on behalf of himself and his wife, and invited me to call on them in New-York, which, however, I never found time to do."

About the time that McFarland got his position in the enrollment office, Abby went home to her parents' briefly with Percy, who was ill. She believed, as did so many, that the country air was a tonic. However, McFarland summoned her back to New York, sending a peremptory demand that threatened to "burn her father's house over her head" if she did not come. She returned to the city, but convinced McFarland to bring her father to New York as well, and give him a job in the office, so she might have some family support. Abby was in the city only a few weeks when a physician said Percy would die if he were not sent back to the country. McFarland relented, and Abby again returned to New Hampshire, staying several months this time. She continued her efforts to remain on good terms with her husband.

Abby to *Daniel*
MANCHESTER, OCTOBER 9, 1863 •

My Dear Husband -

I am very sorry to hear your throat is sore. I presume you will ridicule my prescription, but I will tell you what you had better do. Get some raspberry leaves, and steep them, then sweeten well with sugar. You could get a little tin cup and steep them on the gas. You must gargle your throat and swallow some, and you must use it constantly several days. Now, have the goodness to write me if you do this, won't you dear?

You are wrong, dear, in supposing that it is a matter of indifference to me that you are coming on. That is a real cruel remark. Don't you think so? The reason I didn't say more about it was because I knew it takes time to get a furlough, and you had not begun to get one, and I thought you merely said it to satisfy me. I send my love and many invitations to come.

Have you any objection to my taking a part in some charades the Unitarians are getting up? Doctor Custus's people and Ruth are the chief ones, and they are going to have them at the sewing circle rooms. The word is Falstaff.

With oceans of love and one million of kisses from,
Your affectionate wife,

Abby

Abby to *Daniel*

MANCHESTER, OCT. 13, 1863 •

My Dear Husband -

I went down to the office this morning confidently expecting a letter from you, and was greatly disappointed at receiving none. I hope you have not sent one with an enclosure which has been lost—that is, money in it. I was obliged to walk the mile and a half down yesterday, which was no small amount of trouble, for they were using old Tom. But I walked as fast as he could have gone, which isn't saying much.

I understand you do not read the Atlantic Monthly. Probably you are too busy to read any thing except Herbert Spencer and other such hard books. You know you used to read me some of his works but I couldn't understand them much at first; but when you used to tell me what you had read in the form of a lecture, I could understand it better and remember it longer.

Percy, every one thinks, looks healthier than ever before. His short hair makes him look better; that is, more boy-like and robust. He looks like you almost altogether; doesn't he, dear? I think he will make a bigger man than you. I don't mean bigger in the intellectual sense, but taller. Dear little fellow, his heart is as tender as papa's, and he is your own boy. He is so brisk and he does know so much about words and their meanings. Last night, after I undressed him, he asked me to let him tell me some stories. He recited "Twinkle, twinkle, little star," and, when he repeated the last line, "Like a traveller in the dark," he asked, "What is a traveller?" I explained it to him and said, "When you and I go to New York, we are travellers." "Well," he said, "whenever we stay at home we are untravellers." Wasn't that quite a knowing remark in philosophy?

Do you think there might be another draft riot in New York, dear? I should have been afraid to be there that week last July.

I did feel dreadfully, awfully afraid then that you could have been shot by those Irishmen. They wouldn't shoot you if they knew you were one; but they never would know it from your accent or appearance. You couldn't shoot more than a goosie, could you darling? But I know you would be brave—that is in case of an emergency. You never had much taste for manly sports; for I remember you told me once, when the senior class of Dartmouth went to the White Mountains on a geological tour, they all fished and caught trout but you, and you said you had no pleasure in catching those little things enjoying themselves in the beautiful shining water. It is just like you, and Shelley, too. I thought it was real funny.

Everyone sends much love, and is very anxious to see you. Do, do come soon, won't you. Percy talks a great deal about his dear papa.

Your affectionate,
Abby

Abby was right to be concerned about the dangers of another riot by a mob opposed to the new military draft. The first four-day melee, from July 13th to 16th, had left hundreds dead, including the chief of police, and thousands wounded. Negroes, whom the rabble saw as having caused the war, were one special target, and the rioters showed them no mercy. Even the Colored Orphan Asylum was burned to the ground. The provost marshal's offices—the draft bureaus—were also singled out, and three were torched. Who knew what might happen to the city's commissioner of enrollment and his family the next time?

Nonetheless, in November Abby came back to New York. The family took a room for a few weeks on Varick Street, then moved, in January, to 16 Lamartine Place, off West Twenty-ninth Street. From the time McFarland got his place in the enrollment office in the spring of 1863, until the fall of 1864, Abby went home to her parents three times, sometimes on her own accord and sometimes at her husband's urging, and they lived in eight different boarding houses. It seemed to Abby that if, for one moment, she was peaceful in the possession of a shelter, McFarland's habits or his dissatisfied temper drove him to change.

She did not want to complain during these years. She knew her hardship was nothing compared to that of those on the battlefield. But she did not think she could go on living in such turmoil.

vii

Albert Escapes

1863 – 1865

 Albert leapt from the deck of the blazing ship and grabbed a loose hay bale for a raft. For a few moments, he thought he might still be able to drift on to General Grant. But the rebel forces plucked him from the water, and soon he and his fellow journalists (Junius and Richard Colburn of the *World*) were in a Vicksburg prison camp. They remained full of enough bravado to contemplate their futures with equanimity. The common practice was to "parole" noncombatants, that is, to obtain from them a solemn pledge not to take up arms or engage in other soldierly duty, and then to exchange them for captured Southern noncombatants.

As expected, the reporters were visited by a Confederate major in charge of prisoner exchange, who had them execute parole pledges. But rather than release them straight away, he explained that the nearby prisoner exchange point at New Orleans was inaccessible because of hostilities. Instead they would have to be transported clear across the Confederacy, to Virginia, where a truce-boat could pick them up. They were duly shipped and, being trusting souls, let slip many an opportunity for escape during the two week journey on slow Southern trains, believing that they were on their way to freedom.

For Colburn, this trust was well founded. He was promptly exchanged. But for Albert and Junius it was a different story. Confederate animosity to the *Tribune,* which Albert had experienced before when he was acting as a secret agent, took control of their fates. Not even the personal intervention of the President and the secretary of war could get them freed.

PRESIDENT ABRAHAM LINCOLN,
Telegram to Colonel William H. Ludlow, United States Commissioner of [Prisoner] Exchange, Fortress Monroe, Virginia

JUNE 1, 1863 •

RICHARDSON AND BROWNE, CORRESPONDENTS OF THE TRIB-

UNE CAPTURED AT VICKSBURG, ARE DETAINED BY THE

CONFEDERATES. PLEASE ASCERTAIN WHY THEY ARE DETAINED

AND GET THEM OFF IF YOU CAN.

SECRETARY OF WAR EDWIN M. STANTON,
Telegram to Colonel Ludlow

JUNE 29, 1863 •

YOU WILL EXERT YOURSELF TO PROCURE THE RELEASE OF

RICHARDSON AND BROWNE, TRIBUNE REPORTERS, CAPTURED

AT VICKSBURG. BROWNE'S HEALTH IS SAID TO BE FAILING. IF

THEY ARE HELD AS HOSTAGES OR FOR ANY SPECIAL REASON,

ASCERTAIN AND REPORT IT.

COLONEL WILLIAM H. LUDLOW,
Telegram to Secretary of War Stanton
JUNE 29, 1863 •

I AM MAKING EVERY EFFORT FOR RELEASE OF RICHARDSON

AND BROWNE. MY FIRST APPLICATION WAS REFUSED PEREMP-

TORILY. I HAVE MADE ANOTHER, THE RESULT OF WHICH I

SHALL KNOW AND REPORT TO YOU ON THE RETURN OF THE

FLAG-OF-TRUCE BOAT FROM CITY POINT ON THURSDAY. THEY

ARE HELD IN RETALIATION FOR CITIZENS ARRESTED AND HELD

BY US. THIS IS THE ASSIGNED REASON. THE REAL REASON I

BELIEVE IS THAT THEY ARE CONNECTED WITH THE TRIBUNE

AND ARE HELD TO ANNOY. THE ANTAGONISM OF THE CONFED-

ERATES TO THAT NEWSPAPER IS WELL-KNOWN, AND DIFFI-

CULT TO OVERCOME.

The *Tribune* correspondents were placed in Richmond's Libby Prison for four months, then moved to the nearby, more fearsomely named, Castle Thunder for another five months. Albert's second daughter, Mary Louisa, was born while he was there. Then, in February 1864, they were transported to a newly commissioned prison in a converted cotton mill, at Salisbury, in the western part of North Carolina. All appeals for their release continued unheeded.

The sustained interest expressed in these miserable prisoners by Northerners in high places probably reenforced the Southern will to hold them.

For someone like Albert, for whom action and activity was everything, the enforced idleness of prison while great events transpired outside was a burdensome cross. "Ah, Dick," he wrote to his more fortunate companion Colburn, "it is a heavy hand that has been laid on me." Later he explained, "It is not hunger or cold, sickness or death, which makes prison life so hard to bear, it is the utter idleness, emptiness, aimlessness of such life. It is being, through all the long hours of each day and night—for weeks, months, years, if one lives so long—absolutely without employment, mental or physical—with nothing to fill the vacant mind, which always becomes morbid and turns inward to prey upon itself."

In the tenth month of his imprisonment, Albert's misery was compounded by terrible news from his brother Charles. Lou, whom he had not seen in over a year, had died on March 4. "I am greatly overwhelmed with grief," Charles wrote. "She was in full strength ten days ago. She was taken ill with measles, and congestion of the brain followed. She suffered very greatly during her sickness and was not fully rational at all from the time when the disease first assumed a serious look so that she spoke no parting word to anyone and could leave none for her husband."

"With the death of my wife, hope—the one thing that buoys up the prisoner—is gone," Albert wrote. "That picture of home which had looked before as heaven looks to the enthusiastic devotee, is forever darkened. If the otherwise glad hour of my release should ever come, no warmth of welcome, no greeting of friendship, no rejoicing of affection, could ever replace for me the infinite value of the love I have lost."

Leander was taken in by Charles and Charles's wife Jennie, who had always been close to Albert. The younger children, Maude, little Albert, and infant Mary Louisa, were parceled out to the rest of the family in Massachusetts. Albert tried to keep up with their welfare through correspondence. But then, for no apparent reason, mail from the North suddenly stopped. From early May 1864, a few weeks after

Albert learned of Lou's death, until late November, Albert received no word from home. He kept trying, just to let them know he was all right. "I still go through the <u>form</u> of sending occasional letters," he wrote Charles on November 17th. "We get no letters whatever from home; but we think none the less about the dear ones who are far away on that account. With my warmest love to Leander & Maude, & to all."

Finally, on November 19th, he received a month-old letter from his brother. The news was not good. Leander was no longer with Charles, having been sent for unexplained reasons to live outside the family. Even worse, his baby daughter had died on August 29th, just before her first birthday. Albert had never seen her.

Albert to *Charles Richardson*

MILITARY PRISON, SALISBURY, N.C.,
MONDAY NIGHT, NOVEMBER 21, 1864 •

My dear Brother:-

I write to let you know that after an interval of six months I have again heard directly from you. I had supposed that Le was still with you. Why was the change made? I have had no particulars whatever of baby's sickness and death. How is Maude? Remember I have had no word of her or Le for six months. I trust that Le, even though among strangers, is where special attention is paid to his advancement in study; but above all, where he receives sympathy & affection. I want <u>particulars</u> about him.

> Affectionately your Brother,
> *Albert D. Richardson*

Providence, which had seen Albert through life to Vicksburg, seemed now to be deserting him on all fronts. In October 1864, his seventeenth month of imprisonment, conditions at the Salisbury garrison, which had been unpleasant and tedious, but tolerable, when it held six hundred inmates, suddenly degenerated. Nearly ten thousand prisoners of war were abruptly added to its population. The rebels were now in retreat before the devastating forces of Sheridan in the Shenandoah Valley and Sherman in Georgia, and striving to withstand Grant's siege of Petersburg, only twenty-five miles from their capital at Richmond. The Confederacy's resources were stretched past the breaking point. They could not release captured prisoners, who would have augmented their enemy, but they could barely do more than enclose them. The Salisbury Prison was converted into a horrifying corral of suffering and death.

Junius attempted to paint a word picture of the scene: "Imagine nine or ten thousand scantily clad, emaciated, woe-begone soldiers—unnamed heroes, who had battled for our sacred cause on twenty blood-drenched fields—in an enclosure of five or six acres, half of them without other shelter than holes they have dug in the earth, or under the small buildings employed as hospitals.

"The weather is cold; perhaps a chilly rain is falling, or the ground is covered with snow. There are the soldiers—hundreds of them with naked feet, and only light blouses or shirts, hungry, feeble, despairing of the Present and hopeless of the Future—huddling over a small and smokey fire of green wood, in a crowded tent, whose very atmosphere is poisonous; or standing shivering against the outside of the chimneys of the squalid hospitals, hoping to warm their blood a little from the partially heated bricks; or drawn up in their narrow caves, inhaling the curling emanations of the burning pine, and striving to shelter themselves from the bitter wind; or begging, with pallid and trembling lips, for shelter at the door of those lazar-houses where their companions in arms are lying in dirt, distress, and despair, breathing out their lives at the rate of thirty and forty a day. At any hour one may see men bearing across the inclosure the pallid and wasted figure of a soldier, whom the Rebels had starved or frozen to death with malice prepense.

"The Rebels, apparently not content with the ravages of disease, almost entirely superinduced by starvation and cold, fire upon wretched prisoners whenever the humor seizes them, killing and wounding them without reason or pretext. No one is safe."

SALISBURY MILITARY PRISON, NOVEMBER 1, 1864
BY A.D.R.

By appointment of the prison authorities, Browne and I, and another imprisoned newspaperman (William Davis of the Cincinnati Gazette), were placed in charge of all the hospitals, nine in number, inside the garrison. The scenes which constantly surrounded us were enough to shake the firmest nerves. We could accomplish very little—hardly more than to give a cup of cold water and to see that the patients were treated with sympathy and kindness. More than half the time they were compelled to lie huddled upon the cold, naked, filthy floors, without even the degree of warmth and cleanliness usually afforded to brutes. The wasted forms and sad pleading eyes of those sufferers, waiting wearily for the tide of life to ebb away—without the commonest comforts, without one word of sympathy, one tear of affection—will never cease to haunt me.

At all hours of the day and night, on every side, we heard the terrible hack! hack! hack! in whose pneumonic tones every prisoner seemed to be coughing his life away. It was the most fearful sound in that fearful place. The last scene of all was the dead-cart, with its rigid forms piled upon each other like logs—the arms swinging,

INTERIOR VIEW OF A HOSPITAL IN THE SALISBURY PRISON.

the white ghastly faces staring with dropped jaws and stony eyes, while it rattled along carrying its precious freight just outside the walls, to be thrown in a mass into trenches, and covered with a little earth.

No song, no athletic game, few sounds of laughter broke the silence of the garrison. It was a Hall of Eblis—devoid of its gold-besprinkled pavements, crystal vases and dazzling saloons; but with all its oppressive silence, livid lips, sunken eyes, and ghastly figures, at whose hearts the consuming fire was never quenched.

"That hope deferred which maketh the heart sick" began to tell seriously upon our mental health. We grew morbid and bitter and were often upon the verge of quarreling among ourselves. I remember even feeling a pang of jealousy and indignation at an account of some enjoyment and hilarity among my friends at home.

Our prison was like the tomb. No voice from the North entered its gloomy portal. Believing we had been unjustly neglected by our own government, wondering if we had indeed been forsaken by God and man, we seemed to lose all human interest, and to care little whether we lived or died. But I suppose a lurking, unconscious hope still buoyed us up.

The hope was escape. We were constantly trying to escape. During the last fifteen months of our imprisonment, I think there was no day when we had not some plan which we hoped soon to put into execution. We were always talking and theorizing about the subject. I should hardly dare to estimate the combined length of tunnels in which we were concerned; they were always discovered, usually on the eve of completion.

Junius often declared that they should never escape by tunnel, unless they constructed an underground road to Knoxville—two hundred miles away. Even if they got past the prison walls, the chance of reaching their lines seemed almost hopeless. They were in the heart of the Confederacy. During the ten months they spent in Salisbury, at least seventy persons escaped; but nearly all were brought back. Most of the others were unfortunate enough, or fortunate enough, to be shot in the mountains. Only five had reached the North.

"To walk the same distance in Ohio or Massachusetts," Junius said, "where we could travel by daylight upon public thoroughfares, stop at each village for rest and refreshments, and sleep in warm beds every night, we should have considered a severe hardship. Think of this terrible tramp of two hundred miles, by night, in mid-winter, over two ranges of mountains, creeping stealthily through the enemy's country, weak, hungry, shelterless! Could any of us live to accomplish it?"

SALISBURY MILITARY PRISON, DECEMBER 18, 1864
BY A.D.R.

In November, as winter came on and conditions worsened, we were befriended by a Confederate officer who had newly joined the staff of the garrison. Lieutenant John R. Welborn belonged to a secret organization known as the Sons of America, instituted expressly to assist Union men in escaping to the North. At our first stolen interview he said, "You shall be out very soon, at all hazards."

Browne and William Davis, by virtue of their hospital responsibilities, had been given passes to the outer, less guarded part of the enclosure. I was trying to obtain a similar permit when we learned, on December 18, that the prison Commandant was to be replaced the next day with a much stricter military man. We knew this new man might revoke the passes altogether. Not a moment was to be lost, and we determined to escape that very night.

I engaged several prisoners, without informing them for what purpose, in copying from hospital books the names of the dead. I felt that, to relieve friends at home, we ought to make an effort to carry through this information, as long as there was the slightest possibility of success. The list was appalling. It comprised over fourteen hundred prisoners deceased within sixty days, and showed that they were now dying at the rate of thirteen per cent. a month. It was a fearful revelation of the work which cold and starvation had done.

Lieutenant Welborn was on duty that day. We made him privy to our plan. We proposed to hide ourselves in the outer enclosure. Then, at midnight, we would wrap ourselves in gray blankets, slouch our hats down over eyes, and pass through the outer enclosure as Rebel soldiers when Welborn relieved the guard.

That evening, half an hour before dark (the latest moment at which the inner guards could be passed, even by authorized persons), Messrs. Browne and Davis went outside, as if to order their medical supplies for the sick prisoners. As they passed in and out a dozen times a day, and their faces were quite familiar to the sentinels, they were not compelled to show their passes, and Browne left his behind with me.

A few minutes later, taking a long box filled with bottles in which the medicines were usually brought, and giving it to a little lad who assisted me in my hospital duties, I started to follow them.

As if in great haste, we walked rapidly toward the fence, while, leaning against trees or standing in the hospital doors, half a dozen friends looked on to see how the plan worked. When we reached the gate, I took the box from the boy, and said to him, of course for the benefit of the sentinel:

"I am going outside to get these bottles filled. I shall be back in about fifteen minutes, and want you to remain right here, to take them and distribute them among the hospitals. Do not go away now."

The lad, understanding the matter perfectly, replied, "Yes, sir," and I attempted to pass the sentinel by mere assurance.

I had learned long before how far a man may go, even in captivity, by sheer, native impudence—by moving straight on, without hesitation, with a confident look, just as if he had a right to go, and no one had any right to question him. I think I could have done it on this occasion, but for the fact that it had been tried successfully twice or thrice, and the guards severely punished. The sentinel stopped me with his musket, demanding:

"Have you a pass, sir?"

"Certainly, I have a pass," I replied, with all the indignation I could assume. "Have you not seen it often enough to know by this time?"

Apparently a little confounded, he replied, modestly:

"Probably I have; but they are very strict with us, and I was not quite sure."

I gave to him the genuine pass belonging to Browne. The sentinel looked at it closely, and spelled it out slowly, then refolded and returned it to me, saying:

"That pass is all right. I know Captain Fuqua's handwriting. Go on sir; excuse me for detaining you."

I thought him excusable under the circumstances, and walked out. My great fear was that, during the time which must elapse before I could go outside the garrison, I might encounter some Rebel officer or attaché who knew me.

Before I had taken ten steps, I saw, sauntering to and fro on the piazza of the head-quarters building, a deserter from our service, named Davidson, who recognized and bowed to me. I thought he would not betray me, but was still fearful of it. I went on, and a few yards farther, coming toward me in that narrow lane, where it was impossible to avoid him, was the one Rebel officer who knew me better than any other, and who frequently came into my quarters— Lieutenant Stockton, the Post-Adjutant. Observing him at a distance, I thought I recognized in him that old ill-fortune which had so long and steadfastly baffled us.

When we met, I bade Stockton good-evening, and talked for a few minutes upon the weather, or some other subject in which I did not feel any very profound interest. Then he passed into head-quarters, and I went on. Yet a few yards farther, I encountered a third Rebel, named Smith, who knew me well, and whose quarters, inside the garrison, were within fifty feet of my own. There were not half a dozen Confederates about the prison who were familiar with me; but it seemed as if at this moment they were coming together in a grand convention.

I laid down my box of medicines behind a door, and sought shelter in a little outbuilding. While I remained there, waiting for the blessed darkness, I constantly expected to see a sergeant, with a file of soldiers, come to take me back into the yard; but none came. It was rare good fortune. Stockton, Smith and Davidson, all knew, if they had their wits about them, that I had no more right there than in the village itself.

At dark, my three friends joined me. We went through the outer gate, in full view of a sentinel, who supposed we were Rebel surgeons or nurses. And then, on that rainy Sunday night, for the first time in twenty months, we found ourselves walking freely in a public street, without a Rebel bayonet before or behind us!

The evening was murky, chilly, and rainy. But the air that greeted them as they stepped outside the prison walls was suddenly fresher and cleaner than any they had inhaled in months. "The old worn-out feeling, the inertia, the sense of suppression, seemed to fall from me as a cast-off garment," Junius recalled, "and I believed I could walk to the ends of the Earth, if I could but find the sweet goddess of Liberty—dearest and best of women—at the end of my long, long journeying."

But it was the dead of winter. They were sick and weak from the harsh prison conditions, dressed only in ragged clothing remnants, and barely shod. The escape route was to the west, across the Blue Ridge and Great Smoky mountains, the highest peaks east of the Mississippi. They knew it would be difficult, but the journey proved nearly twice as long and infinitely more severe than even they had conceived. Albert, Junius, and their compatriots spent weeks on the road. Their shelter was a barn if they were lucky or the open woods if not. Their food was the meager fare that the war-ravaged region could offer.

They did have help. Luke Blackmer, a sympathetic local attorney, put them up in his barn, only a quarter mile from the prison, the night of their escape and all the next day. This threw the search parties off their trail; they were looking miles away when their prey was barely outside town. As they passed through the countryside, black field-slaves were their source of refuge. In the mountains, there were many white Northern sympathizers who helped them, sometimes so many that they could walk down the open road in daylight. For the final, most arduous and most dangerous part of the trek, they were guided by Dan Ellis, a fearless and resourceful Tennessee woodsman who won deserved fame for his heroism in leading out escapees. Albert extolled the virtues of Captain Ellis, and he, in turn, contributed to the legend of Albert. "He attracted my highest regard with a sort of magnetic enchantment which was entirely irresistible," Ellis wrote in a post-war book on his adventures. "Whenever I gazed into his intelligent face, the bright beam of intellect which sparkled in his eyes seemed to say, 'I once dwelt in Arcadia.' "

It seemed that Albert's luck had returned. Whenever things were the most dismal, whenever it seemed that they had no chance, some savior appeared. On one dramatic night, when a force of rebel Home Guard was closing in, a teenage girl on horseback led them to safety. What a tale Junius spun around that event! It inspired a popular "Song for the 'Nameless Heroine'," which contributed to the fame of the intrepid escapees.

> *Weary and hungry, and fainting and sore,*
> *Fiends on the track of them,*
> *Fiends at the back of them,*
> *Fiends all around, but an angel before.*

Albert and his comrades could never have made it through without support from others. But for the most part they simply struggled along, always driven by a greater fear of what lay behind than ahead. And the thought of home.

Strawberry Plains, Tennessee, January 14, 1865
by a.d.r.

Our journey—originally estimated at two hundred miles—had grown, in view of our devious windings to three hundred and forty miles by our moderate estimate. At ten o'clock on the morning of our twenty-seventh day, came our great deliverance. It was at Strawberry Plains, fifteen miles east of Knoxville. Here—after a final march of seven miles, in which our heavy feet and aching limbs grew wonderfully light and agile—in silence, with bowed heads, with full hearts and with wet eyes, we saluted the Old Flag.

Remembering his capture, and his Tennyson, Richardson immediately telegraphed the *Tribune:*

> *Out of the jaws of Death;*
> *out of the mouth of Hell.*

viii

After the War : Abby

1864 – 1866

 While the war continued, McFarland at least had a regular income from his government position to support his family, which had now grown to four. A second son, Danny, had been born in May 1864, while Abby was at her parents' house. The new mother did not look forward to struggling with two children, including an infant, and McFarland's temper in a boarding-house room. But McFarland promised to find something outside the city.

Abby to *Daniel*

MANCHESTER, JUNE 1, 1864 •

My Dear Husband -

I hope to get away next week and return to New York. I hope in looking for a boarding house in the country you will get high ground; besides mosquitoes, which are so thick on low land, there is always fog and miasma. Baby is going to be too bright and active to lie on the bed and sleep.

Percy is homesick for you. He ate breakfast with us this morning and he said, "I used to get good things at my papa's office. I use to get shrimps and cream cakes and pies. Papa used to leave me all alone while he went and brought them." He wants to see you very much. I shall meet you in Boston shan't I dear? I think I shall take the girl on with me that Sarah Gould spoke about.

You will find baby very much prettier. We have not got any name for him yet. You named both Percy and darling little Jessie, and we all thought you might name baby also. We all suggested that you might call him after yourself, and we might give him a middle name. Poor little Percy appears as if he felt cast off since baby was born. When we spoke of calling him Daniel, Percy said, "I ought to have had papa's name, because I am the oldest."

Till I see you, I am your loving wife,

Abby

McFarland could not find a country boarding house. But Abby returned to New York anyhow, and found critical support from new friends. She had met Charlotte Sinclair at one of the readings arranged by Mrs. Cleveland. The two women took to each other quickly, and Charlotte, who was dismayed at Abby's domestic situation, tried to help her in discreet ways. The well-connected Mrs. Sinclair had helped influence Speaker Colfax on McFarland's behalf. She also arranged a paid reading for Abby in one of the parlors of her house, and solicited ticket purchases from her friends. In the fall of 1864 she came through with the greatest favor—a temporary solution to Abby's housing problem. Abby could stay the winter, rent-free, in the Sinclair's farm house in Croton, a rural town up the Hudson within commuting distance of the city by train.

The family lived in Croton all winter. In the spring, when the Sinclairs wanted to make use of their country house, Abby rented a cottage nearby, and stayed through the summer. "Here," she recalls, "Mr. McFarland's conduct was more endurable, for he was away nearly all day, and the quiet and pleasantness of the country when he came there, I fancied had a good effect on him."

Abby was not idle while at Croton. She tried her hand at writing.

This was the profession she most respected, and she dreamed of a career with her pen that might be more satisfying and more financially rewarding than her readings. A respected Boston firm, Hurd and Houghton, accepted her efforts and agreed to publish *Percy's Year of Rhymes*, which she had written over the summer.

Her publishing contract was heartening, but this book of poems would not produce much income, and the end of the war that spring meant the end of McFarland's employment. By the fall, the family was back to basics in trying to support itself. Abby began making plans to resume her readings, which she had not been able to do while living in Croton. This displeased McFarland. When he had envisioned his wife as a theatrical star under his careful tutelage, he had been enthusiastic about her performing. But Abby's readings were not stardom. They were a way of eking out a living, and everyone knew that she did them only because her husband could not support her. So he swore at, but he did not stop, her.

ABBY, FROM HER AFFIDAVIT

I returned from Croton to New-York, to occupy some small rooms over a stable in Thirty-Sixth-st., which Mr. McFarland had hired. All the Fall and Winter of '65 I made a desperate struggle for life. I had my two babies—the youngest just weaned; I had this man half of the time coming home intoxicated, and I had nothing but my woman's heart and hands to look to for support. I gave all the readings I could. I did all my own housework when at home. I took faithful care of my children, but I often sank into such utter despondency of heart as only God knows and can pity, when he sees the poor human soul sinking under it.

Mrs. Sinclair knew of my troubles and tried to help in any way she could. In April 1866, she and some other friends arranged a reading at Steinway's Rooms, on Fourteenth-st.

Abby's supporters booked the hall and advertised the reading in the newspapers. Mrs. Sinclair thought it was a wonderful performance. Abby read from Spenser's "The Fairy Queen," and *Macbeth;* and she recited Whittier's "Barbara Frietchie," and Robert Browning's "How they Brought the Good News from Ghent to Aix." The program, titled "The Poets of Two Centuries," included works by other living poets—Tennyson and Longfellow—and those of the sixteenth century.

They had hoped to attract a large audience. The hall was well filled, with almost two hundred attending, but it was not a commercial success. Abby's friends had bought most of the tickets themselves. They did not tell Abby this, however, and were able to give her $150 as proceeds of the evening.

ABBY, FROM HER AFFIDAVIT

Mr. McFarland abused me in his usual violent way for giving this public reading. He argued that it disgraced him as a gentleman in the eyes of the public for his wife to read in a city where he had acquaintances. He made this an excuse for getting grossly intoxicated on the evening of the reading. He collected the whole receipts, and gave me only $25 to pay my fare and the children's to my father, who had now moved back to Massachusetts, reserving the rest for his own uses.

In May, Mr. McFarland came on to my father's, bringing with him $1,000 in money. He had got this money from a wealthy owner of oil lands in Pennsylvania, residing in New York City (whose name he did not like to mention), by threatening to expose him for some irregularity in paying his income tax. He also told me he had "several other men under his thumb in the same way." The manner of getting this money was inexpressibly shocking to me, and I told him so, and we quarreled over what he was going to do with it and how we were going to sustain ourselves over the fall and winter. He answered me in his usual brutal manner, and I said no more about it.

It was agreed, however, that I should go for the summer to a small farm-house at Shelburne in the White Mountains, and that he should pay the board there for myself and the children.

Abby knew that Mrs. Oliver Johnson was also going to be spending the summer at Shelburne and could provide some company. Mary Ann Johnson was an older woman, about the age of Abby's mother. Her husband was then editor of the *New York Independent,* a liberal weekly. He had been an associate of the great abolitionist William Lloyd Garrison, and has been described as "the wheelhorse of every humanitarian movement for almost half a century." He was as active a supporter of women's rights as he had been of abolition. Mary Ann was a woman to be reckoned with. At one time she was assistant matron of Sing Sing female state prison, and she was known for her lectures to women on anatomy and physiology.

Abby enjoyed her summer at Shelburne. McFarland's niece, Mary, the daughter of his brother, Owen, also came to stay with her and help with the children. The northern New Hampshire farming village was close by the line of the Grand Trunk Railway from Portland to Montreal. It had acquired a modest reputation as a bucolic resort, thanks in part to Josh Billings's favorable comments in the New York papers. Accommodations were in farm houses or in small converted homes, the largest of which accommodated only thirty-five guests. There was not much in the way of diversion, and the black flies could be overwhelming. But compared to living in fetid New York with McFarland it was heaven. Abby felt some guilt at the expense, but rationalized that the cost—$210 for board and washing for the entire summer—was far cheaper than a boarding house in the city.

In September, McFarland came up to the White Mountains himself. He told her that, as usual, he was out of money. But, also as usual, he had a scheme. He had acquired rights to a patent-gas invention that would make his fortune. In the meantime, he needed a little cash. He sent Abby to Boston, to the offices of her publishers, to see about an advance on *Percy's Year of Rhymes,* which was due out that fall. She got fifty dollars, of which McFarland took half. With the other half, he sent Abby and his niece to stay with his brother in Newark.

But Abby could not be concerned about McFarland's petty manipulations now. She had many talks with Mary Ann Johnson on the long, quiet days at Shelburne, and the accomplished older woman had emboldened the young twenty-seven-year-old to pursue a career more actively. For the fall of 1866, Abby was excited about a new prospect that had come her way over the summer, thanks to the assistance of another new friend, Lu Calhoun.

Lucia Isabella Gilbert Calhoun was a notorious woman at a time when female success in the masculine world unavoidably meant notoriety. When the war ended in 1865, Sidney Howard Gay of the *Tribune* was searching for a correspondent to attend the grand ball celebrating the end of the war. He had the idea it should be someone who might have a different view of the festivities than usually presented, someone who might have a ladies' perspective. A mutual friend showed him samples of daily letters that Lucia Gilbert (then in her midtwenties) had written to her brother in the army. Gay was impressed. Young Miss Gilbert had the ability to go on about virtually anything, making the most mundane event seem like a coronation at Versailles. Gay gave her pen a chance on the grand ball and was amply repaid. For her next assignment, as a test, he asked her for an exposé of poor conditions in New York slaughterhouses. When she produced a report just as vivid as that of the ball, this loquaciously talented young woman became a permanent correspondent. She began to write regularly for the *Tribune,* becoming, it is said, the first American woman to so occupy the editorial pages of a major metropolitan daily newspaper.

L. G. Calhoun had thus established her career as a writer and editorialist, appearing in Oliver Johnson's *Independent* and other papers as well as the *Tribune,* by the time she met Abby in 1866. But the two women were the same age and had similar interests. Their friendship blossomed. Lu assumed the role of wiser sister, advising Abby on how to make a life for herself. As L. G. Calhoun, she had proved that women could succeed, and she thought that Abby could do the same, if only she were given the chance. Lu was not one to stand off when such a challenge presented itself.

Mrs. Calhoun to *Abby, in Shelburne, N.H.*

NO. 77 CLINTON PLACE, NEW YORK
SUNDAY EVENING, 24TH JUNE, 1866 •

My Dear Mrs. McFarland:

It was a good inspiration which led you to write me, and to believe that I wanted to hear from you. A dozen times since you went away I have sat down, with the express and absolute purpose of writing you, and then some dreary manuscript interposed and my interesting pen labored till it was so tired that it had no power of purpose left. Now that consumes time and patience, and exhausts the forces without building any monuments of progress.

Revising, correcting, and mending, comparing, regretting. Eminently useful, greatly easier than writing, of which I am not fond, but rather dreary. I have not written so very much since you went away. Besides my work for the Tribune, I do a certain class of book reviews for the Independent.

Beyond that I go about with hands so very full that I have seldom opportunity to take up private letters. For, as I daresay you know already, but as it is the central fact of the universe it will bear repetition, I am housekeeping! Mr. Calhoun and I attained that blissful condition, to my extreme surprise, on the 1st day of May. We heard of the house but two days before, took it, and bought one tea-kettle at once. For myself, I am most pleased.

I enjoy the freedom and largeness and hospitality of a home, and as we must live in shells through all this mortal pilgrimage, it is so much more comfortable to have them of the largest and pleasantest. But for this ignorant present, I would center myself with you in the smallest farmhouse that ever took root in a cleft of hills. You know I am a Cockney of Cockneys; know nothing of the heart and wonder of country-life; never have seen the mountains in my life save a scattered peak or two. But all through the soft spring and passionate summer an eagerness for woods and waters possesses me.

Everybody is out of town. Mrs. Ward has gone, and the Sinclairs went last week, and everybody else whom I knew had gone before, except Mr. Richardson, who has a room here, and is so delightfully agreeable and good-natured that not even this dreadful weather makes him cross, which is saying a great deal for his Christian discipline. Mr. Greeley has almost finished his book, and then he is going away. Probably to Saratoga, to trip the light fantastic toe! You know what it is like there of course—the congregation of the vulgar, and the assemblage of the snobs.

I hope that you will study toward the stage, if not for the stage, this summer. That goal seems to me so inevitable, and so desirable, if you cultivate your very great gift at all, that whenever I think of you, I wish you were in your rightful place. The Drama is the beautiful art, and you are worthy to be its prophet. My own dreams of serving it will never be more than hopes now, but whenever I see brave young feet set toward it, and thoughtful brows bent thitherward, I say, "God speed," from my inward soul.

Ever and always believe me affectionately yours,

Lu. G. Calhoun

Mrs. Calhoun to *Abby*

AUGUST 16, 1866, SUNDAY AFTERNOON •

My Beloved Friend:

It is after dinner and I am bilious. You have been very good to take so much trouble in making enquiries for me about rooms at Shelburne. I want to see you and thank you with my lips and eyes; and yet it is quite possible that I may not be able to come at all. You know we are housekeeping for the first time in three years, and the expenses are terrifying; but I knew Mr. Calhoun wanted to do it, so I thought we could manage, and when I began to receive a regular salary I resolved not to ask him for anything for my personal wants. Therefore, I have taken care of myself entirely for the last six months. But I have been away for the *Tribune* three times, and though the paper pays my traveling expenses and my board bill, still I had to dress more than I should at home; and I am forced to buy many things which I should not otherwise. Moreover, I was obliged to put all my sewing out, because I have not had time to do it, and my clothes, and dressmakers' and seamstresses' bills this summer have been over $200. Then I took one of my sisters, who was not well, to Saratoga, and that cost me almost $50; and I pay the school bills of the others, which are $90 a quarter, and altogether I have no money just now. Of course, if I were to ask Mr. Calhoun, who is the best man in the world, he would tell me to go, but I know he can't well afford to let me just now, and I don't want to break my resolve.

It will be my Birthday in a few days, you know; I shall turn twenty-eight on the 20th. This life has wings does it not? I am determined this year to do my exceeding utmost to make money. It is the one potent servant, the comforter and consoler and helper. In its uses I mean; of course, not in itself. And you—I hope your desire and purpose for the stage has not faded or been trampled out by hard hoofs of necessity. Have you had any encouragement?

Of course I know that the life is by no means an easy one. I know that I counsel you to discouragement and toil, and contact with coarse people and sights. But if I had half the confidence in my powers that I have in yours, I should have been on the stage months ago; and I know that I should not have failed; I think you have so many gifts, your beautiful voice, your changing color, your varying, soulful face, your earnestness and freshness of nature, your love for your art—and in your love for your art, and your love for your children, you have also the highest incentive. Dear child, I wish I could make your path straight and smooth to the highest success, but only that success is highest to which we make our way with pain and toil.

When you come back we will have a long talk about this

matter, and see if we cannot make one eager ambition give place to excellent doing. J. Stuart might be induced to place you on his staff at the Winter Garden. They have absolutely no lady there. That Miss Johnson is a chambermaid of the most hopeless order, and how Edwin Booth can play with her passes my understanding. Now, if ever, women of power are needed on the stage, and I believe way can be made.

When are you coming home? We must see much of each other this winter. I hope you will bring back health and strength from those far hills, and a whole harvest of freshness, to be used all winter as need calls. With the spirit of prophecy upon me, I foretell that this winter will be a crisis to us both, and I hope a long season of good work in the right direction. I am ever freely yours,

Lu. G. Calhoun

Did you ask me once what was my name? It is the pretty Italian name Lu-ci-ia. but everybody mispronounces it so I like the diminutive better. Please use it.

Mrs. Calhoun to *Abby*

SATURDAY, SEPTEMBER 1ST, 1866 •

My Dearest Child:

Do you know what is my panacea for all my woes? Mr. Richardson. Nobody is half so kind and unselfish as he; and when I am "stuck," as the newsboys say, I just tell him, and his clear, common sense and kind heart always finds a way into smooth paths again. Therefore, if he were here I should just trust him with the whole story, and send him to see J. Stuart, whom he knows very well. Alas, he left for Kansas on Wednesday, and my right hand is wanting; so I must alone do the best thing—I cannot at this moment tell what, but my inspiration will come in the course of the day. It always does. I never met

Stuart but once, when he was very courteous. He would not remember me now; but if it is the best thing for me to go and see him, I shall go. Perhaps I <u>should</u> write Mr. Gay for his assistance or at least an introduction.

Ever and always, my beloved, yours fully;

Write often,
Lu

Mrs. Calhoun to Sidney Howard Gay

SEPTEMBER 8, 1866 •

My dear friend,

Will you send me a note of introduction to Stuart of the Winter Garden? I have a dear friend who wishes to go on the stage this winter. Stuart has seen her, and thinks she has ability. But it is absolutely necessary that she should obtain a country appearance before she can hope for an appearance in New York. I want Stuart to tell me how she can obtain this country appearance. She is too frightened to see him herself, and does not know him. As I have nothing to ask for myself, I shall be much more helpful to her, than she could be to herself. This is no girl's fancy of hers. A helpless husband, and two babies make it a terrible necessity. She has very decided capacity, and much training for the stage. None, for any other vocation. If this hope fails her, she must teach, for which she is totally unfitted of temperament.

You must not, unless you think it best, tell Stuart just why I want to see him. I think I will enclose a card in the note asking him to luncheon, as it would be so much easier talking with him here than at the Theatre where, I am told, he lives. And besides, if he sees me in my own house he will not think me an assentress.

Please write such a note as will please Stuart much, and send it to me at once. My friend is coming to New York in a few days, and has set all her hopes on this bit of advice, and I am a hundred times more anxious for her than I could be for myself.

> Ever most faithful,
> L.G. *Calhoun*

Mrs. *Calhoun* to *Sidney Howard Gay*

SEPTEMBER 12, 1866 •

My dear friend,

Your note-to-Mr. Stuart, which was charming, and quite perfect came duly and was forwarded, with visiting card, and invitation to luncheon. I received a very kind reply, saying that potentates never lunched, but would be happy to visit at the appointed time. So he came, and gave me his company, during which I had become a pipe for Fortunes's finger, etc. I met him with inward trepidation and outward calm, wondering at my own daring in asking this man big with theatrical events and success, to consider the poor, little theatrical foundling I had hidden in my heart. However, I made a dash. It recalled the days of my first interviews with you, when I went into your little room with throbbing pulses, . . . O, how afraid of you I was for weeks, and weeks! . . . But to return to Mr. Stuart. He was very kind, very attentive, thanks to you—said my friend should have an opportunity to play with Booth this winter, but ordinary parts, as Gertrude, Camilia, Lady Anne, Jessica. Or, if she preferred a country engagement he would use his influence to gain her a small role. She owes her good fortune to you, for I should never have had the assurance to approach Mr. Stuart without your aid, and she would not have spoken for herself.

Mr. Richardson is ill in Omaha, Nebraska, with lung fever. I am anxious about him, but there is nothing to be done, but to wait with patience. He is a noble, honest soul, and has been the kindest friend to us.

> Ever yours,
> *Lu*

Mrs. Calhoun to *Abby*

THURSDAY, SEPTEMBER 27, 1866 •

My dear Abby:

Hurrah, my darling! All my wheels are turning the right way, and the world moves. Mr. Stuart has just moved. He answered the sacred letter I proposed you write. Booth was with him when it reached him, and he read it to that divine man, who feels interested in you. I quote the words of the potentate, and if you play such parts as the queen in Hamlet, and others, at first, you can have an engagement with the miracle here! this winter!!! under an assumed name!!! Or, if you don't want to do that, Mr. Stuart will give you an engagement in the country; but I advise here first by all means.

My darling, I could not be happier if I had discovered a gold mine. Maybe we have. Think of playing with Booth. I believe I should die of that rose in aromatic pain if such a privilege were mine. My dear, this is such a good omen. Youth, and hope, and beauty, as poor Miss Flite used to say, but there is no sad moral in this case. I hope this will reach you in Boston, but if it does not, it will be only because you will be here where I can tell you all the wire-pulling I have done.

I am so delighted. In all my prayers hereafter I shall name Mr. Stuart by name. Nobody could be kinder than he, and he wants you to come and see him as soon as you are here. And Booth! he had talked about you, and himself proposed to bring you out to see Naples and then die.

My darling, I put two loving arms about you and give you the heartiest and hopefulest blessing you ever had in your life. Come at once. If you should come on Saturday, and don't have time to come and see me, go to church—Mr. Frothingham's, Fortieth street, near sixth avenue—on Sunday morning, and sit with me, pew No. 89, and we will talk it all over afterward.

Ever devotedly,
Lu

Abby, from her affidavit

Shortly after I came to Owen McFarland's house in Newark, (where my husband had sent me after Shelburne) I went to the Winter Garden, and my engagement was made certain at a salary of $20 per week. I was going to appear with Mr. Booth!

However, I had to get away from Owen's house. He was worse, if possible, in his fits of intemperance, than Daniel. I stayed there three weeks in scenes which would baffle description, in daily and nightly fear of my life from this terrible madman, all of whose family held him in supreme fear.

I wrote to Mr. McFarland, who still remained behind in Massachusetts and New-Hampshire on his gas business, that I could not and should not stay any longer at his brother's. He came down to New-York shortly after this, borrowing money in small sums of my father to pay his expenses, and took me from his brother's to a wretched boarding-house in Amity-st. near Sixth-ave. This was October 1866. He left me at this house, with my two babies, informing

WINTER GARDEN THEATER.

me that he should probably not be back very much of the time during this winter.

McFarland was surviving on what he could cadge in loans. His latest business, which consisted of selling rights to a patent device that supposedly improved the illumination of gas lights, was, as all of his ventures, more full of promise than results. "If you can spare it, I wish you would send me about ten dollars," he wrote to his father-in-law this fall. "I have not much doubt that I shall make some kind of a negotiation yet in Manchester. Two persons have told me that they will each go $1,000 on the basis of $15,000 for rights in Manchester. The fact is that scarcely anybody knows anything about the thing. I am going to have the newspaper men see it and mention it in their local columns as an item of important news to the people of Manchester. If the big bugs don't take the thing I think I can get a number of smaller bugs to go in for it."

Daniel continued to live in the future. But Abby existed in the present, and that was worse than ever.

ABBY, FROM HER AFFIDAVIT

I was so worn out by the anxieties and the terrible weeks I spent at Newark that, by the time we moved back to New-York, I was broke down and was ill. I was at a strange boarding house, alone with my two babies. While there, Mrs. Calhoun called and found me in this condition, and coming home, she wrote a note in which she told me in the most delicate manner, that whenever I wanted money her purse was at my service. The same day Mrs. Sinclair called, and shocked at the wretched and desolate condition in which she saw me, took me and both my children to her house.

As soon as I was there and had begun to recover, Mr. McFarland came back and made his preparations to come there, too. As gently as I could I told him Mr. Sinclair's house was overfull, and if he were coming back to town I must get a place somewhere for all of us. It was then about two weeks before my engagement began at the Winter Garden. Mr. McFarland instructed me that I might get board for myself and the children but only occasional board for himself, as he should be absent about the gas business most of the time. I then engaged board in Macdougal-st., in a very respectable house, where I had a small attic-room for all my family.

As soon as I got here my health again gave way, and I was ill in bed nearly two weeks. It was only by sheer force of will that I got up from bed and dragged myself to the theater to begin my engagement. During these two weeks' illness, Mrs. Sinclair and Mrs. Calhoun visited and ministered to me. Both of them sent me nourishing food from their own table, by their own servants. They sent me money, and gave me the lovingest sympathy that woman ever gave to woman.

I had already got an engagement to write for *The Riverside Magazine,* and one day during this illness, when Mrs. Calhoun found me sitting up in bed, weak and exhausted, finishing a child's story, with my two noisy little children playing at my bedside, she took it away, and interested the managing editor of the *Independent* in my work, so that he sent me word he would take some of my stories for his paper.

I have been most fortunate in my friendships, but I never knew any woman more loyal to affection, more overflowing with tenderness, more ready with helpful sympathy than Lu Calhoun. My whole nature, usually reticent, went out to her confidence and friendship, and it was well rewarded.

To the women, brave and noble beyond expression, whose sympathy has forever refuted the slander that women are not generous to one of their own sex—to them, I lay bare my heart. Of all my women friends from earliest girlhood, I know of not one who has fallen off from me in my great trouble. Not a single one. If it had not been for their unswerving trust and love and sympathy; for the readiness they have shown to help me bear up under heavy burdens, I believe I should have been utterly crushed. I have accepted their loving sympathy as the one compensation for all the unspeakable misery of my lot.

ix

After the War: Albert

1865 – 1866

Albert had escaped from prison. But the repercussions of his horrendous confinement lingered on. His health, which had previously been robust, was now so erratic that he could not work consistently. He had contracted pneumonia—it had been almost unavoidable given prison conditions—and had suffered badly from it in the weeks before the escape. Somehow, through force of will or adrenaline, his body triumphed over the effects of the disease during the trek through the mountains, but it laid him flat again as soon as he reached safety. He also grumbled to Sidney Gay of "twinges of rheumatism making me wince and some tenderness of the feet, caused by walking and frost bites the first week of the trip." All this precluded Albert from writing a report for the *Tribune* on the derring-do of his escape. Instead he sent one by his coescapee William Davis that had been published in the Cincinnati *Gazette*.

These infirmities did not however stop Albert from pursuing the matter highest on his conscience, doing something about the prisoners who had been left behind. He wrote to Gay on January 19, only five days after reaching freedom, "Junius, Davis & myself start, about the close of the week, for Washington. The situation of our prisoners of war at Salisbury is so utterly horrible, that we could never rest in our beds again if we omitted any possible efforts for their relief. It is our first duty, & I feel it as the heaviest obligation that ever rested upon me. We have very minute & explicit information on the subject (which our official positions in charge of the hospitals enabled us to gain) facts & figures—names & dates. Hopeless as the task seems we do believe we can do something.

"I tell you confidentially (for we don't want any of the facts published till we can get them all grouped strongly together, & put in such shape that they will make some impression on the public by their accumulation of horrors) that almost <u>25 percent of the whole number of prisoners in Salisbury died in sixty days.</u> I have in my pocket the names of some 1500 of those who died, which I will forward you, when I get them copied legibly, exclusively for <u>The Tribune.</u> Of this more hereafter."

On the issue of Salisbury Prison, Albert could not maintain reportorial detachment. He was appalled by a harsh new administration policy of resisting prisoner of war exchanges on the callous ground that these exchanges benefitted the Confederacy more than the Union. To Albert, who had seen what it had done to thousands of men, this policy was profoundly immoral. He had to *do* something about it, not just write about it. He badgered congressmen and administration officials and testified before the Congressional Committee on the Conduct of the War. He found a sympathetic ear in the Christian Commission, a YMCA-sponsored group that had been providing material and spiritual support to Union soldiers throughout the war. After speaking to its convention in Washington, Albert wrote Gay, "The narration made a profound impression. Almost every person in the hall was in tears, and a resolution was adopted pledging the Commission to work in the matter unremittingly till something is accomplished."

Using the celebrity generated by his dramatic escape, Albert went on a lecture tour to drum up support for liberalizing the prisoner-exchange policy. He spoke to the Christian Commission again at the Academy of Music in Philadelphia. Though he ached in "every joint in my body" from rheumatism, he carried his message to cities and towns throughout the Northeast. He would pause for nothing, not even to return home. "I feel a great anxiety to see the children, Father & Mother, & you and yours," he wrote to his brother Charles on February 1. "We can talk when we meet of domestic arrangements for the next few months. My present impression is that I will make no changes not immediately necessary till the lecture season is over."

In part he was possessed by a cause. In part he needed the lecture fees—a hundred dollars in cities such as Providence and Albany, seventy-five dollars in towns such as Bangor and Concord. But he also wanted to drive himself, to keep busy, so that he did not have to think about the emptiness he felt in his heart.

Albert to *Sidney Howard Gay*

PORTLAND, [MAINE] THURSDAY
FEB. 23, 1865 •

My dear Mr. Gay:

I am sorry that the pressure of letters inquiring about Salisbury prisoners has kept me from writing for the Tribune. I am getting a warm reception on this lecture tour. A splendid house of 2,200 here, and Tremont Temple & Boston Theater were both remarkably filled. At Franklin, among my own people, when I rose in the crowded Church & saw the handkerchiefs go up to the eyes of fully half the women in the house, I think I first realized how wide & deep is the sympathy which has been awakened.

Alas! that my nearest one & dearest was not there to share it! Three nights in my desolate house, surrounded by her books, & pictures & writing at her desk, with everything then just as she left it—have taught me more even than I knew before, how dark it is there, now that the perpetual sunshine of her presence is gone—how dull it is, when her abounding humor no longer enlivens it—how bitter it is with her love forever lost.

I have been reading some of her letters, written just before my capture (which had not been sent.) One of the first passages in them makes me almost think I hear her voice again, it is so like her.

"Leander came home from school today covered all over with mud from head to foot—the result of one of those accidents which <u>will</u> occur to the most quiet children when mud-puddles fly up & splash them in the face! I have indicated to him that if such a catastrophe again befalls any mud-puddle in his immediate vicinity, he shall not be allowed to take cold for want of sufficient circulation of blood on the surface."

I speak in Bangor tonight, here tomorrow, Haverhill, Mass. Saturday, Providence Monday, Chelsea Tuesday, Albany Thursday, & then go West.

Yours most truly,
A.D.R.

All this travel was more than Albert's health could bear. In Albany he nearly fainted on the platform. He had to cancel two months of western appearances, was laid up in bed for weeks, and was so debilitated he had to rely on a stenographer for correspondence. But his efforts bore fruit. Prisoner exchanges were resumed, and most of the Salisbury inhabitants were released by the end of February. Events on the battlefield soon made all these efforts moot, however. By April, General Stoneman's raiders had liberated Salisbury Prison and Lee had surrendered at Appomattox Courthouse. The war was over.

For Albert, as for the country, the end of the war was the beginning of a new life in a world where the old rules and priorities no longer applied. When the fighting had begun, four years before, he was still in the flush of youth, twenty-seven years old. His career, steadily successful, was maintaining the same westward trajectory he had set when he left home as a boy. His family was growing, as it should, with a devoted wife and children ensconced in a safe home. It was the life of a happy, dauntless young man, on whom fortune had only smiled.

Now Albert had emerged, at age thirty-one, into a midlife more intricate and perplexing. He faced the responsibilities of fatherhood alone, with three children—Leander, age nine, Maude, age five, and Albert, Jr., age three—the youngest of whom he barely knew, having been in the field or in prison since his birth. His health—and his boyish, buoyant faith in humanity—had been compromised by his prison ordeal. He longed, as he had written Gay during the war, for some way to settle into "simple, quiet descriptive writing," and tend his family, who were temporarily living with his parents in Massachusetts.

Book writing seemed to offer Albert what he needed. He continued to submit occasional articles to the *Tribune* and other journals, but he devoted his primary efforts to producing a volume on his war-time experiences, and continuing to think about his future.

Albert to *Mrs. Charles Richardson*

TRIBUNE OFFICE, MARCH 20, 1865 •

My Dear Jennie,

What can I do to remind you that in these sweet Spring days, which to me are so full of bustle & work, I bear you constantly in my love. I can at least, now I have cleaned the last letter off my desk tonight send you a little of my aggravated and hopeless scrawl.

I am beginning to get at it a little on the book; but make slow work of it. I have an excellent stenographer; and after tomorrow shall "rush" it. Have contracted to give the printer 450 to 500 pages before April 20; and so far have given them just 2! I will pour it on them when I begin!

I lecture in Hoboken tomorrow night. My lung has largely recovered. I am not so strong as I used to be tho! Can't do so much work: get tired more easily.

I am very comfortable here. Have a nice parlor & bed room all to myself; with my desk & books in it; pleasant front view; and a bath room with hot & cold water. I am all alone, as I like to be. Take my meals at the Astor House.

Everyone is very kind to me. If I have <u>any</u> sense left after all the absurd petting I have had and am having, it will be a profound wonder. Do give me a sharp punch when you see the vanity or folly coming out to the surface; & ask Charles to.

How is little Maude. I should like to have her to look at when I feel despondent. She is very droll.

Fisher spent some hours with me the other day. He seemed very glad to see me in his way. It is a very cold way to me. All the New England ways are cold ways. I never can feel at home there, anywhere except at father's house; & there it is because I am the baby still. I feel at home everywhere else— here, in Cincti, St. Louis, Chicago, anywhere where I have friends. But New England is like a wet blanket to me. The shell is too thick. I don't exactly know what the matter is; I suppose the tremendously cold, freezing manners. And yet I like perfect quietness and undemonstrativeness in men. I have no fondness for those excitable gentlemen who kick up their heels & go through life with a noise and a row. People call me very quiet. Lou used to say to me in our early married life, "I wish you would manifest a little excitement on some subject,—just for variety's sake."

Still I don't believe I am quite such a walking refrigerator as so many New England people seem to me. I wonder if it is that which has made me feel, all my life, like an alien from my own race—from all of it except mother. I don't want people to throw their arms around you, and bellow; but if they love you & are glad to see you, I want them to show it somehow—in their eyes, or somewhere in their faces—& make you feel it. Knowing it isn't enough.

Well, well; "Something too much of this."

With love to all, I am, as ever,

Affectionately Your Brother,
Albert

In a matter of a few months, he completed his opus: *The Secret Service, The Field, The Dungeon, and The Escape.* It was successful beyond his highest expectations, generating a remarkable sale of one hundred thousand copies, and further boosting the fame and popularity of its author. Junius's ironically titled version of the same events, *Four Years in Secessia*, also did well, but Albert's was thought to be the superior work.

Albert immediately commenced work on its successor, *Beyond the Mississippi—Life and Adventure on the Prairies, Mountains, and the Pacific Coast*, which was to combine his prewar travel and adventures with new and updated material. He had fresh insights from another wandering journey in the west. But this time he went not as a lone correspondent riding Indian ponies over the mountains. Schulyer Colfax, the speaker of the house, had invited Albert along on a cross-country junket for the summer of 1865, as a guide and companion for himself, Lieutenant-Governor William Bross of Illinois (a journalist and part-owner of the *Chicago Tribune*), and Samuel Bowles (the well-known editor of the *Springfield Republican*).

Colfax, the man who had secured McFarland's appointment as commissioner of enrollment two years earlier, was a rising star in the Republican Party. He would continue as speaker until 1868, when he was elected Vice-President with the all-conquering war hero, Ulysses S. Grant. While McFarland had tried to ingratiate himself with Colfax, and failed, Albert easily became Colfax's friend and political intimate. The speaker was a former newspaperman and shared Albert's enthusiasm for opening the West. They enjoyed each other's company immensely.

The Overland Mail and Stage Line, which was still the primary means of travel west of Missouri, paid for everything, and Albert relaxed in his role as an "illustrious dead-head." He was "in clover," he said. In Denver Albert visited some old friends and reported on the momentous changes. What he remembered as a scene of "Arapaho squaws, log cabins & dirt floors," was now one of "pianos, well-dressed ladies, Brussels carpets & silver ware, & two or three kinds of wine at dinner." Governor Bross apparently saw it differently. Albert wrote Gay that the governor "may be less impressed with our prospects than I am; he made his will, paid his debts, & had solemn religious services at his house before leaving!"

Bowles recalled how companionable Albert was, entertaining them on their long stage rides with anecdotes from his previous travels. But, noted Bowles admiringly, "notwithstanding his long bohemian life, amid rough people and in out-of-the-way places, Mr.

Richardson imposes on you with the style and air of a man who has had a very narrow escape from the pulpit, and cherishes a natural hankering for it yet. He does not chew tobacco, disdains whiskey, but drinks French brandy and Cincinnati Catawba, carries a good deal of baggage, does not know how to play poker, and shines brilliantly among the ladies."

Once in the West, the old bug bit Albert again. He "loved to do descriptive letters more than anything in the world," he wrote to Gay, and he sent a steady stream of them back to the *Tribune*. When his companions boarded a steamer on September 3 for their return to the East—one-way by stage having been enough for them— Albert stayed on through November, exploring Yosemite, Montana, and Idaho. He wanted to see all the new territories, especially those he had not seen before.

For a while he was the prewar Albert. But his lungs constantly bothered him. He did not have his old stamina. The sharp sea winds in San Francisco "cut me down badly," he told his friend Gay. He drove himself on. The weaker he became, the more he felt the need to stay in the fresh, tonic-laden air of the West. He had to finish this trip so that his book could be comprehensive, and he probably knew in his heart that he might never again have such an opportunity.

When he finally returned east for the winter, Albert went to his children and family in Franklin with a melancholy heart. His sense of adventure was sated, and his sense of family starved.

Albert to *Sidney Howard Gay*

FRANKLIN, MASS., JAN. 28, 1866 •

Dear Mr. Gay:

For five days I have been engrossed in the letters, papers, & other articles left by my dear wife, which I have never had the heart to look at before. It has been full of painful & bitter memories. I think I <u>meant</u> to be a tender & kind husband to her; but I was always selfish, often exacting, & sometimes harsh & unjust. The memory of two or three occasions of the latter will fill me with bitterness & self reproach to the last hour of my life. When I think of the perfect loyalty, the undying patience, the utter & unselfish love, for which I made so poor a return, & above all of that last terrible week, when she went down to the dark valley <u>alone,</u> I almost wish that I were among those untroubled sleepers who rest beside the old Salisbury garrison.

I did not mean to trouble you with my personal griefs, but only to say this. In looking over the papers which she left, I find many letters from you, & I see, for the first time how prompt, how kind & how sympathetic you were to her, who needed kindness & sympathy so much. I can make you no return but my poor thanks, but I shall never, <u>never</u> cease to be grateful. May Heaven reward you for it if your time ever comes to drink the bitter waters.

> Always yours
> *Albert D. Richardson*

Albert knew the time had come for him to settle down. His plan was to take a house in Fordham or New Jersey, then developing as suburbs of New York. There he could provide a proper home for his children, and he could live and work where the air might be better for his health.

These plans had to be postponed. The remainder of 1866 was a trying period for him. He was striving to finish *Beyond the Mississippi*. He knew that tens of thousands of workers were laboring on the transcontinental rail line, simultaneously pushing it east from California and west from Nebraska, laying as much as two and one-half miles of track a day. The vast project symbolized the American spirit that Albert wanted to capture in his book, which had grown to almost six hundred pages, with over two hundred engraved illustrations. "Soon we shall ride from New York to San Francisco in one week, without change of cars. Around the world by railway, with two ocean ferries!" he would proclaim on the final page. But his health was not cooperating. He developed an inflammation of the eyes in June and could not read or work for most of the summer. In the fall a recurrence of his pneumonia, while he was inspecting the progress of the railroad in Nebraska, laid him up for two weeks. "I am very hard worked indeed," he wrote to Governor Bross in November, "and a little afraid of breaking down before I get through with this book. It weighs on me like a mill-stone, but if I can last just two or three weeks longer, I will snap my fingers at fate."

Albert was still living alone in rooms in the city. He was a popular social guest, and frequently dined at the homes of his friends, including the Calhouns (Lu and her husband, with whom he boarded for a time) and the Sinclairs (Samuel and Charlotte).

It was at the Sinclair house, one evening in the spring of 1866, that he first met Abby Sage McFarland. Mrs. Calhoun had spoken glowingly of her talented new friend, but Albert had not yet had the pleasure of her acquaintance. That evening, when he heard Abby give a reading, Albert could only agree with Mrs. Calhoun's praise. The paths of the two would cross again from time to time at similar social occasions. McFarland, who knew of Albert's friendship with men in high places, was pleased to have his wife develop the connection. He imagined the popular author could be helpful to him in his business endeavors.

X

Abby Escapes

Abby had thought that the fall of 1866, with the publication of *Percy's Year of Rhymes* and the inauguration of her career on the stage, would be a bright new beginning. But instead she had to struggle with McFarland and her health. Her life seemed to go from one crisis to another. Again her friends, who now included Albert Richardson, came to her assistance.

One such occasion occurred on an afternoon in late November 1866. Abby was lunching at the Calhoun's with several other friends of Lu, Albert among them. It was an informal and friendly meal. Abby had made her stage debut the previous evening, and Lu proudly told everyone of her protégé's appearance in *Hamlet* with Edwin Booth. The Miss Cushing listed in the program, Lu informed them, was really their luncheon companion. Abby demurred. She had only a bit part. Besides, she told them, her performing had created a problem. Despite her use of a pseudonym, her landlady had learned of her new profession and had immediately ordered her to move out. The landlady did not want any actress in her house.

Everyone was indignant at the landlady's attitude. Albert volunteered that some vacant rooms were available at the house where he lodged, No. 61 Amity Street. "If you came to look, and liked them," he offered, "I would speak to my landlady of your acting. I'm certain she would not object." The next day Abby called at Albert's boarding house to look at the rooms. Amity Street, where Abby had lived earlier that fall, was a section of what was otherwise Third Street, parallel to and just one block south of Washington Square. The rooms were more expensive than she could afford, but the neighborhood was congenial and very convenient to the theater, which was on Broadway just below Amity. Abby found another place nearby, at No. 86 Amity Street, and moved in about the 16th or 17th of December, 1866.

ABBY, FROM HER AFFIDAVIT

On the 20th of December I had an engagement to read at Salem, Mass., before the Lyceum Lecture Course. My mother had written us that if I would bring on one of the children she would take him and take care of him for an indefinite period, because she feared I had too much to do with the two children and all my other duties. So I concluded to take my youngest child Danny to my own home at my father's, on this journey to Salem.

I played at the theater the night before starting for Massachusetts, and was obliged to sit up nearly all the night to get myself and my child ready. About 1 o'clock in the night Mr. McFarland came home in a state of beastly intoxication. He was past talking then, but toward daylight, while I was getting ready to take the morning train for Boston, I roused him, and told him I had been intending to take Danny home, but now I thought I would take both the children and leave them with mother till I could do something better, and come back and separate myself from him entirely, that I could not possibly work as I was doing and bear his habits any longer. On this he professed great penitence, begged me to try him once more. Said he would do better if I would give him this one trial, &c., &c. I did not believe him, but I hardly knew what to do, and I finally went off with Danny to my mother's. This was the morning of the 19th. I read in Salem the 20th, returning to New-York the 21st, and going to the theater the same evening.

At New Year's time I foolishly allowed Mr. McFarland to draw a two weeks salary from the theater, which had been lying over because the money I had earned at Salem paid the necessary board-bill, and he went again and got drunk, and remained so for two or three days. At this time I made up my mind I would do something. On the afternoon of January 2 I wrote a long letter to Mrs. Calhoun, to whom, in all of my acquaintance, I had never spoken of Mr. McFarland, except incidentally, telling her some of my troubles.

In this letter, which it cost me terrible pain and humiliation to write, because my habits of concealment were so natural and difficult to overcome, I glozed over some of the worst facts. I tried, with all the humanity and justice which was in my nature, to speak most gently and impartially of this unfortunate man.

Abby to *Mrs. Calhoun*
JAN. 2, 1867 •

My Darling and Comforter:

I have seated myself with the intention of writing you a long, long, letter; of telling you some things which I have never before told to any one; but which, kept secret and brooded over, seem to eat out my heart and consume my life day by day. I was miserably unhappy yesterday, all the latter part of the day. Yesterday morning, after I had got all ready to go to Ms. Sinclair's for the New-Year's Day, after I had kissed Percy "Good by," and had my parcels in my arms ready to take them over, some little impatient words I said irritated Mr. McFarland, who is very sensitive and quick-tempered. It arose from my asking him to help me carry some of my bundles, and his resenting it, and our both getting a little bit angry. I did not say half as much as I hear women every day say to their husbands, without its being remembered on either side. I should not have remembered it one instant, but he does, and I went away without smoothing out the snarl. It was perhaps a little perverse, but I got so tired of constantly smoothing and coaxing. But all day I was nervous when he did not call with Percy as he had promised, and I was very anxious. I could not get away in the evening without showing how uneasy I was, so I stayed. When

I got home, I found Percy in bed, hugging up a book with which he had got himself asleep—alone. After an hour or two of agonizing waiting, waiting—listening for footsteps, and dreading to hear them—which are only a few of the hundreds of hours I have spent so—he came in, two-thirds intoxicated and very morose. I asked him why he could so spoil my day, and cause me so much unhappiness, and he answered that "I had treated him outrageously, and he should spend the New-Year's as he chose."

Two weeks ago—the morning of the Tuesday before I went to Salem to read, you remember—I got utterly discouraged, and I said something, not reproachful, to Mr. McFarland about my feelings. One cannot always keep up, you know. There was no unkindness between us, only when I sink a little in hope he sinks in despair. That night he did not come home to dinner, and I was obliged to leave my babies when I went to the theater, awake and alone. All the evening I was burning with anxiety to get home. He did not come for me, and I went home alone after I got through the play. I found him in a beastly slumber, from which I could not rouse him; he had been drinking all day. I was to start that next morning for Massachusetts, and it made me almost crazy. Next morning he was in sackcloth and ashes for his conduct. He wept, and begged me to forgive him—not to tell my father and mother, and swore he would vindicate himself before me by a different life this year.

Dear, I try to write these things coldly and mechanically. I want to do so, so as not to be unjust, but I must write you. I feel I must let you know something of my inner life, and of the struggles that no one can see, or I shall die.

You know, my darling, when I was married I had not much experience of life, or judgment of character. When Mr. McFarland asked me to marry him, I said "yes," without proper deliberation. I was not in love with any one else; everybody got married, I thought, and I never questioned whether I was sufficiently in love or not. I thought I was, and did not reason. After I was married and began to know Mr. McFarland, I found him radical to the extreme in all his ideas. He seemed to have many heartfelt schemes of philanthropy and lovely traits of character. He had beautiful theories, and he believed he acted on them, when he did not, and was often cruelly unjust to me and my motives. He was madly jealous of me from the first—a jealousy which seemed to me to have its root in a radical want of confidence in woman's virtue. A bachelor experience had made him believe women were not always chaste, I think; but to me, who was as chaste as ice and as pure as snow, if ever women were chaste, these things were <u>horrible</u> outrages. They struck the first blow at the tenderness I felt for him, which might have ripened into a real affection, I have no doubt.

This was the first shock—the second was the discovery that if anything annoyed him, if I was impatient or a little cross (as I think all women are at times, and I know my temper is naturally sunny), or if business cares oppressed him, or a hundred other annoyances which might trouble one, then as a refuge from any of this he would drink liquor, and come home under its influence.

This is an awful thing to say, dearest. To drag out eight or ten years an existence with a man whose whole nature overflowed with passion, who by turn adored and abused you, and who wanted to absorb both body and soul, and to feel nothing but a feeling of pity.

I <u>want</u> to do Mr. McFarland justice, and I pity him more than I pity myself. His condition and his suffering are worse, perhaps. He had noble theories and not strength enough to realize them. The mistakes that he made embittered and still embitter him. He meant his life to be noble, and it <u>is</u> a failure. I am glad and proud to say that for the last years he has ceased to be jealous of me or my feeling toward any man. I should never be anything but a chaste woman in my relations with men, but his feeling has made me more than prudent, and I have been always <u>most</u> reserved. I have never had any sentiment so warm as friendship for other men, and my actions would bear the most jealous scrutiny.

My darling, I have spent hours and nights in scenes before which tragedy grows pale. I have no words to speak of them.

I have tried and do try to do my duty. I have the most sincere pity for this unfortunate man; my heart bleeds for him. I try, Heaven knows, to be as patient as I can. With all my troubles, my life is now as unhappy as his. My heart and soul are my own; he cannot touch them. I pity him, but I do not love him enough to let him wound me to the quick.

I don't know what to do—what course to take. I want to be advised. I dread my future so much and I have my babies to think of besides.

<u>Don't</u> come to me after reading this; I fear I shall repent writing it.

Yours always,
Abby

P.S.—I just went down to breakfast and left him in bed. When I came up he was gone! I shall be so anxious till night.

ABBY, FROM HER AFFIDAVIT

A short time after I moved there, I found the boarding house at No. 86 Amity-st. intolerable, for various reasons, and removed to No. 72 Amity-st., taking the back parlor and extension-room for my rooms. They were very comfortable. I took these rooms sometime in the first or second week in January. At this new place, besides going nightly to perform my part at the Winter Garden, I wrote during all of my spare moments, being then engaged to write regularly for *The Riverside* and the children's column of the *Independent,* and endeavoring to do work for other papers; and I also did all the cooking for three persons, a large part of the washing and ironing for three, and all the sewing, mending, &c., for my family. I had little time for anything but work.

Somewhere about the last of January or first of February, Mr. Richardson came to lodge at this house. He came because there was a good room vacant, and he was obliged to move his lodgings, which were in the vicinity. He told me that he did not wish to move far, as he expected to leave the city altogether very soon. I introduced

Mr. Richardson to Mrs. Mason, the lodging-house woman, but beyond that had no interest or influence in getting him installed. If I had any feeling about Mr. Richardson's coming to take a room so near Mr. McFarland and myself, it was one of aversion, from the fact that he could not be there without knowing something of my unhappy life, and I felt keenly that such a knowledge would pain and humiliate me. But I could not control the event.

I saw Mr. Richardson there often, and he did me many kindnesses. A few weeks earlier, during the time we were staying at No. 86 Amity-st., Mr. McFarland, who fancied Mr. Richardson had some influence in the Pacific Railroad, had sent me to call on Mr. Richardson to ask for his aid in getting a place as a clerk or something of that kind on the railroad. Mr. Richardson obliged by providing a letter of introduction to Mr. George F. Train of the railroad, which I believe Mr. McFarland presented without result.

Now that we were neighbors, Mr. Richardson called sometimes at my room, which was next to his, but from its situation, and the fact that it was my sleeping-room, parlor, and dining-room in one, it was in no sense a private room. My boy Percy, who was then seven years old, was always with me, and Mr. Richardson's calls were made usually in the afternoon about the time he got through work, and oftener after Mr. McFarland had got home from downtown.

On the fourth of February Mrs. Sinclair and Mrs. Calhoun went to Washington. Just before they left Mr. McFarland had a terrible and unusually dangerous attack of rage, of which I told Mrs. Calhoun. Since I had written that letter to her a few weeks previous, she was more than ever my confidante. She said she was afraid to go away and leave me with that man, for fear he would kill me, and asked if she might tell some of our friends about his conduct, so that we could have some advice in the matter before she went away; but I felt as if I could not consent to this, and told her so. Mr. Oliver Johnson told me afterward that Mrs. Calhoun did speak to him and his wife of her great anxiety for me, and her fear that Mr. McFarland would murder me in some of his paroxysms.

After Mrs. Calhoun and Mrs. Sinclair were gone, I devoted myself more closely than ever to my work. On the evening of the 19th of February, when Mr. McFarland came in from the Custom-house (where he had been employed as a clerk since the 1st of February, through the influence of the Sinclairs), I was standing at Mr. Richardson's door in the front hall. He was just handing me some manuscripts which he had offered to lend me to make use of, if I could, in some literary work. Mr. Richardson's room was used as his working-room; and at this time, as at all parts of the day, he had with him a stenographer, a messenger-boy, and an artist, who were engaged in his literary works.

When Mr. McFarland came in he objected to my going to Mr. Richardson's room, to which I replied that "I had not been in, was not in the habit of going there, and even if I had been in there, it was not a private room, but an office, in the day-time." With this the matter dropped, and I supposed this was all of it; but in a few moments Mr. McFarland commenced to say something again on the same subject. I saw he was in ill humor, and I supposed he wished to make anything the pretext for one of his passions, so I said little or nothing. From this he worked himself up into a great fury, in which I left him to go to my necessary work at the theater. When I returned he continued in this rage and I spent a terrible night with him.

All through the next day (the 20th) he remained at home abusing and tormenting me. He used to me expressions which I never could forgive or endure; and still harping on the fact of my being at Mr. Richardson's room, asked me before Percy, who was all the time present: "Did Mr. Richardson ever kiss you? Have you ever been in his room alone with him?" and other questions which I considered insulting and unpardonable. He was under the influence of liquor all day, remaining at home, and going out every little while to the nearest bar-room to drink, and then coming in still more furious. At last he declared he was willing to be separated from me, and that I might go home to my father's and leave him. When I assented to this, he wanted to bring in some of my friends to talk the matter over before them, but I refused to take counsel from any one until my father could be sent for. I only prevented him from rushing out and calling in some of my friends by representing to him that he was then so intoxicated that his cause would be prejudiced by that fact.

On the evening of the 20th, before going to the theater, I secreted his razors, his pocket-knife, my scissors, and all articles I considered dangerous—as I frequently did on such occasions—and left him. While I was at the theater, I wrote in my dressing room to Mrs. Calhoun, then still in Washington, telling her what I was suffering, and my fears for my safety. I felt that Mr. McFarland might murder me in one of his outbursts, and it was right that she should know the very worst. I was frank to the utmost. She and Mrs. Sinclair answered that letter a few days later, with two noble and womanly letters in the same spirit. But I did not need to wait on advice from my friends. I had already made my own decision.

When I came home Mr. McFarland was still raging. He frequently had made threats of committing suicide, often going out of doors with that avowed purpose. On this occasion, about midnight he bade me an unusually solemn "eternal farewell," and told me that this time he was certainly going out to destroy himself. He had done this so many times that I said nothing, and made no effort to detain him. At the door he hesitated, and asked if I had nothing to say "in this last parting." I said, "I can only say that I am hopelessly sorry for you." He went out, and in a few minutes returned, as I knew he would, cooled and sobered by the cold night air, and then, as mildly and firmly as I possibly could, I began to talk with him as I had resolved to do. I told him decidedly that I should leave him forever, that I had borne with patience for many years great outrages from him; that he had made my life miserable, and had often put me in great dread of my life; that I could not endure it any longer; that by his outrageous conduct for the two days past, and by the language he had used when he found me at Mr. Richardson's door, he had added the last drop to my cup of endurance, and I should go away from him at once. On this he groveled at my feet in the most abject penitence. He wept and sobbed, and begged me to forgive him. He confessed that he had wronged me, that no woman would have borne with him as I had done, and about daylight went to sleep exhausted.

My mind was firm. The next morning I did not allude to my purpose, but after seeing Mr. McFarland leave the house for the Custom-house, I went to Mr. Sinclair's and placed myself under the protection of his roof.

I sent my other child, Percy, off to stay at father's in Massachusetts. Two days later, my father came down to New York, and arranged a council with Mr. McFarland. On the 24th of February, 1867 in the presence of Mr. and Mrs. Oliver Johnson, Mr. Sinclair, my father and Mr. McFarland, I announced my absolute determination to leave him.

I never afterward saw Mr. McFarland, except once or twice in the presence of others.

XI

The Paths Converge

ABBY, FROM HER AFFIDAVIT

On the last night of my life with Mr. McFarland, the night of the
20th of February, it happened, as was most unusual, that Mr. Richardson was in his room the whole evening. He almost always spent
his evenings at the house of Mrs. Gilbert (Mrs. Calhoun's mother),
in Newark. He has since told me that he heard the greater part of
what had passed that night, as was unavoidable from the position of
his room, and that he feared he might be obliged to call for help, or
himself interfere in my behalf against Mr. McFarland's violence.

The next day, when I left Mr. McFarland, I found Mr. Richardson
at Mr. Sinclair's house when I arrived. No one else was present but
Miss Perry, Mrs. Sinclair's older sister. Mrs. Sinclair had not yet
returned from Washington. Under ordinary circumstances I should
have controlled myself until I could see Miss Perry alone; but worn
out as I was by the misery and excitements of the last two days, and
the fact that I had still been obliged to keep at work at home and at
the theater, I broke down, and burst into tears as soon as I entered
the room. As soon as I could speak I began to talk to them both. Mr.
Richardson said very little. I remember he said, "This is a matter in
which I cannot advise you, but whatever you make up your mind to
do, I shall be glad to help you."

He *did* help me in ten thousand ways in which I never should have permitted him to take part if I had the slightest knowledge of the feeling which was to grow up between us. He helped me make the arrangements to send Percy home, which was the first thing I was anxious to do. He telegraphed for me to one or two friends, and wrote to Mrs. Calhoun and Mrs. Sinclair of the step I had taken, which I asked him to do at once. All these things which common prudence would have prevented him from doing if there had been any guilty secret between us or any relation except the simple one on his part of sympathy toward a very wretched woman, he did warmly and unreservedly.

Two days later, on the evening after the family council in which the separation was confirmed, Mr. Richardson called at Mr. Sinclair's and stayed an hour or two with the family. He told us all that in a few days he was going to Hartford to finish his book. I was going to Massachusetts the 7th of April, when my engagement expired at the theater, and I thought if he went away in a day or two I might not see him again, so when he arose to leave that evening, I went to the door to say—what I could not say before others—that he had been *very,* VERY good to me. That I never could repay him, but that God would surely bless him for it.

I could not say this without strong emotion, and while I spoke, he said: "How do you feel about facing the world with two babies?" I answered: "It looks hard for a woman, but then, I am sure I can get on better without that man, than with him."

At this Mr. Richardson, still holding my hand, which I had given him to say "good night," stooped down, and speaking in a lower tone so that he could not be heard through the door into the parlor, said these words: "I wish you to remember, my girl, that any responsibility you choose to give me in any possible future, I shall be very glad to take." Those were his exact words. And with this he went away without a single word more being said by either of us. I turned and went up-stairs and said nothing to any one that night.

It may have been two days later that Mr. Richardson called again. It happened that I was in the parlor alone when he came in. In the talk which took place then, he told me that during the storms of the last few days of my life he had become interested in me and very fond of me. He said I was the woman of all the world he had seen to whom he would gladly entrust the care of his motherless children; that my prudence and reserve during all our acquaintance when he knew I was unhappy had won on him greatly.

Then he looked at me very directly, so that our eyes met, and he said, "I *love* you. If in any future, however far off, you could be free to marry, I want you to know fully this feeling."

What could I say? Mr. Richardson had all my respect for his chivalry and generosity before he spoke thus. When he spoke, all my heart went out to him as freely as the river flows toward the sea. The formal separation from Mr. McFarland in which he seemed to release me from the bondage in which he held me, had to me the moral effect of a divorce. I had a feeling which perhaps no one can understand. It was as if a millstone had been cut off from my neck, and left me as free and unbound as I ever felt in girlhood. Mr. Richardson seemed to me in every respect the opposite of the miserable man who had so long tormented me. His goodness to me, his unusual strength of character, united with his tenderness and sympathy, made it absolutely impossible not to love him.

While he waited for me to say something to answer what he had said, I did not think of the imprudence of it at all. I only asked him earnestly if his chivalry and a generous impulse to assist a woman in trouble had not led him to mistake this for a warmer feeling. He laughed at this. He advised me to tell my friends all he said and take their counsel.

Our talk at most was not a very long one, and within a few days he went to Hartford. It was early in March 1867. I did not expect to see him again for an indefinite time.

XII

McFarland Acts

ABBY, FROM HER AFFIDAVIT

After Mr. Richardson's departure I went back from Mr. Sinclair's house to my old room in Amity-st., where my trunks and wardrobe still remained. It was convenient to do this, and my lady friend Lilly Gilbert went to spend the nights with me. She is the sister of Mrs. L.G. Calhoun and was then (and still is) the fiancée of Mr. Richardson's friend, Junius Henri Browne.

Two nights after I returned to the Amity-st. rooms, Mr. Richardson unexpectedly came from Hartford, intending to go to Washington for a day or two. He had written me several letters during his stay at Hartford, which I had received and answered. He arrived in New-York on the 12th of March, and on the evening of the 13th, when I went out of the theater after the performance, I found him there waiting for me. He was asked to call for me by Mr. Browne and Miss Gilbert, who usually took me home, and who, on that night, were gone to the opera.

It was only three short blocks from the stage door of the theater on Mercer near Amity to the rooming house. The couple moved briskly in the rain. Albert had his hat pulled down and was holding an umbrella forward of them, so he could not see very far ahead. As they were approaching No. 72, they heard footsteps behind, and a voice cried, "Libertine!"

It was McFarland, only a foot away and holding a pistol. He fired one shot at Albert, which hit its mark, and then two more that missed. Albert shouted for Abby to run and she fled. He lunged for the gunman and wrestled him to the ground. Two policemen were there in moments. They disarmed McFarland and took both him and Albert to the police station.

Fortunately, Albert had only a flesh wound, on his inner thigh. They took him to the Sinclair's house to recuperate. Abby remained in New York with Albert and took care of him for the five days that his wound kept him in bed. Then she resigned her position at the Winter Garden, where she no longer had the nerve to perform, and returned to her parents and two sons in Massachusetts. Five days later, the theater burned down.

Though Albert's lawyer tried to convince him otherwise, he declined to prosecute McFarland for this attack. He said he wished to avoid needless public scandal about himself and Abby. Albert felt McFarland was "half a madman," but also that he had done wrong to speak of marriage with Abby so soon after her separation. "Of course," he wrote to Junius, "the fault is in no sense hers. She is a helpless woman, so nervous with apprehension and terror of him that she starts wildly whenever she hears a door-bell ring, and she turned naturally to one who offered her sympathy, shelter and affection at such time. *I* ought to have been more prudent but the fact of my love was there, and I never sought to evade it or deny it. I simply told the truth about the matter."

ABBY, FROM HER AFFIDAVIT

After I went back home, terribly hurt by the scandal which had been caused by the shooting of Mr. Richardson in the open street, I wrote to him telling him that I feared—and that the thought grieved me inexpressibly—that in a moment of romantic generosity he had offered me his love, and that the events had proved that such an offer on his part becoming known had made an enemy of McFarland, who had proved a more dangerous man than I should ever have believed him, and that I released him from any allegiance or fancied allegiance to me in my misfortune, which at best would only be sacrifice on his part. To this letter of mine, of which I can only remember the substance, not the words, Mr. Richardson wrote me in answer the following letter.

Albert to *Abby, in Massachusetts*

MARCH 31, 1867 •

My Love:

If Heaven shall ever grant to me the last blessing of calling you mine, by the most sacred name of wife, it will compensate me for all waiting and sorrow. And, precious, should one of us go hence by unalterable destiny before that blessed hour comes, it would still be blessed and full compensation to know that you had loved me; that you had found in my poor nature somewhere hidden any worth that deserve that.

And, precious, about our immediate situation. There isn't a bit of any sacrifice or generosity about it on my part. Once for all, remember that. Partly from my own rashness, partly from things neither of us could control, you and I are in a little boat on a high and somewhat perilous sea. If I had any sense, you would not have been there. But I believe devoutly in the proverb that a man who isn't a fool part of the time is one all the time. It was foolish, imprudent, cruel to let you be on such a craft with me, when patience could have avoided it. But I loved you and took no counsel of reason.

Well, darling, here we are in the little boat, waves high, some sharks, some pirates. For me, it is nothing. I have faced all perils in life and death before, and familiar faces don't disturb me. And I am not a bit afraid to die; so I am not afraid of anything in life. But, precious, for you my heart reproaches me. I am sorry when I should have been your helper and comforter and shield, to have brought you into such a storm. But, darling, if I live, I am going to see you safely out of it. If I should not live to go into harbor with you, the Father will take care of your sunny head.

But, precious, let us take our chances. I have been in rougher waves before, and ridden them safely. Let us exercise the best seamanship we can, provide for all contingencies as far as possible, and then keep the set of mind which defies fate and fears nothing but guilt, knows how infinitesimal all these petty things of life are, and feels sure that infinite love and absolute justice rule the world.

My darling, in all that I am or do, or have or hope for in life or death, you are irrevocably interwoven. I regret nothing that I have done, save just to the extent that it has affected or marred your happiness. My whole heart, my whole life, go out to you. I think I see a happy future, sunny days, love of children, love of home, good to others. I <u>know</u> I see a loyalty nothing can shake, a trust that is absolute, a love that is utter and vital.

Your loving
Albert

xiii

The Struggle for Freedom

 Abby remained secluded in Boston with her two sons, even though that meant separation from Albert, and giving up New York and her theatrical aspirations. She feared that McFarland's mad rage might fall on her and the children. If she remained distant, and firm in her resolve to leave him, she hoped he might eventually accept the inevitable and cool down.

But McFarland would not forget. He launched a verbal offensive against Albert, telling everyone how this libertine had seduced away his wife and destroyed his family. "I will never see them married," was McFarland's ominous warning to anyone who would listen. And he extended his attacks to Abby as well.

ABBY, FROM HER AFFIDAVIT

Mr. McFarland assailed me in every way possible to harass a woman. I hardly have one friend in New-York or New-England whose house he did not enter to force them to listen to his story. He assailed my character with epithets, which I should blush to repeat, and which he knew, in his own consciousness, I would die a thousand deaths rather than deserve.

He went to my rooms at Amity-st., and, gaining access by such representations as poisoned the minds of the landlady and the servants against me (to whom, of course, I had said nothing about my affairs), he broke open my trunks, took out all the private correspondence I had preserved during my whole life, rifled my writing-desk and portfolio, and even searched the pockets of my dresses. He took not only my letters, but all my accounts and receipts by which I could show what money I had earned, the notices and advertisements which I had preserved of my dramatic readings, and even robbed me of all the mss., and odds and ends of literary labors, some of which I had a long time had on hand, and from that day forward I never saw any of my private papers of all kinds. He also succeeded in intercepting two or three more letters from friends out of town.

Albert and Abby felt that patience was the best strategy for dealing with this man who threatened their lives and happiness. They believed, with good reason, that McFarland was irrational and that any counterattack they might make, such as a prosecution for attempted murder or for slander, would fuel his mania. Best to ignore him, and let it burn out. This was the Puritan, stoic approach, dictated by their upbringing.

McFarland, however, would not be ignored. He carried his battle to the courts of Massachusetts. At the end of March 1867, he commenced habeas corpus proceedings against Abby, seeking to gain custody of his two children.

Albert stood by her. He arranged for former governor John A. Andrew of Massachusetts to represent her in the habeas corpus case. When Mrs. John F. Cleveland (Greeley's sister) was approached by McFarland to act as intermediary, she turned to Albert to deal with the settlement proposition. McFarland proposed that if Abby would give up the two children to him he would interpose no obstacle to her remarriage. McFarland did not really think Abby would desert her sons. He rather thought that by forcing her to choose between Albert and her children he would cause Abby to realize the error of her ways. He thought she would return to him.

McFarland was wrong. With Albert's encouragement, Abby simply refused the offer. She was not about to give up her children, but she was not about to give up her freedom from an oppressive marriage either.

When the negotiations stalemated, McFarland's lawyers pressed forward with the case. They took depositions of forty-three witnesses in New York for presentation to the Massachusetts court. It appeared that the matter might actually go to trial. Abby despised the thought of the publicity this would generate. Even worse, she feared the outcome of the trial. Her lawyers advised that the husband normally had preference in obtaining custody of children, especially when the wife had left him. McFarland's failed pistol attack on Albert would certainly count against him, but that was not violence toward the children. Unless she could show that he was a threat to his sons, she might lose custody. If she prevailed, on the other hand, McFarland's friends warned her that he would go utterly and hopelessly mad, and take such actions as they could not predict or be responsible for. With these fears plaguing her, her principal lawyer, former governor Andrew, suddenly died.

ABBY, FROM HER AFFIDAVIT

At last, weary and worn out with more contests than I can describe here, pursued by his revenge, in the form of anonymous letters, by spies set to watch my footsteps, by all that can wear down a woman's courage and heart, I made a compromise with Mr. McFarland. It was agreed that all proceedings should be stopped by a division of the children, and that he should take Percy and I should keep Danny in my charge. Hitherto I might have been imprudent in allowing myself to love a good man, and to allow him to confess that he loved me, when we had no legal right to admit it to each other, but I had never felt any sense of guilt about it, for I knew I meant to do the best I could. But now I confessed my baseness, my want of courage, in giving my boy, nursed at my breast, and dearer to me than my life, to compromise with my sworn foe. My remorse in letting the child go without letting the legal proceedings take their course was terrible. But I was very weak. I was in Boston, where I had no friends except my family. Most of all, Mr. McFarland came to my mother and promised, with a solemnity which seemed like truth, that he would put my child in school, that he would consult my wishes in choosing a place for him, that there should be no bar between me and the little boy. So I let Percy go in November 1867.

Albert knew that this was not the end of the matter. "What new thing may set McFarland on the war-path I know not," he wrote Junius on December 1. "You will remember that on the first occasion apprehending violence from him I decided not to arm myself because I did not want the blood of any man, and particularly of this most wretched man, on my hands. I have the same feeling still. It would be too horrible for the poor children who are hers and bear his name—too horrible for *her*—too horrible for *my* children. So, if he attacks me again, I shall mean to run a very great risk rather than do deadly harm to him. Indeed, I hardly know which would be the worst under any circumstances—to kill him or have him kill me. I *could* have taken his life before, when he first attacked me, with his own weapon with the most perfect ease, but I have always been glad that I did not.

"What the upshot will be Heaven only knows. You and I have faced death and seen the sweet sleep, the precious, perfect *rest* it brings, too often, to hold it in any special terror. If I go before you, I know there is no need of commending to your tenderest friendship the sweet and gentle soul whose love has blessed me, and whom unwittingly I have brought to bitter grief, instead of helping as I had hoped, her hard and grievous life."

By the spring of 1868, though a year had elapsed and the habeas action had been settled, it was clear that McFarland's wrath had not abated. He continued to badger people with his catalog of the abuses he had suffered at Albert's hands, and he now put this litany into another lawsuit, this time against Albert for alienation of affections.

About the same time, Abby learned that McFarland was not living up to his promise to educate Percy properly.

ABBY, FROM HER AFFIDAVIT

I heard the child was not in school, was not going to be there, that he was dragged from one lodging house to another, till I became so anxious I came to New-York to see him. When, accompanied by Mr. Runkle, my lawyer in New-York City, I went to the lodgings where Percy lived, I was met by Mr. McFarland with such a storm of outrage and abuse as I will not try to describe.

After this outrageous scene, which nearly broke my heart, my friends all said one thing—that I must at once take legal steps to get free from Mr. McFarland. I decided very soon to go to Indiana. The laws there, as I found on consultation, permit a divorce for drunkenness, extreme cruelty, and failure to support a wife. I was told that adultery was the only ground on which a divorce in New-York was obtainable. I knew beyond a doubt that Mr. McFarland had committed adultery while I lived with him as his wife. I had been offered proof that he had committed that crime against marriage once I had ceased to live with him. But I repeat now what I said then, with all my soul upon my lips, that I considered his treatment of me, his personal abuses, his terrible profanity, his outrages of all kinds, an infinitely greater sin against me and my womanhood than if he had committed again and again, unknown to me, the crime against the marriage relation which was the only cause the New-York courts hold just grounds for divorce. My opinion in this remains unchanged even while I write. So I went to Indiana that summer, 1868, to obtain my freedom.

Indiana was, to many Easterners, the wild and woolly West, a place wide open to all kinds of improper things, including divorce. The feral image suggested by the state's name—*land of Indians*, with all that Indians connoted to Eastern sensibilities—may have had some meaning. However, in order to take advantage of Indiana's liberality Abby had to establish residence by living there for a year to eighteen months. With Danny at her side, she left her family home in Massachusetts and went off to live in this unruly place.

Albert remained in New York, working on a biography of General Grant, who was then the Republican candidate for President. But Abby was not far from his mind. He frequently traveled west, doing research for his book, keeping up with his interests in Kansas and Colorado, and visiting his friend Sidney Howard Gay, the former managing editor of the *New York Tribune,* who had moved to Chicago to fill the same role on the *Chicago Tribune.* He asked Gay to help out Abby.

Albert to *Sidney Howard Gay*

FORDHAM, NEW YORK, SEPT. 14 1868 •

My dear Friend:

You will like the people of Chicago, but you must get used to their ways. They are intense, slashing, and particularly vehement in denouncing whatsoever or whomsoever they don't like. But they are very warm hearted, & love their friends with just as much zeal as they hate their enemies with.

Like all the Western people they have two very strong dislikes.—1. For men who are mean pecuniarily, & 2. For settlers from the east who give themselves any airs of superiority. You are neither of these, so I don't see how you can fail to like & be liked.

May good fortune attend you & your days again be bright and fruitful.

>Always faithfully yours
>*A.D.R.*

P.S. If you ever get near Indianapolis please do stop over there & call on Mrs. A.S. McFarland at Mrs. Foote's, 18 East Michigan St. She would be delighted to see you & of course knows all about you. It would cheer her exile, too. By the way, she is writing clever juvenile stories - chiefly historical sketches of the discovery period of American history with the view of weaving them with a juvenile history she is to prepare for my publishers.

If you happen to want one or two for a juvenile department of your paper - (one or two on Western early discoveries & life) write her & see what she can do. She writes often picturesquely & cleverly. I suppose tho, you have no juvenile department.— <u>Please regard her being West as confidential.</u> It was not absolutely necessary that she go there—but she did so to make assurance doubly sure. There is hope of getting the evidence needed for her release here—but it is not certain. She has been there 6 or 8 weeks.

As the months wore on, McFarland pressed his lawsuit against Albert for alienation of affections. The complaint in this action did not mince words. It baldly asserted adultery—that the defendant Richardson "did maliciously and wickedly . . . debauch and have illicit and criminal intercourse with" the wife of the plaintiff. McFarland was also touting this claim to anyone whose ear he could capture. Albert finally lost his patience. Two full years had elapsed since the McFarland separation and Daniel's first attack on him. Yet the man would not give up.

Albert decided to challenge McFarland in the way he knew best, not by filing a lawsuit, or striking a blow, or firing a shot, but by publishing a statement in the newspaper. The *New York Tribune* for March 15, 1869, carried a "card" from Albert, telling his side of the case. He rehearsed for those readers who might not have heard it, the story of McFarland's attempt on his life back in March 1867, and of McFarland's monomania thereafter on the subject of his wife and family. "He," wrote Albert referring to McFarland, "seems to have devoted himself chiefly to slandering her, and reading an alleged copy of my letter, with many dramatic accompaniments, to every acquaintance or stranger who will listen to it. He ends his tale claiming that if ever I marry her he will kill me on sight." Albert closed by throwing down the gauntlet: "Mr. McFarland has now filed a legal action against me, based on this letter, seeking damages for my alleged interference with his marriage. Whatever fault there was in my holding a loving attitude towards this lady who had very recently separated from her husband, was solely mine, and I shall not try to palliate it. Whatever sum twelve unbiased men may determine that I owe this antagonist I shall with alacrity pay, if it comes within my modest means. And finally, whatever violence he may rethreaten or reattempt, should the lady ever be legally free during my life-time she will certainly become my wife, if she will accept so poor a man as I."

It was good that Albert knew how to wield a pen, because he was in no shape to defend himself otherwise. He continued to suffer from recurring pneumonia and an eye inflammation that kept him at home, unable even to write his own letters. He managed nonetheless to maintain a running correspondence with Sidney Gay on the prospects of starting a newspaper in Chicago. The project was apparently well advanced. It was to be, Albert said, a paper to advocate the causes in which they believed, "the best possible freedom for women, the best possible freedom in trade." Gay was hunting up possible backers, and Albert was trying to recruit Junius and Lu Calhoun, among others, as correspondents.

In the midst of all this, he kept after Abby's interests, urging his friend Whitelaw Reid, who was the new editor of the *New York Tribune,* to offer her book-reviewing work and to publish an article by her on "attempts from the earliest times to get to the Indies." It is "quite graphic and spirited," he wrote to Reid. "The author," he added vaguely, "is one in whom I have special interest." The *Tribune* accepted this article, "Eastward to the Indies," and also a later article by Abby, "Westward to the Indies," to accompany the opening of the transcontinental railroad that summer.

Abby made a living turning out articles and reviews for the *Riverside,* the *Independent* and the *Atlantic,* as well as the *Tribune,* for ten to twenty-five dollars a story, while living quietly in Indianapolis with little Danny. In October 1869, after she had been there sixteen months, her lawyers felt it was time to file for divorce. They brought the action in Morgan County, a rural district outside the city, where things could be kept quieter. Notice was published in the local paper, but it is questionable whether Daniel McFarland saw or knew of it. In any event, although he did know where she was living and why, he did not appear at the divorce proceedings.

Abby's parents came out to testify for her, as did her dear and loyal friend, Lu Calhoun. At a hearing on October 14, they told of McFarland's drunkenness and his abuse and exploitation of Abby. One time, they said, he had held Danny out a window and threatened to drop him, and another time he sent two ruffians to Indiana to kidnap the boy. The most persuasive testimony, according to local newspaper reports, was that of Mrs. Calhoun, who with "her glowing face and impressive manner detailed act after act of petty tyranny and abuse most foul on the part of McFarland." By the time she finished, no judge could disagree with her rhetorical conclusion, "Would any woman with the key turned in the lock be safe with such a man?"

ABBY, FROM HER AFFIDAVIT

Within a week, my divorce petition was granted by the Superior Court of Morgan County, Indiana, and on the 31st of October, 1869, I returned to my father's house legally set free from my first marriage bond.

During the long time, almost three years, that ensued between my former separation from McFarland and my legal divorce, my acquaintance with Mr. Richardson had been most carefully guarded. We agreed, and all our friends agreed, that we had been selfish and foolish. After I returned to my father's in March, following Mr. Richardson's wounding in the first shooting, I did not see him except twice—once when he came as an emissary from Mrs. Cleveland with a proposal for settling my dispute with Mr. McFarland, and once when I was most sorely grieved and troubled, just after Percy went away. When I went to New-York in the Spring of 1868, before I left for Indiana, I saw him occasionally in the presence of friends of his and mine. During all my stay in Indiana, and in all his frequent journeyings West, I never saw him once, and he carefully avoided passing through the city where I stopped, to give no shadow of a cause for scandal.

But on the 31st of October, 1869, I came home *free*. On November 17, 1869, Mr. Richardson came on to his mother's house in Franklin to Thanksgiving. On Thanksgiving evening I met him at the railway station, as he came from his aged mother's, whose youngest son he was. For the first time since he was shot in 1867, I walked with him in the street. In all that time we had entered no place of amusement together, and had only once met accidentally at one evening party at the house of a mutual friend. It seemed as if for the first time I had a right to talk freely and unreservedly to him, so carefully had our acquaintance with each other been protected. Nothing definite was planned about our future. We could afford to wait until events shaped themselves. His health and strength seemed to have returned, and he was in boyish spirits. "I feel as if I could leap a five-barred gate at one bound," he said. "I have never felt like this since the days in prison."

Albert was indeed feeling much better. He had recovered sufficiently to attend the opening of the transcontinental railroad, ride the train on to San Francisco, and travel throughout the West once again during May and June, writing a series of travel columns on his trip for the *Tribune*. He returned to New York briefly in August, then returned to the West again for September and October. Albert was busy and exuberant. He got in some buffalo hunting in Kansas, "with keen enjoyment," thought the sport was, he acknowledged without a trace of guilt, "slaughter or disappointment." He even tried to encourage the social life of his editor and bachelor-friend Whitelaw Reid: "Miss —— whom you met with me the other Sunday, inquires longingly for you. She has two sisters, both apparently as bright & attractive as she, & their home is <u>very</u> pleasant." But most important, he continued working on his newspaper plans with Sidney Gay. Albert loved the West and saw it as a place where he and his new wife could begin a fresh life together. The day after his reunion with Abby, Albert returned to New York. She planned to join him shortly.

But less than a week later Abby got a terrible telegraph message. Albert had been attacked by McFarland again, this time right in the office of the *Tribune*. She took the night train to New York.

XIV

The Vigil at the Astor House

•ASSASSINATION

A TRAGIC SCENE IN THE

''TRIBUNE'' COUNTING ROOM•

New York World

NOVEMBER 25, 1869

Albert D. Richardson, the well-known writer and journalist was today shot in the counting room of the *Tribune* office. Dan Frohman, a clerk in the office, was about to hand Mr. Richardson his mail when a man who, for some minutes, had been standing at an inside desk at the other end of the counter, suddenly rushed towards Mr. Richardson, aimed a pistol at him and fired. The man who committed this cowardly deed is named Daniel McFarland, a shiftless vagabond who, although having no connection with the *Tribune*, has been allowed the freedom of the office. He is the same man who in March, 1867, assaulted and shot Mr. Richardson in Amity street.

The wounded man was removed to the Astor House, accompanied by a number of his friends.

•*THE ATTEMPTED ASSASSINATION*•

New York Tribune and
New York Sun
NOVEMBER 26, 1869

As he was carried to the Astor House, Mr. Richardson was at first in great distress, vomiting blood and bile so freely as to lead to the apprehension that his liver had been wounded. As the night wore on, however, under the influence of anodynes, his paroxysms ceased, and he slept. Gentlemen from the editorial staff of *The Tribune* sat up with him all night, with other personal friends, to administer to the wants of the sufferer. Dr. Swan was also within call. Early in the morning Mrs. Sage, formerly the wife of McFarland, and her mother arrived from Boston to keep watch and ward in the sick chamber.

They found him smiling and reading the papers about his attack. "Mack has improved as a marksmen," he commented grimly. His condition, though critical, is now very encouraging.

•CONDITION OF MR.

RICHARDSON

HOPES OF RECOVERY•

New York Tribune and
New York World

NOVEMBER 27–28, 1869

As soon as the day had fairly set in, there was a constant stream of visitors to his room. The effect of so many visitors some expressing their sympathy by a few kind words or a hearty grip of the hand, some by a bouquet of violets, or some other flowers, while in one sense gratifying, rather excited and wearied the patient, so that in the early part of the afternoon the following notice had to be posted:

MR. RICHARDSON'S CONDITION IS NOW CRITICAL, AND WILL BE FOR SOME DAYS, AND HIS RECOVERY IS LARGELY DEPENDENT UPON PERFECT REST AND QUIET. CONSEQUENTLY WE PARTICULARLY REQUEST THAT HIS FRIENDS WILL REFRAIN FROM CALLING AT HIS ROOM OR VISITING THE HALL OF THE FLOOR WHERE HE IS LYING, UNTIL THE CRISIS IS PAST.

JUNIUS HENRI BROWNE
WHITELAW REID

During yesterday afternoon, the doctors made a careful and thorough examination of the wound, and ascertained that the ball had lodged in the fleshy part of the back, having passed completely through the stomach, and was in such a position that there was no immediate necessity to extract it.

Mr. Richardson's condition improved for a time. His pulse was strong and good. But toward evening he became more restless and excited, and showed a strong inclination to talk in a confused and rambling manner. He developed a fever, and his pulse became weaker and more rapid. He could retain nothing in his stomach, so the doctors supported him with injections of milk.

• *MR. RICHARDSON BETTER* •

New York Tribune and
New York Sun

NOVEMBER 29, 1869

On Monday morning Dr. Sayre was summoned, and for an hour between 8 and 9 a.m. he probed the wound and removed the ball, bringing up a quantity of purulent matter, and opening a channel where it was possible for the festering from the wound to discharge itself. He found the ball more deeply embedded than he had anticipated. It is a large conical ball, and remains in Dr. Sayre's possession. The use of chloroform or ether was thought to be inadmissible, but the sufferer bore the operation with great fortitude and without a single complaint.

After the ordeal, his soiled underclothing was then for the first time removed, and Mr. Richardson soon fell into a gentle sleep from which he awoke greatly refreshed. About noon he had still further rallied. His pulse fell from 126 to 96. They gave him injections of beef tea for nourishment, and threw a little rum in a fine spray upon his face to cool him.

The interest in Mr. Richardson's condition was so great that a bulletin is being posted in the *Tribune* office every two or three hours. The surgeon now says there was no internal hemorrhage, so that the principal danger is peritonitis. The next forty-eight hours will be critical.

•*A. D.   RICHARDSON   DYING*•

New   York   Tribune   and
New   York   Sun

NOVEMBER 30, 1869

After the operation, in spite of the most assiduous care, Mr. Richardson's strength slowly but too surely fell. Injections of beef tea and brandy were constantly administered. He has not consumed anything for four days because his stomach will not retain it. On Tuesday morning there appeared to be no improvement in his condition. His pulse was 145 and very weak, he was nervous and restless, and his mind at times rambled, though generally he was lucid. There is hardly a ray of hope that he can recover.

ABBY, FROM HER AFFIDAVIT

As soon as I arrived at the Astor House, Albert asked me, if there should be no hope of his recovery, whether I would marry him at once, and I said I would. He wished to be married that I might have a firmer legal right to take charge of rearing his three orphaned children; and also because he could die more peacefully having made me his wife. As for myself, if I had ten thousand lives, I should have been more than glad to have given them up for him who was dying for the crime of having loved me. His lightest wish in the matter would have weighed with me against all other motives in the world. So, when it became plain that he must go away from all the hearts that yearned to hold him here, we decided to proceed.

Lu Calhoun had alerted two of New York's most famous ministers, the Reverend Henry Ward Beecher—the Great Divine—and the Reverend Octavius Brooks Frothingham. They were now summoned.

At 5:30 P.M. Tuesday afternoon, November 30, the fifth day after the shooting, a small crowd of friends and family gathered in the room at the Astor House to witness a heartbreaking ceremony. Junius was there and, of course, Dan Frohman, who remained sleeping in the corridor. So were Lu and her sister Lilly Gilbert. Albert's brother Charles attended for his family, and Abby's mother for hers.

The groom lay on his back, propped up with pillows. Abby sat in a chair by the bed, their hands clasped. "Our father," said Rev. Frothingham, "may it please Thee to bind together these two hearts,

THE DEATHBED MARRIAGE, AS DEPICTED
IN *THE RICHARDSON-MCFARLAND TRAGEDY*.

and though the hands may not hold each other through the journey of life, may they still be one before Thee, to whom life and death, the world to come and this world are the same."

Rev. Beecher spoke the crucial phrases.

"Do you take the woman whom you have by your side now, in this hour, standing near the heavenly land, and renew to her the pledges of your love? Do you give your heart to her, and your name? Is she before God and before these witnesses, your beloved, your honored and your lawful wife?"

"Yes," the dying man answered in a clear and firm voice.

The minister turned to Abby.

"Do you accept him as your head in the Lord? And are you now to him a wife sacred and honored; bearing his name? And will you love him to the end of your life?"

"I do . . . and I will."

"Then by the authority given me by the Church of Christ I do pronounce you husband and wife; and may the blessings of Almighty God, the Father, the Son and the Holy Spirit, rest upon you and abide with you. Amen."

• *S C E N E S   A T   T H E   D E A T H - B E D* •

New York Sun

DEC. 1-2, 1869

All the next day, Albert lingered in his bed, saying goodbye to his friends and family who clustered about his bedside. At 9 o'clock in the evening, he lost consciousness, but was revived on and off by small doses of brandy. Between 3 and 4 o'clock in the morning he became momentarily conscious, and pronounced the name of his new wife, who stood before him. His sufferings were evidently very severe. He frequently gasped for breath, and gave utterance to low moans. At half past four he sank into a quiet stupor, but continued to breath. A stillness reigned in the room. The muffled tinkle from the bell of a street car was heard, followed by the dull roaring of milk carts on Broadway. The bell of St. Paul's struck five. Before its last vibration had melted away, Mr. Richardson drew a last gasp.

Albert was thirty-six years old. He and Abby had been married for sixty hours.

BOOK TWO

The Trial

XV

The Mood

Junius Henri Browne to *Sidney Howard Gay,*

Managing Editor, Chicago Tribune

ASTOR HOUSE, TUESDAY, 4 P.M., DECEM. 14TH, 1869 •

Dear Gay,

During the terrible six days that our friend lay at the Astor House, I was in no mood to write, and supposed the information that we furnished the public would keep you advised of his condition. I knew from the first the almost necessarily fatal character of his wound; but I would not and did not surrender hope until I saw the stamp of death on his face. Thru all of his sufferings he bore himself with a calmness and courage almost superhuman. All my sorrow could not repress my admiration for the noble fellow. I hope when I take the train for the cemetery that I shall be half as philosophic as he. There was a good deal of the stuff of which heroes are made in our departed friend.

His desolate widow, how my heart weeps for her. She is one of the best and purest and truest of women; and, if I understand myself, nothing shall prevent me from being her steadfast friend. I feel for her as for a stricken sister especially since the shameful slanders of the Press have been heaped upon her.

Could anything be more infamous than the course of the

newspapers? I expected no decency from the <u>Herald</u>, <u>World</u>, or <u>Express</u>; but I did think the <u>Sun</u> would at least be charitable. The insinuations, the falsehoods, the one-sided statements they have published make me hate New-York which in the main is made up of thieves and Irishmen. If I could I should leave the country never to return. One is almost forced to conclude that the race of gentlemen is dying out in America.

> Sincerely and sadly
> *J.H.B.*

The press had indeed jumped on the incident as though it were a major event, upstaging such matters as the opening of the Suez Canal. LAMENTABLE TRAGEDY proclaimed the *Times* on page one, column one. But even more than a news story it was an occasion for editorial posturing. Albert's old friends at the *Tribune* and the *Independent* (still edited by Oliver Johnson) urged quick justice—meaning a murder conviction. But this was not the popular view. Other papers saw better circulation gains in trumpeting the cause of McFarland.

Junius's grievance about the *Sun* was well founded. For the first few days after the shooting the paper had been sympathetic to a dying fellow journalist, and to Abby, whom it described reverently: "Her whole aspect suggests a high tone of mental and physical harmony. Her voice and expression denote exceeding gentleness and modesty, and she shrinks with pain from the publicity to which she has been subjected." McFarland was portrayed as a drunk prone to violence, and a man with "the habit of opium eating for the purpose of drowning his sorrows." But on December 2, the *Sun* suddenly set on the dying man. A PUBLIC OUTRAGE ON RELIGION AND DECENCY it asserted in a lengthy editorial. Albert was now condemned for luring Abby away from her husband. As for McFarland, if he was guilty of any crime, it was only the crime of poverty. The next day, the front-page news story was Albert's death, but the editorial page did not pause for compassion, continuing with condemnations of "free-love follies" and "hymeneal mummery." A notice to news dealers on page 1, column 1, a few days later explained the *Sun*'s change of heart. The dealers were advised that the editorial on A PUBLIC OUTRAGE was so popular it had sold out the paper, and that it was being reprinted in the weekly edition, which should be ordered in advance.

There was no stopping the *Sun* now, as it began dredging up whatever it could to paint Albert and Abby as adulterers, and sell papers. Quoting such evidence as the allegations of McFarland's brother, "Abby went reading just to get a chance to paint her face, pass for a beauty, and get in with that free-love tribe at Sam Sinclair's," the *Sun* abruptly transformed the lovely, high-toned Abby into "a woman who had not regard enough for herself or her children to keep her, while married to one man, from shameless adulterous intercourse with another." By the end of the week, Abby was a woman of no talent, and McFarland was a distinguished Shakespearian scholar and an elocutionist.

James Gordon Bennett's *Herald*, always competing with the *Tribune*, could not resist joining in: "The Socialistic circles of this metropolis, composed mainly of people nominally married, are on the eve of a thorough and merciless overhauling, and the Richardson–McFarland affair will hasten this." The paper conceded that Albert was "everything claimed for him by his friends—talented, pure and high minded." But he was nonetheless guilty of breaking up a marriage that had produced ten years of "uninterrupted domestic happiness." Abby, too, came in for scorn. "Richardson, with all his charm of manner, would have failed to seduce from her allegiance a woman truly loyal to her husband. Is there any sane respectable citizen of New York who would care to see the wife whom he had lived with for ten years, and the mother of his children, quit the privacy of a happy domestic life to strut in gaudy costume on the stage of a theatre? Her head was turned with vanity. Such is life where instincts are perverted."

The Richardson–McFarland case became a *cause célèbre*. As with all such matters, the *cause* was not the individuals involved—not Daniel McFarland, or Albert Richardson, or Abby Sage, who were mere mortals—but something grander. This time it was the state of marriage. Adultery was the only ground for divorce in New York, and the mass of popular opinion thought this was just fine. But feminist reformers wanted easier access to divorce to enable them to escape from enslaving marriages.

Women seized on the case to advance their position. While the *Herald* was editorializing against Albert and Abby, the news pages of the same paper covered the opposing view. "The recent shooting of Mr. Richardson is an unfortunate occurrence that illustrates the fundamental problem of marriage, inequality of rights between husband and wife," said Mrs. S. F. Norton, speaking before the feminist Reform Club. She advocated a new kind of marriage, with equality. "Abby Sage was a woman mentally cultivated to outgrow her husband," Mrs. Norton explained. "The knowledge she acquired from year to year would in all probability have brought with it sufficient wisdom to have enabled her to bear the disappointment of her husband's non-development for the sake of her children and society. But he put it out of her power to do so by committing acts of violence against her. This changed her feelings from resignation to active contempt and resistance against a fate which she could see no just reason for submitting to. She earned their bread. What could she do? In such circumstances, free love is perfectly proper, since love itself must be free." What the Reform Club wanted was "a right of divorce whenever bondage is hateful and intolerable."

It was a visionary idea. The speaker who followed Mrs. Norton applauded all that she had said and complained that women could not even do this at the theater—express their approval with applause—unless the male portion of the audience took the lead. The right of spontaneous female applause was on the Reform Club's wish list, along with no-fault divorce. The times may have been progressive in some ways. When a delegation of American Jews asked President Grant to intervene with Czar Alexander II of Russia to avert the latest pogrom, the President responded sympathetically. "It is too late in this day of enlightenment," Grant said, "to persecute any race, color or religion." But attitudes toward women had not yet moved into the new age.

Egged on by the press, the public began to take up sides, and most people seemed to see it as the *Sun* and the *Herald* did. Either you were for the lovers—meaning you were for immorality—or you were for McFarland—meaning you honored the right of a husband to defend his family. Even thoughtful intellectual journals such as *The Nation,* which was not given to rabble-rousing, sided with the avenging husband. For this elite publication, the issue was one of controlling "sexual passion." If a person merely assisted in bringing about a separation and divorce with a thought of marrying one of the parties, he or she was "for all the purposes of a moral judgment, guilty of adultery, and ipso facto exposes himself or herself to the social penalties of the community." This was absolutely necessary to protect the institution of the family and the sacred interests of children. "So it is with Mr. Richardson," *The Nation* pronounced.

The staid *Times* chimed in with anxiety about the THE DISGRACE OF INDIANA—THE DIVORCE LAW. "A man in New-York," said this newspaper of record, "becoming tired of his wife, or a wife preferring some more wealthy or attractive suitor, can, on going out to Indianapolis and spending a pleasant winter, and giving notice in some obscure paper, be henceforth at liberty to follow 'elective affinities' and marry again. We already know of a young couple that entered into marriage here, as they might form a partnership for a dance. They know it can be almost as easily broken by a Western Court." Thus, said the *Times,* "the high sanctity of that tie which has been an inheritance of our race since the time of Tacitus is now trampled in the dust and made a vulgar thing."

The deathbed marriage (tagged "the unholy marriage" by the *Sun*) provoked most of the criticism. As touching as this wedding may have been to those who loved Albert and Abby, it was not an effective strategy for courting public favor. George Templeton Strong, whose diary records the feelings of an enlightened, well-to-do New York lawyer of the time, gives a sense of the reaction in his entry for December 4, 1869: "The Reverend Henry Ward Beecher's indiscretion in marrying Albert D. Richardson, on his death bed, to the wife of his murderer—for she was his wife, barring a worthless Western divorce—is pretty generally denounced. It tends to turn the tide of feeling that was running very strongly against McFarland, the murderer, and may save his neck by no very logical process. I fear there is a good deal of rather lewd practice among the women of the upper middle strata. A newspaper correspondent this morning thinks so and takes high moral ground about it, and also complains that it diminishes the legitimate profits of the poor girls who make their living that way! The *New York World* attacks Beecher with great bitterness. That's no new thing, of course, but this attack is really damaging. It seems a rule that these popular sensational 'free thinkers' of the pulpit and platform, such as Beecher, Frothingham, and others, have a screw loose somewhere. They are brilliant, clever, astute talkers, efficient in business—'men of the world' and of affairs, far more than ordinary clerics; yet every now and then their common sense gives way and lets them down, with a grievous fall, into some flagrant disastrous blunder, like this one."

Henry Ward Beecher had made religion safe for capitalism. To a country founded on Puritan asceticism and self-denial, he preached a doctrine that glorified wealth earned through hard work. This was a theology for the times. The population was moving from farms to cities, and the industrial and commercial expansion of the gilded age made old values obsolete. The Plymouth Church in Brooklyn, built for the Great Divine, seated three thousand, and it was full each Sunday of devotees who came to assuage their guilt. Beecher himself tried to set a good example. His home was luxurious. He carried uncut gems in his pockets, which he loved to fondle. But he also led his parishioners down the road to social reform and embraced the crusades of the day. Rifles, known as Beecher's Bibles, went from the Plymouth Church to free-state settlers in Kansas before the war, and a slave once was brought to its pulpit so that parishioners could bid to buy her freedom. After the war, Beecher adopted the cause of women's suffrage. By coinci-

REV. HENRY WARD BEECHER.

dence, on the same day that Albert was shot, Beecher had been elected symbolic head of the American Woman Suffrage Association, as it strove to link its future to abolitionist ideals.

Beecher was a celebrity. He knew it and he made sure of it. So when Mrs. Calhoun asked him to perform the deathbed marriage of the famous and popular journalist Albert D. Richardson, the minister hardly thought twice. This would be an event covered in every newspaper. It was, he thought, important enough to deserve him.

Octavius Brooks Frothingham, who conducted the wedding with Beecher, was another religious muse. A disciple of and successor to the late Theodore Parker (who had married Abby and Daniel twelve years before), Frothingham advocated a "rationalistic system of theology," in opposition to traditional dogmatism. His cousin, the writer Henry Adams, thought "he distressed his father and scandalized Beacon Street by avowing a skepticism that seemed to solve no old problems, and to raise many new ones." But Frothingham's Independent Liberal Church offered a spiritual haven for those who rejected the religiosity of their childhood, and could not quite bring themselves to abandon God.

Their "blunder" in marrying Albert and Abby put these moral leaders on the defensive. The Great Divine tried to evade responsibility, pleading ignorance in the matter. He said he did not know the circumstances of the divorce. Frothingham was more forthright, or more brazen, propounding from his pulpit an elaborate justification of "elective affinities." As he explained it, "The doctrine is simply this. That men and women are united not only on the animal plan of passion but on the rational plan that they belong to each other, not by force of any animal magnetism, but by force of culture; not by the strength of any sensuous affinity, but by the strength of mutual harmony and sympathy of purpose."

It was a refined idea, but no one knew what it meant. The notion of elective affinities in romantic relations had been given currency by Goethe sixty years earlier in a novel of the same name, written while the writer was in the throes of an affair with a much younger woman. Goethe derived the title from a theory of chemistry that purported to explain how substances react and form new compounds when they are combined. That did not seem to be what Rev. Frothingham had in mind.

This was a time full of radical ideas about relations between the sexes. The utopian notions of Charles Fourier and his followers— that society should be organized in agricultural communes, in which wealth was distributed equally and sex was offered without marriage—were tantalizingly discussed. Such august citizens as Horace Greeley had actively supported a Fourierite community in Red Bank, New Jersey, before the war. For much of the public there was little difference between elective-affinity advocates, Fourierites, radical advocates of free love, and suffragettes. All wanted to deviate from the security of the traditional family norm, and all were equally threatening.

XVI

The Assassin

McFarland was quickly indicted for murder, a capital offense, on December 8, just six days after Albert died. But the trial was delayed. Albert's friends had supposed that the process of justice would be swift. What could be simpler, or plainer, than the truth: McFarland shot Richardson down in cold blood, in full view of many witnesses. Dan Frohman, who had been right there and seen it all, kept asking Junius and Mr. Sinclair why the villain had not been brought to justice. Their only answer was that with the press and public reaction being what it was, the district attorney felt the trial should be put off until the public temper was more calm. Albert's allies did not disagree. At least "the wretch who did the deed is safe in jail, and harmless there," wrote Mrs. Calhoun to Sidney Gay. "I think we are all relieved." Her husband, who was a lawyer and legal advisor to the *Tribune*, persuaded her that there was a reasonable chance for a fair trial and just verdict, eventually.

In the meantime, Albert's supporters, led by Junius, began to raise money to employ legal counsel to assist the district attorney, whom they thought could do with a little help. They succeeded in retaining Noah Davis, a former judge who was serving as congressman for the upstate twenty-eighth District. He was an experienced lawyer, and they thought he might have the right combination of political and legal skills for the case.

Abby took comfort in these efforts of her friends.

ABBY, FROM HER AFFIDAVIT

As the trial of his life approaches, I commiserate with Mr. McFarland deeply. I know that death, which seemed so infinitely sweet and peaceful and blessed when I turned from Mr. Richardson's deathbed, is to this unhappy man the most terrible of horrors. I hope with all my heart that he will escape that most barbarous penalty of a barbarous law.

When I heard that Judge Davis had been engaged to assist the prosecution in the case, I went to him and said, "In this case I have only one interest. The man on trial is on trial for his life, but I am no less on trial than he, and for something dearer to any woman than life could be. The best friends I have are assailed with me, good people who have befriended both the prisoner and myself. If you can only let in a little light of truth in all this cloud of abuse and calumny I beg that you do it. For the rest, I hope that this man will not be convicted, and no one is more willing to believe him insane than I." Judge Davis promised to do all he could do to the end I asked.

Junius understood Abby's feelings. But he could not tolerate the idea of an acquittal. "We know the best sentiment is with the murdered man," he wrote Sidney Gay, seeking money for the prosecution-aid fund. "The murderer must not be acquitted if we can prevent it." Gay apparently agreed, sending four hundred dollars.

In Court

New York Herald

APRIL 4, 1870

MCFARLAND ON TRIAL

*The Ordeal in the Present—The
Agony in the Past*

COMMOTION IN THE COURT ROOM

After long and vexatious delay, the celebrated McFarland case is now before the courts for trial. No homicide committed in New York for a number of years has caused such intense excitement.

It could have been Barnum's the day Tom Thumb first appeared. The delay of four months since the shooting had hardly diminished public curiosity about the case, and the newspapers made certain that any slight cooling of interest was quickly fanned back to a hot flame. Every paper had not only reporters there but stenographers to take down testimony, so they could provide readers with a verbatim transcript. This was *the* story of the moment, to be played for all it was worth.

"Seldom has the Court of General Sessions presented such an aspect as it did yesterday," continued the *Herald*. "Everyone was alive with expectation. The McFarland trial is evidently the acme of criminal sensations. People feel on both sides of the question. They feel and they cannot conceal their feelings. Eyes flash with interest and excitement. Standing room is regarded as a luxury and people buoyed up with excitement deemed it a pleasure to enjoy the privilege of standing and enjoying a look at poor McFarland, whose domestic infelicity, and its well know *denouement* have given him such unenviable notoriety. His trial will certainly be handed down, whatever its final result may be, as an authoritative case in American jurisprudence."

Daniel McFarland himself, the center of it all, was carefully dressed for the occasion in a dark-brown frock coat and pants, with a freshly laundered shirt front, dark necktie, and standing collar. He showed no emotion. He sat there, a man accused of open and notorious murder, with a clear conscience and cheerful prospects. The groundswell of public support and acclaim he had received since the shooting had convinced him of the rectitude of his actions, and his lawyers had given him reason to believe that an acquittal was likely. His demeanor, the newspapers all said, was calm and his face had, if anything, a hopeful look.

To embellish the scene, McFarland had his ten-year-old son at his side. Percy had been staying with his Uncle Owen in Newark while his father was in jail. The defense lawyers, understanding the emotional appeal it would produce, arranged for the boy to sit by the accused at the trial. He ran happily up to his father as the prisoner was brought into the court room from the Tombs. During lulls in the proceeding father and son chatted casually. The boy gave little sign of comprehending the seriousness of the pending charge, or, if he

THE TRIAL

OF

DANIEL McFARLAND

FOR THE SHOOTING OF

ALBERT D. RICHARDSON,

THE ALLEGED SEDUCER OF HIS WIFE.

BY A PRACTICAL LAW REPORTER.

CONTAINING A COMPREHENSIVE HISTORY OF THE CASE, THE PRELIMINARY MOVEMENTS;
OPENING AND CLOSING SPEECHES OF THE COUNSEL; THE DISPOSITION OF THE
PARTIES IMPLICATED, TOGETHER WITH THE LETTERS, ETC., OFFERED
IN EVIDENCE, WITH FULL AND UNABRIDGED TESTIMONY OF
ALL THE WITNESSES; TOGETHER WITH THE EVIDENCE
SUPPRESSED BY THE DAILY PRESS,

WITH A PRELIMINARY ESSAY ON MEDICAL JURISPRUDENCE BY DR. WM. HAMMOND,
AND
THE *Ex Parte* STATEMENT OF MRS. M'FARLAND.

NEW YORK:
AMERICAN NEWS COMPANY,
No. 119 Nassau Street.

did, his father and the lawyers had convinced him there was no cause for concern.

Mr. McFarland may have been an object of immense interest, but the crowd wanted even more to see *Mrs.* McFarland–Richardson. When any attractive woman was sighted, a buzz of questioning started. Much of the attention was focused on a mysterious lady in black who sat upright and rigid in the first row. Her face was covered by a veil so heavy no one could make out her features. This veiled lady was the subject of endless speculation, many supposing that she was the infamous *femme fatale*.

Abby denied it. She had resolved firmly to stay away from the trial unless summoned as a witness. Given the proclivities of the throng in attendance, she had reason to fear what they might have said, or done, had they seen her. And the proceedings themselves, with all the details of the tragedy rehashed, and with Percy, whom she missed desperately, sitting beside his father, were not something she had any desire to share. She was staying nearby, however, at a house Albert owned in New Jersey. "She is manfully brave and strong," wrote Mrs. Calhoun, "but I fear this life is over for her." Abby had her plan, however. She sat down at Albert's old desk and began carefully writing out her view of the facts. It would be ready for publication if the trial did not give her and Albert a fair hearing.

Abby's father, William Sage, was in attendance, as was Albert's brother, Charles, and his good friend Junius. Young Dan Frohman, who was destined to testify for the prosecution as an eyewitness to the shooting, was also there, sitting beside Junius and bearing witness for his lost idol.

As the proceedings got underway with jury selection, it was immediately evident that the lawyers for the two sides presented a contrast. The lead prosecutor, District Attorney Samuel Garvin, was a New York Supreme Court judge for a term before being elected district attorney. He stood six feet tall and had a cool demeanor. Dressed in a full black suit, Garvin was a commanding presence, reminding spectators more of a United States senator than a prosecuting attorney. But his abilities as a lawyer were suspect, at least in the eyes of Albert's supporters. That was the reason Noah Davis had been lured in as cocounsel. Former judge, now congressman, Davis was a stern man with a forceful personality and a broad knowledge of the law. He was known for being a close logical reasoner, "as full of precedents as Euclid is of problems." Most of his legal experience, however, had been in more bucolic regions, in the western part of the state near Rochester. Whether he was ready for the rough and tumble of a New York City courtroom remained to be seen.

Their chief antagonist, John Graham, was a short, broad-shouldered man. His appearance was most notable for a full, florid-complexioned face framed by a light gray goatee and "an ill-made wig of Scotch red hair that hid nearly half a forehead more remarkable for width than height." Observers seemed to find his bubaline appearance odd and even comic. But, quite the opposite of the D.A., Graham's skills far surpassed his image, and his reputation at the bar was impressive. "In speaking," said the *World*, "he is quick but deliberate. His sentences are sharply cut. For invective it would be difficult to find his superior anywhere in the world."

Graham also knew well the terrain he was about to travel in defending McFarland. He had been associate counsel in the famous *Sickles* case, where Congressman Daniel Sickles, a former Union general, had shot down his wife's paramour, Philip Barton Key, the son of Francis Scott Key, on a Washington sidewalk. In that case the lawyers had successfully invoked a defense of temporary insanity to win acquittal on a murder charge. The other lawyers in the case had been Edwin M. Stanton, later Lincoln's renowned secretary of war, and, as senior counsel, James T. Brady, the most famous criminal lawyer of the time. Brady was so revered that all the New York courts adjourned for the day out of respect when they learned of his death. Graham wanted to succeed to Brady's status and he saw the McFarland case as his first opportunity to prove he was worthy. It was no secret that Graham's strategy was to use the *Sickles* insanity defense for McFarland and to invoke the precedent of that case, with all its prestigious overtones, in aid of his current client.

Graham was assisted by Elbridge T. Gerry, whose grandfather was a signer of the Declaration of Independence. Gerry was famous for his scholarship. He was reputed to have locked himself up for a fortnight before the case to prepare himself. Courtly and polished, Gerry reminded one reporter of "those descriptions of the *ancien regime,* of which the Adamses are perhaps the best living representatives."

Even in the simple process of jury selection, Graham demonstrated he was master of that quintessential legal strategy, arguing any side of any point. At times Graham went too far. He asked one man, a Mr. Wentworth, if he had formed any opinion on the case. Wentworth said yes, but that he would be governed by the evidence. Graham then asked, "Is your opinion adverse to the prisoner?" When Mr. Wentworth said that it was *favorable* to the prisoner, Graham struggled to get him as a juror. "It is only a ghost-like transitory opinion that flitted through the man's brain, and should be counted for nothing," Graham argued. Or, at most, "He is only indulging in the legal presumption of innocence." However, Mr. Wentworth was excluded.

With all this legal maneuvering, the selection process went slowly. Graham did not want anyone who was part of Octavius Brooks Frothingham's congregation or was in any way sympathetic to it. He challenged men simply because they attended any Unitarian or reformist church. And he did not want men from the Sinclairs's class or circle, whom he obviously suspected would be supportive of Albert. To their good fortune, the defense did not have to worry about women, since this unenfranchised sex was not allowed on juries.

In comparison to the defense lawyers, the prosecutors were almost complaisant in the jury-selection process. They objected to someone like Mr. Wentworth, of course, but not much more. Nonetheless, the process continued for three days.

Despite Graham's strenuous efforts, the group chosen seemed fair enough. The jurors were, for the most part, ordinary merchants and tradesmen. None were part of the literary set that Graham opposed, but none were men of apparent Irish descent or loyalties, who might be expected to side emotionally with McFarland. And there was one exceptional juror, Mr. George C. Howard, an actor and theatrical manager who had once produced and played in *Uncle Tom's Cabin.* His wife was famous for her portrayal of Topsy, a little black girl, in the play, and his daughter Cordelia had been Eva. Such a man might be expected to be sympathetic to Albert and Abby. Their supporters, who had been dumbfounded by Graham's machinations during the selection process, even had reason to feel encouraged that the jury might be more disposed to the prosecution than to the defense.

The prosecution opened on the fourth day. "The excitement continues unabated," reported the *Times*, "and long before the hour of eleven the corridors and steps leading to the General Sessions Court-room were thronged with people anxious to gain admission." McFarland was brought in about a half hour early and sat calmly in his seat. Percy came soon thereafter, and was greeted with an affectionate filial salute as he took his place at his father's side.

The case presented by Garvin and Davis was straightforward—a blunt, unadorned presentation of the facts of the shooting and death.

Dan Frohman

Being first duly sworn, sayeth:

I was working in the Tribune office, in the counting room, on November 25th. I saw Mr. McFarland in the office about fifteen minutes before the shooting. He was standing at the subscription desk. He was doing something—drumming on the desk or something of that kind. He had the position one has when writing. He stood there ten or fifteen minutes, until Mr. Richardson came in. I did not look at him more than once.

Mr. Richardson came in about 5 o'clock. He came in the Spruce st. door. I noticed him when he was at the middle of the floor coming toward my desk. As soon as I saw Mr. Richardson I knew what he was coming for, and I started to get his letters, as there were two there, and I don't know whether I got hold of them or not when I heard the shot fired.

I then saw McFarland go out through the Nassau st. door. I also looked around for Mr. Richardson, and went out in the square to look for him. I went along Park Row for a while, and I went back and found him in the editorial rooms. Dr. Swan was probing the wound, and Mr. Richardson was lying on the sofa. They took him to the Astor House, and I went over myself.

On cross-examination, Dan was candid, admitting that he later learned, while at the Astor House, that Albert had a pistol with him. But he was firm in saying "I never saw a pistol in Mr. Richardson's hand," in the *Tribune* office. The press reported that he had "presented his statement without hesitation, and put his language in clear terms," and besides that, he was "a decidedly good-looking young gentleman of eighteen years."

DAN FROHMAN, IN 1872.

The entire prosecution case took only a day and half and involved no revelations. The only unexpected event occurred when Graham attempted to argue that Albert's friends, who so carefully attended him, were the cause of his death because of their ministrations. The court would have none of this argument, but it gave everyone some warning of what might be in store from the defense lawyer. He was going to miss no opportunity to shift the blame from his client.

When it was announced that the defense would begin on Friday, April 8, with its opening statement and dramatic disclosures, the crowd reached a new high. The police finally got matters under control, but whenever the door to the courtroom had to be opened to admit someone, the crowd pressed forward again and the police had to struggle to restrain it.

The defense's opening statement did not disappoint. For almost two hours it held the audience in thrall with the story of Daniel McFarland's painful life, "a humble birth, a struggling youth, a man who had been overtaken by sorrow and calamity brought on by the unholy, reckless, and lawless passion of a bold, bad libertine; of a sensitive mind laid in ruins by wrongs accumulated upon him by a wife-seducer and child-robber sent into eternity by the hand of a husband and father wronged in a moment when the angry waves of a great sea, overwhelming it, turned away his reason."

The lawyer spared no adjective, no hyperbole. He painted his picture of McFarland as a good, honest, and hardworking family man doing his best in a hard world. But it was not enough for his wife, who "dreams of triumphs upon the stage and in society," and "pants for more refinement—a higher intelligence."

In the end, so the story went, it was too much for McFarland. He had a family history of insanity, and that devil took over his mind: "Gentlemen of the jury, virtuous women and honorable men the world over, in this the hour of Daniel McFarland's trial, stand by him. As you love and honor your wives at home, stand by him. As with a parent's affectionate love and the care you would guard your daughters, stand by him. As you regard the safety of your dear sisters, stand by him. As you revere the gray hairs of good old mothers living, or sainted ones gone to their rest in that heaven where adulterers cannot enter, and there pray for you, stand by him. By the hallowed ground of a peaceful home, by all that is sacred, pure, precious, and holy in this life of probation; stand by him. Let your verdict tell that here in our city, upon the false footsteps of those who would prostitute our sisters or our wives, shall surely follow, with unfaltering step and stern resolve, an implacable Nemesis."

Some newspapers thought the defense lawyer "had shot his arrow of righteous indignation" too far. But the spectators followed every word and broke into applause at each outpouring of emotional description. McFarland was their man, and his lawyer was their hero of the morning. This was theater just as much as the night before when Edwin Booth played Macbeth at the new Winter Garden. Only now the audience was ready to join in exclaiming, "Lay on Graham, and damn'd be him that first cries, *'Hold, enough!'* "

There was no similar reaction in the jury box. While the spectators knew they were there to enjoy themselves, and were free to show their pleasure, the jury had a different role. Its obligation was to restrain emotion, to sit in judgment. So the jurors sat immobile. But Graham had accomplished his purpose in the selection process better than Albert's allies realized. Every man on this jury was a husband and a father. They were not merely men, they were *family* men.

The defense had a simple strategy. They knew this was not just a murder case. In the public's mind, the trial was not of Daniel McFarland for the killing of Albert Richardson. It was of family tradition, threatened by new ideas. McFarland's lawyers saw that they had to make McFarland the common man, acting out of desperation to protect all that he, and the jury, held dear. They also had to make Albert the libertine, and Abby the fallen woman.

XVIII

The Intercepted Letter

New York Herald

APRIL 8, 1870

THE
MCFARLAND TRIAL

The First Trace of the Tempter

THE INTERCEPTED LETTER FROM RICHARDSON TO MRS. MCFARLAND AND THE ELOPEMENT

Long before the hour fixed for the opening of the Court of General Sessions, a crowd of probably two thousand persons had congregated in and about the old brown stone building in which the trial of Mr. McFarland is being held. A large number of respectably dressed females were among the most clamorous for admittance; and several of them, who did all that their persuasive powers

could to induce the officers to let them in, had little babes in their arms.

The rough and tumble crowd of court loungers were also out in considerable strength, and the atmosphere in the hallways was heavily laden with the delightful odor of Fourth ward whiskey and molasses, as a most odoriferous matter of course. This portion of the would-be spectators, however, did not seem to have much influence with the court officers, and but very few of them succeeded in squeezing their precious carcasses into the room.

The greatest excitement on this first day of defense testimony came when McFarland's lawyers produced a notorious "intercepted letter" that Albert had written to Abby shortly after her marital separation, from his temporary residence in Hartford. As Mr. Gerry of the defense team began to read it in a loud, clear voice, the *Herald* reported "there was a stillness of death in the court-room, and nothing could be heard save the ringing tones of the counsel's voice, as he emphasized every word of the extraordinary epistle. He did not read it hurriedly, but slowly and deliberately, and as he went over sentence after sentence of the letter he would ever and anon stop for a short time and look steadily at the jury, as if to study the effect on them of what he was reading."

Albert to Abby

HARTFORD, MARCH 9, 1867 — 4:50 P.M. •

Darling Abby,

I received two hours ago, darling, yours of yesterday.

At noon I mailed you the Atlantic for March to No. 72. You should be back living there by the time it arrives. This letter I send in care of Mr. S., hoping that you may get it tomorrow.

Don't be disturbed about your family, little girl. Families

always respect accomplished facts (my hobby, you know). I once outraged mine a great deal worse than you ever can yours, and they are the straightest sect of Puritans—but Time made it all correct.

So you couldn't go to Mrs. M.'s till Monday, and couldn't have my room. Be patient, little girl, and <u>you</u> shall have to give, not take, orders about my room.

Learn all you can about the material and contents of the new book within the next few weeks; for we may want to announce it in my book. Please remember that it <u>ought to have</u> plenty of humor, and that it <u>must</u> have some horrors. If you recoil from them you shall not have to do them.

Darling, I smiled at my being "pining and hurt" about my former lady friend. Why, I am like a man who has got rid of his elephant, and am lighter hearted than I have been for years; indeed I felt as if a weight had been lifted from me, even before your sweet love came to sweeten and bless my life. I was not pining. All the trouble with her was that she thought she could not let me go. Long ago, when she and I first came together, I said to her, we will make no vows to love each other always—of that we cannot tell. I will only exact that you tell me the <u>perfect</u> truth whether it keeps us together or separates us, and she replied, God helping me, I will. She tried to, but the leopard could not change its spots, and she did her best and was very tender and loving, and I have nothing in the world to complain of. If you had not come to me, little girl, it would have made no difference. <u>That</u> scene was ended long ago.

Our news will rather startle Mrs. S., won't it, darling; I think she will like it in the end.

What a goosie you are about my coming home. <u>Of course,</u> I shall come, whenever my business compels or will let me. What judgment shall you fear, doing no wrong? The circumstances make it right and unnoticeable, and I will not stay away for 40,000 Mrs. Grundy's. I will not neglect my work to come; but it is quite possible I may have to come next week. I have not been waiting for you darling all these years to wear haircloth and serve seven years now; I want you always. A hundred times a day my arms seem to stretch out toward you. I never seek my pillow without wanting to fold you to my heart for a goodnight kiss and blessing, and the few months before you can openly be mine will be long enough at best. No grass shall grow under my feet, but I never let public opinion bully me a bit, and never mean to; so, sunbeam, I shall come whenever I can, and stay as long as business will permit. I will decide about the summer just as soon as I can, darling; can probably surmise by Monday or Tuesday.

Darling, I should be <u>afraid</u> if you had fascinated me in a day or a week. The trees which grow in an hour have no deep root. Ours I believe to be no love of a noon-day hour, but for all time. Only <u>one</u> love ever grew so slowly into my heart as yours has, and that was so tender and blessed that heaven needed and took it. My darling, you are all I would have you, <u>exactly</u> what I would have you, in mind, body and estate, and my tired heart finds in you infinite rest, riches and sweetness. Good night my own, my love, my wife.

Burn this—will you not?

Your loving,
Albert

Rumors about this letter preceded the trial, and everyone knew its thrust, but most people had not seen it or heard the particulars. The details exceeded everyone's expectations. This was sensation. The newspapers all carried the full text. The reaction of the audience was "positively tremendous and utterly indescribable," said the *Herald*'s reporter. The last damning line in the letter, "Burn this—will you not?" was added in pencil somehow dramatizing its guilty quality. It embodied the spirit of the letter as the audience heard it.

The mention of a new book in the letter was of particular interest. The *World* had printed a lengthy story, without attribution, claiming that Albert and Abby had traveled together to Hartford to see about interesting his publisher in a book she had written. This trip was said to have been made during the winter of 1867, presumably while Abby was still living with McFarland. This rumor was never confirmed, and Graham never mentioned it. But the reference in the letter gave some credence to the rumor, and the public naturally suspected the worst.

Garvin and Davis might have challenged the introduction of this damaging letter, since it seemed of questionable relevance to an alleged murder two and a half years after it was written. But they did not utter a word of objection.

Abby never had a chance to burn this intercepted letter; she never received it. It was sent to the *Tribune* office, addressed to *Mrs.* McFarland in care of Mr. Sinclair, since she had taken refuge under the Sinclair roof. But *Mr.* McFarland just happened to be at the *Tribune* office when it arrived, and the mail clerk (not Dan Frohman in this instance) handed the letter to him.

McFarland kept the letter for his own. He read it again and again, obsessively. He brooded over it. He began badgering people with it, reading passages to them, soliciting their sympathy for himself and their enmity for Albert. Matters became still worse when McFarland learned of Abby's activities in moving back to their old lodgings at No. 72 Amity Street and her involvement with Albert there.

MRS. MARY MASON

Being first duly sworn, sayeth:

I keep a boarding house at No. 72 Amity street. I know Mr. McFarland and his wife. They had rooms in my house for three or four months at the beginning of 1867, just before they separated. Mr. Richardson also had a room in the house.

Shortly after Mrs. McFarland left her husband, and he too moved from my boarding house, she came back and asked me to let her have her old room again. This was the first week in March 1867. She said the gentleman's family, Mr. Sinclair's it was, where she was staying were coming back from Washington, and she wished to have the room until the termination of her theater engagement. She was performing at the Winter Garden, I believe. I told her I could not let her have the room because my husband was using it.

She then asked if she could have Mr. Richardson's room while he was away. There was a lady with her whom she called Miss Gilbert, and whom she introduced as Mr. Richardson's intended. Mrs. McFarland said Miss Gilbert had told her Mr. Richardson was away in Hartford publishing a book, and that he would be away about six weeks. She said Miss Gilbert would sleep there with her.

I would not let her have Mr. Richardson's room, but finally agreed she could have her old room, the back parlor adjoining his room, in a week's time.

Abby moved back to her old room on March 11, just after the fateful letter completed its errant trajectory into McFarland's hands. The next evening Albert unexpectedly returned from Hartford.

Junius Henri Browne

Being first duly sworn, sayeth:

Lilly and I escorted Abby home the night of March 12 after her performance at the Winter Garden. We did not attend the performance, but waited there for her in the tiny vestibule by the Mercer st. entrance, sitting on the rough little board seats.

We returned to Abby's room and sat for a while conversing when, at about half-past eleven or twelve, Albert knocked at the door. He had let himself into the house with his night key. I said "Come in." He entered and shook hands with me. I remained there about fifteen or twenty minutes, and Miss Gilbert let me out. She was to stay with Abby for the night.

Lillian Gilbert

Being first duly sworn, sayeth:

I first met Mrs. McFarland through my sister, Lu Calhoun, and she and I became good friends. I accompanied her to Mrs. Mason's when she went to see about getting her old room back and I agreed to spend the nights with her. She planned to stay there for several weeks, until her engagement in the theater was completed. That is how I came to be at the room with Mr. Browne and her on the night of March 12. I had also slept there on March 11, the first night that she returned to the house on Amity st.

Although Mr. Richardson was occupying the room next door to Mrs. McFarland, he was away in Hartford and had not been expected to return for three or four weeks. But he had sent a telegram that afternoon saying he would return early, so we anticipated his arrival.

Mr. Richardson arrived some time after 11 o'clock, and I saw Mr. Browne out a little after 12 o'clock. Mr. Richardson returned to his room about the same time and we all retired. I spent the night with Mrs. McFarland.

The next morning, about 9 o'clock, Mr. Richardson rapped at the door to the room and asked if he might come in. Mrs. McFarland was not there at the time. She had gone out to purchase something for breakfast. I said, "The room isn't prepared, you can't come in yet; I will prepare the room, and then you can come." He went away for about fifteen minutes, and then knocked again. Mrs. McFarland had not returned. He came in and stayed about ten minutes until she arrived. He spoke with us only for five minutes and then said he had to go downtown to breakfast. He did not ask to breakfast with us, nor did we invite him.

At that time, I had no knowledge that there was an attachment between Mrs. McFarland and Mr. Richardson. Mr. Richardson's calling at her room seemed to me only friendly. If I had thought that she had gone there with any improper intention I should not have gone with her. I believed then, and I believe now, that there was nothing between them until after she left her husband. I believe that his love was caused by her troubles and misfortunes then, and that it never had any existence before.

After breakfast, I returned home to my mother's in Newark.

KATE MCFARLAND

Being first duly sworn, sayeth:

I am the wife of Mr. George McFarland, a brother of Daniel McFarland. On the afternoon of March 13, 1867, I went to call on my brother-in-law at his rooms on Amity st. I did not know then of the troubles between him and Mrs. McFarland, or that he had moved away. I found Mrs. McFarland there, with Mr. Richardson in her company. She was arranging her false curls in his presence. They both seemed very much confused and embarrassed. At first she could not speak, and she did not introduce him to me. He remained only a few moments after I came in. Before leaving he said he hoped to meet her again before he left the next day. She replied that he certainly would if he came around to Mrs. Sinclair's.

Kate soon found her brother-in-law and told him what she had seen and heard. He wasted no time in acting.

PATROLMAN THOMAS CULHANE

Being first duly sworn, sayeth:

I am a member of the Metropolitan Police—I mean the new police, the police of the City of New York. I am the police officer who took the pistol from Daniel McFarland on the night of March 13, 1867. With officer Leery, I took him and Mr. Richardson to the station-house. We summoned a surgeon for Richardson.

Shortly thereafter, Mrs. McFarland came to the station-house. I was standing with McFarland at the desk. He seemed to be very much excited and nervous. But she walked right by him, and inquired after the wounded man. I pointed at McFarland and asked her, "Is this your husband?" She said, "Yes, he was once my husband, but not now." She rushed into the room where Richardson was being attended to by the surgeon. She called him "Dear," and she stood there while the surgeon removed the ball and dressed the wound. He was wounded in the groin.

"Where heroes are never wounded," interjected Graham. "People that look men in the eye never get a wound there."

PATROLMAN CULHANE (CONTINUING)

Mr. McFarland stood by my desk this entire time. I have a recollection he acted like a man in something of a daze, like he did not realize the position in which he had placed himself.

Afterward, Mrs. McFarland asked if I could get a coach for her. I did, and went with her and Richardson in it to the house on Amity st. She went in and brought out some clothing and a bottle of whiskey. She said to him, "You had better take some liquor, it will do you good," and when they were going on in the coach, she laid her head on his knee right so, and said, "My dear, how do you feel?"

We took him to No. 8 West Washington place and carried him up to a bedroom. It was Mr. Sinclair's house. He and another gentleman helped us. I think it was Mr. Runkle. I left them there.

XIX

A Luscious Woman

New York Times

APRIL 11, 1870

THE MCFARLAND TRIAL

---

*The Defendant's Mental Condition
Previous to the Shooting*

The sixth day of the trial of Daniel McFarland for the alleged murder of Albert D. Richardson was an unpleasant one, the rain falling copiously during most of the day, but notwithstanding this fact the approaches to the trial chamber were completely packed with persons anxious to gain admission, if even for time sufficient to take one look at McFarland. As usual, McFarland, little Percy, and the brothers of the defendant were early in attendance.

The testimony for the defense this day was very important, and almost wholly directed to prove the condition of McFarland's mind.

Mrs. Mary Oliver

Being first duly sworn, sayeth:

I am the daughter of the late Francis McFarland, who was a first cousin to the prisoner, Daniel McFarland. They had the same grandfather. I remember when my father died; there is a record in the family bible. "Departed this life, Sunday, 13th of September, 1847, at 5:30 P.M., Francis McFarland, aged 40 years, 9 months and 22 days." Father was ill for eighteen months or two years before his death. He took fits of crying and melancholy. He did not attempt violence to any one but himself. He often tried to strangle himself. His spirits were very depressed. On two occasions he attempted suicide. This was previous to his being sent to the insane asylum.

We were compelled to send him to the asylum, on Blackwell's Island, because he got so desperate we could not manage him. I accompanied him there, and I saw him twice during his confinement. On both occasions he was very violent and desperate; he had on a strait-jacket both times. He remained in the asylum a couple of months. About that time he got helpless. He became paralyzed.

As he could not do any harm to himself we took him home. We could then manage him there. He lived but a short time longer. I watched him during his last illness. He died biting his flesh and gnawing his shoulders.

At first the implication of this sad story was obscure, but suddenly Mrs. Oliver pointed to McFarland, and blurted out, "My cousin there looks enough as my father looked then to be him."

The insanity defense had begun.

John D. Billings

Being first duly sworn, sayeth:

I am an attorney-at-law and friend of the accused. I have known him ever since the Fall of 1859. He was engaged in the business of real estate at that time—buying and selling land in the West, in Wisconsin, I think.

I saw Mr. McFarland perhaps twenty-five times over the two years after his wife left him. Usually he was very excited and voluble. He hardly met me on any occasion or came to my office but what he commenced to talk about Mr. Richardson taking away his wife and children. He read me that letter from Richardson to his wife. On all those occasions he would talk incoherently, and appeared in an abnormal condition. He never talked on any other subject, never, to my knowledge.

I remember one instance. It was about the 27th March, 1867. He came to my office, 80 Broadway. He said he had been to Boston in reference to proceedings to get his children. When he came in he sat down in a chair, commenced to cry, and began telling me of his troubles. As he did so, he would sit in his chair a spell, then get up and walk backward and forward, put his hand to his head and pull his hair, and say, "Oh my children; my God, what have I done that they should hate me?" Then he would cry and say, "I love my children and wife, and, Oh God, they have taken her away from me." I tried to calm him down and found I could not do it. He was in such a state of excitement of mind that he could hardly be considered rational.

I saw him again several months later, on the last of July or the first of August, 1867. He told me he could not bear the thought of his children having some other father besides him. It made him frantic, wild. "I would rather be in my grave than as now; if I cannot have my children restored to me I would rather be in my grave." He said he spent all he had, between $3,000 and $4,000, pursuing a habeas corpus case trying to get them; and that he had commenced a civil suit against Richardson as well, because he wanted to show the community all the facts. He wanted to show that Richardson was a libertine and a thief. He said he understood Richardson to be a wealthy man, and would use all the money necessary to accomplish his purpose in fighting against him in regard to his children.

I then put my arm around him and felt his pulse. It was 115 or 117. He said it had been so for three or four months. His face was very red and dry and he looked as though he had a heavy fever. He was going down to Staten Island for his fever. He said he could not and would not sleep. He looked haggard and pale, as though he had not had any sleep, as though care-worn, and very negligent in his dress.

I saw him on the street again two years later at about 4:20 o'clock on the day of the fatal shooting, less than an hour before the central event. He had never looked so peculiar, or been so distant. It was nearly opposite the New York Hotel, in Broadway. I was alone, going up town; he was going down town. When I first noticed him, he was three or four yards away, and I observed that he looked somewhat different from the way I had been in the habit of seeing him. He had on an overcoat, his hands were in the pocket of the coat, his head was down, and his hat was pulled over his eyes.

I stopped him, and said, "Mac, how do you do?" He looked up and said, "Oh, this is you." I said, "Mac, what is the matter?" He said, "Why, what do you mean?" I said he was looking very strange, and asked him if he had been sick. He said, "No." I asked where he was going. He said, "Down town." I said, "Isn't it late to be going down town?" He said, "No." We went around again on this line of conversation, and I became more worried about him. I asked him again where he was going, and he said, "To the Park Hotel, to see a gentleman who expects me there, before he goes to New Jersey." I tried to change his mind, but he said he must go see this man. Finally, he said he must go, "for the stars will be out pretty soon," and he passed off down the street. He had a peculiar look. He was very pale and his eye was glassy. He looked sorrowful, as though under heavy pressure. So convinced was I that he was not in his right mind, that I asked him to go with me.

JOSEPH P. NONES

Being first duly sworn, sayeth:

I am a notary public and lawyer. I have been in the Navy and sailed with Admiral Decatur from 1815 to 1817, in the expedition against Algiers, Tunis and Tripoli. I first met McFarland about the middle of May 1867, when I was appointed by the court in Massachusetts to take testimony of witnesses for the habeas corpus case he had instituted to get his children back.

I saw him as much as four or five times a day during that period, and I never considered him anything better than a madman. He stated that his mind was destroyed on account of the separation. He always spoke of his wife affectionately, and I told him he was a fool for doing so.

A murmur of approval went through the audience at this remark.

MR. NONES (CONTINUING)

He frequently talked of suicide. I would reason and moralize with him, tell him how weak and foolish it was to talk so. I told him to "keep a stiff upper lip." But I might as well have talked to the winds; he went on as any fool might.

During this time, on June 7, 1867, I took the deposition of Richardson in connection with the habeas corpus case. I had a private conversation with Mr. Richardson immediately after he gave his testimony. He sat there on my sofa and we spoke in a friendly way. I asked why he was keeping McFarland's wife and children from him. Richardson said he could not help it, that she did not want to live with her husband any more and that he, Richardson, would have her divorced and as soon as she was divorced he would marry her. I asked him what kind of woman Mrs. McFarland was, and he asked, "Have you ever seen her?" I replied, "Never." "Well," he said, "she is an intellectual, lovely woman." Maybe it was "rather a very luscious woman" or "a very voluptuous woman," one or another of these phrases, I think it was "luscious." He said, "I cannot help it, if you saw her you would say the same thing."

I repeated this conversation the next day to McFarland. I was immediately sorry I had done so. He went on like a madman, wept like a child, wet his head in the basin, pulled his hair. I did not know what to do with him. I thought I should have to send him home in a carriage. He was to be a witness in another suit I was connected with; but I postponed that suit several months because I could not trust him on the stand.

It was now the sixth day of the trial, the second day of the defense. The jury had heard more than a dozen defense witnesses who, like Messrs. Billings and Nones, spoke of their experiences with McFar-

THE MCFARLAND TRIAL. SCENE IN THE COURTROOM.

land in the years preceding the assassination. Now Graham wanted to go a step farther and introduce various letters and conversations to which McFarland had not even been a party. It was a critical point in the trial. Judge Davis immediately objected, and Recorder Hackett seemed skeptical about allowing such evidence. Graham rose to the occasion.

JOHN GRAHAM

Now if your Honor please, it seems to me that there is enough out in this case to show that Richardson was engaged in fighting Mr. McFarland. It seems to have been one of the burdens of Mr. McFarland's complaints not that he was fighting his wife but that he was fighting the temptation that Richardson had thrown about her.

If your Honor please, a very important part of this defense is to show what kind of delusion this man was under at the time. If this was a delusion on his mind, am I not entitled to establish the facts of it from the evidence? Are we not entitled to show that he reasoned to himself that Richardson was the man that prevented the return of his wife?

The recorder ruled for Graham. Since McFarland's sanity was in issue, any conversation could be admitted into evidence *"if it was repeated to McFarland, whether the statements of that conversation were true or not,"* so long as it might bear on his mental condition. It would not be introduced as truth, only as providing the basis for the defendant's frenzy. With the jury already sympathetic to McFarland's point of view, Graham hardly cared about this fine distinction. He was now free to paint for the jury the sordid picture of Albert and Abby as Daniel McFarland perceived it.

XX

Private Letters

New York Times

APRIL 13, 1870

THE MCFARLAND TRIAL

More Epistolary Evidence

The Court-room was crowded, and ladies thronged the trial chamber in greater numbers than at any time before. Over fifty were present, some fair in appearance and others who probably were fair some time ago. The most careful inquiry fails to show that these women assemble for any other purpose than merely as spectators, and that one in a dozen is or expects to be a witness in the case. They are treated courteously by the officers, have good seats, and as a matter of course, comport themselves with decorum. They do not stand up to the obstruction of the view of other spectators, nor stretch their necks upward and around in order to satisfy their curiosity.

There had been a celebration at the Academy of Music in Brooklyn the previous evening, commemorating the ratification of the fifteenth constitutional amendment guaranteeing voting rights to all races. Everyone in the audience, which was half white and half black, joined in a spirit of great fellowship. The Reverend Henry Ward Beecher proclaimed they had completed "the fruit of the tree of liberty," and the newly elected black senator from Mississippi, Hiram R. Revels, spoke on the bright prospects for his race now to work out its own future in a democracy.

It encouraged even feminist reformers. Perhaps the world was progressing and perhaps their cause would be next. The McFarland trial, however, was not giving them much hope.

In the courtroom this day, Elbridge Gerry, the defense cocounsel, took the floor again for a dramatic recitation of letters from Lu Calhoun and Charlotte Sinclair to Abby. He spared "no expression which allowed of full and telling emphasis" said the *Herald*. The presentation began with the letters sent at the end of February 1867, just as Abby was leaving Daniel McFarland. These were in response to Abby's letter, written from her dressing room at the Winter Garden, telling of her fears for her life at McFarland's hands and her resolution to leave him.

Mrs. Calhoun to *Abby*

WASHINGTON, FRIDAY MORNING,
FEBRUARY 22, 1867 •

My Darling Child—

What can I say to comfort thee? My heart bleeds over thee. Would I could enfold thee for ever more. My precious, you must make your decision. It is profanation for you to stay with that man. You shall not. No woman ought to put her womanhood to open shame as you have been forced to do for yours. It is most cruel, most devilish. You cannot work, you cannot advance, you can make no certain future for yourself and the children while you stay.

My darling, you will leave him scathless; the world is more

generous than we think about these things. I think you could live—yourself and Percy—for what you earn now, and if you can only be free so that you can improve, your salary will be increased. Oh, do leave him my darling. It is so wrong that you should stay with him.

Thine ever,
Lu

Mrs. Sinclair to *Abby*
WASHINGTON, FEBRUARY 21, 1867 •

My dearest friend—

Mrs. C. read your letter to me this morning and I am almost heart broken for you. My dear, what are you going to do? Whatever you decide upon of course your friends—your true friends—will accept. But I do hope you will act with firmness and decision. Do not for one moment longer entertain that morbid idea that you are responsible for the life of one who is sure to break you down completely, and ruin, perhaps, your children, if they continue to live with him. Those dear boys must be taken care of, and who can do it but their own mother?

My dear Abby, I love you like a sister, or I should not write this. I have no doubt of your success on the stage, but should you find that too trying for your health, you can do equally well by writing. I think you write better than almost any one I know, and should you give your time to it, I have no doubt of your exceeding any American female writer in a very short time.

I must suggest one thing, and that is get Percy away from his father as soon as possible. You know Percy now believes in him, and the longer he remains with him, the more intensified will this feeling become, and of course the longer will it take to erase it.

How is dear little Danny? I wish he could come to Mary's birthday, the 9th of March. You must come and bring Percy.

Now my darling, do write soon. Remember that Fear is your

friend. I hope you will not neglect her in my absence. I shall hope for something definite.

> Your devoted friend,
> *C.A.S.*

This presentation of letters continued for some time, as Graham and Gerry expanded their range to the period during the summer of 1866 when Mrs. Calhoun was urging Abby, then up in the White Mountains for the summer, to pursue an acting career. Everyone enjoyed listening to this part of the reading; Mrs. Calhoun's letters were so charming and full of poetic sayings. "My darling," she counseled Abby while urging her to the stage, "there is more glory in plucking bright honor from the pale-faced moon than in being petted with sugar-plums of ease." Or, she reflected, "Ah, well, life is nothing but the use we make of it, and it is better to get false teeth for people who need them than to gather the apples of Olympus for one's self."

The audience savored every word and they learned in no uncertain terms how strongly Abby's friends endorsed her decision. As for McFarland, the *Times* reported he "sat with bowed head, his face pale and evidently much affected." The *Herald*, more dramatically, said he "buried his head in his hands."

Abby was furious when she learned of this court-room scene featuring her friends' letters. This was what she had implored Judge Davis to prevent. These letters were private. They had been stolen by McFarland when he broke into her trunks at 72 Amity Street. But Graham had established the idea that anything bearing on McFarland's state of mind was acceptable, even purloined letters having nothing to do with Richardson. Judge Davis did not even try to object to their introduction. He insisted only that the full text of the letters be read rather than just selected excerpts, which the court accepted. After Gerry finished with his selections from each letter, Davis simply rose and read the balance.

He did not seem to understand how these letters, so full of feminist support for a woman to leave her husband, would be perceived by the family men on the jury.

McFarland's Medications

New York Times

APRIL 14, 1870

THE MCFARLAND TRIAL

*Testimony of Physicians
Who Prescribed for Defendant*

**REASONS ASSIGNED BY
MRS. MCFARLAND FOR LEAVING
HER HUSBAND**

The trial of McFarland was continued before pretty much the same throng that has been assembled from day to day since it began. One of the ladies, with a view perhaps to familiarize her infant to scenes of this character, brought her child with her, and the presence of the young heir or heiress would doubtless have been unnoticed had it not commenced to prattle. This unusual sound so disturbed the serenity of the occasion that the little cherub was removed to realms below.

A new elevated railway had been inaugurated the day before, and those who wished could now have an "airborne" ride to court, at least as far as Cortland Street. One skeptic was said to have promised that the thing would fall down. But the handsome wooden car rolled over tracks padded with India rubber for a smooth and quiet sixteen-minute ride from Thirtieth Street. The only difficulty seemed to occur on the streets below, where horses reared in fear as the transport rumbled overhead.

Not everyone took the airborne route, but the curious masses continued to flock to the trial. Some, such as Mrs. Norton of the Reform Club, were profoundly interested in the issues at stake. But most aspired only to shocking revelations, believing that the lurid portrait painted in the defense's opening address would be fleshed out in prurient detail. That was not on this day's agenda, however. Instead they saw McFarland's medical history developed.

DR. JOHN WARD

Being first duly sworn, sayeth:

I am a physician. I know the prisoner quite well. I made his acquaintance in 1863 when I began attending his family.

I never had occasion to prescribe for Mr. McFarland before 1867. In April of that year, he came to me for medical advice. He was in a great deal of nervous agitation; he said his wife had left him. His pulse was running 110. His skin was hot. His face was flushed and he had suffused eyes—a wild eye. There was considerable tremor about the eye. He was very restless, moving continually about. Yet there were no indications of liquor about him. I thought he was under a state of great mental excitement. He said he had had no sleep for two weeks, since his wife had left him. I judged he had congestion of the brain, that is, an excess of blood in the brain from too much mental agitation. I saw him during 1867 and 1868 perhaps two hundred times. He always had the same restless manner, the same quick pulse, and the pupil was contracted, showing evidence of disease action of the brain.

His visits became less frequent at the end of 1868, but he began coming to me again in March 1869. His manner was very much agitated, as of a man suffering terribly in his mind. From the Spring of 1869 to November, I think I saw him every two days; sometime twice a day. His symptoms were continuous and he always alluded to his family trouble. His pulse was 120 from April 1867; I never knew it lower than 110; I saw it reach 130.

Such a pulse denotes great excitement. Alone it does not denote cerebral disease, but joined with the wild eye, the cold skin and the insomnia, they are unmistakable signs of brain congestion.

In the Spring of 1869 I went once out with him and walked with him a half mile to calm him. He had alluded to suicide, and I feared he would take his life. He said, "I dream of my wife and children. I see my wife in Richardson's arms, and I cannot bear it. My children cry out to me and they implore me to do something. I tear Richardson from my wife and clutch him by the throat. I squeeze my hands with all my might. His eyes bulge before me and he flails about. But then I spring out of bed in a cold perspiration, and everything is unchanged. This happens over and over, sometimes twenty times in a night. My God, Doctor, can't you give me something. I can't rest. I can't go on like this!" I prescribed morphine for him in grain doses and told him to take the powders whenever he could not sleep. He told me he was taking forty grains every night.

I would not have dared give him grain doses if he had been only ordinarily excited. I would have given him belladonna. I rarely use morphine. It affects the system by reducing pulsation. I only resort to it in extreme cases.

From the 18th to the 24th of November, 1869, I saw him every night; on the 23rd he followed me to the St. James; he wanted something to quiet him. He said he had walked the streets continuously.

I saw him for the last time on the 24th of November, 1869, the night before the shooting of Richardson. His excitement and tremor had been continuous over the previous days, but on the 24th they were heightened. He came to my office about 7 o'clock in the evening and remained there about fifteen minutes. He was in a muscular tremor, with his eyes flashing and glaring like balls of fire. I asked him what had happened. He said, "I have been roaming; I have been to the ferry looking for my boy; I must have my boy." I told him to quiet himself. He said, "I cannot live. I am in a horrible condition. I cannot take care of myself."

"I have that terrible impulse upon me that I have had before," he said, which I took to mean he was contemplating suicide. I had never seem him in such a bad condition before. I gave him two grains of morphine. I told him to take one when he got home—on going to bed—and if that did not relieve him, to take the other in the course of an hour.

He put out his hand to me. It was shaking so that I laid it on the table. His pulse was running on 120. He said, "Richardson is going to take my child away; I must have my child; I can't live without my child." I left with him and we walked down Fifth avenue to Tenth street.

I have only a general knowledge of mental alienation. I am not an expert. But my impression that day was that his mind was diseased and that he was irrational.

On this one day in court, five physicians, plus a druggist, appeared. They all said essentially the same thing. Dr. Egbert Guernsey, McFarland's long-time physician, saw his patient in August 1869, prescribed a "powerful narcotic," and thought there was an "existing insanity," because his tongue evidenced a nervous disease. Dr. John Miner began prescribing "coffee and a preparation of opium" for him in September 1869. Dr. James O'Rourke saw him in November 1869. McFarland told O'Rourke he was taking a grain of morphine every three hours. This medical man prescribed more morphine "as much to get rid of him as for any other reason." He thought McFarland was not insane, but that he "was not sane on the subject of his domestic troubles." Dr. Francis Hermann, the druggist, gave him morphine powders about once a week. He issued the drug even though McFarland appeared "irrational," because "Mac showed the prescription each time," and it was Hermann's duty as a druggist to comply. The prescriptions were apparently open ended and refillable, and McFarland had several from different doctors. Only Dr. George Taylor, the proprietor of the Swedish movement cure, did not prescribe morphine. He told McFarland to take the country air, and use whiskey as "a quieting medicine."

McFarland seemed to have more doctors than most doctors have patients. He saw Dr. Ward professionally, and Dr. Maurice Mattson, Dr. O'Rourke and Dr. Clark informally, the day before the shooting, and he was seeing Dr. Miner frequently.

The next medical witness was a relative of the defendant. He added his professional prescription to the list, telling how he sent Percy off to the druggist to fetch powders of morphine when McFarland was sleepless and agitated. But he also added some telling personal anecdotes.

DR. WILLIAM C. McFARLAND

Being first duly sworn, sayeth:

I am a physician and a nephew of the prisoner, Daniel McFarland. I have known him since 1852 or 1853, several years before his marriage. In January and February 1866, I boarded in the same house as my uncle and his wife—Mrs. Gates' on Thirty-sixth st.—and saw them every night at dinner. They were exceedingly affectionate, and Mrs. McFarland told me that he was generous and gave her all the money she needed. I had never heard of any trouble between them until I visited at their rooms on the Monday before she left him, in February 1867. They had had a disagreement about something. My uncle spoke of the ingratitude of women. He told me if ever I got married not to marry while I was poor.

I did not see either of them again until two days after the separation, when I went to see her at Mrs. Sinclair's, No. 8 Washington place, where she was stopping. It was Thursday, the 22nd. My uncle was then still living at No. 72 Amity street. He occupied the back room and Mr. Richardson occupied the front room. I asked Mrs. McFarland her reason for leaving her husband.

She said he had commenced drinking. "Has he got on sprees?" I asked. "No," she said, "but he gets drunk about once in four months." I urged her to return to her husband, but she said, "I am too proud a woman to go back." I asked her if she had any doubt as to her husband's love for her. She said, "No, he loves me impossibly much. He thinks the sun rises and sets on my head." Then she implored me to go back to Mr. McFarland, and stay with him. She was afraid he might destroy himself. She made me promise I would stay with him that night. She said her father was coming to New York on Saturday, and that they would hold a conference with Mr. McFarland and settle the matter.

I went back to Amity street about an hour afterward, and communicated the result of my interview with his wife to him. He seemed very much affected. He was crying when I saw him and he burst into tears when I told him of the conversation. I stayed with him that night and the next.

I may have been the person who first put the idea in my uncle's head that Richardson was the cause of his troubles. On the second night I stayed with him, just after Mrs. McFarland had left, I told him that I thought Richardson had been instrumental in seducing his wife away. I also told him of a conversation I had had with her some two months earlier. She had told me, "I want to be an elegant lady. I want to gain my place among the literary people and the *elite* of New York. All I need for this is money."

The masses in the court room nodded knowingly to each other. It was what they wanted to hear, and since it was a conversation "communicated to the defendant" the prosecution could do nothing to block it.

While Judge Davis did nothing on cross-examination to refute this blot on Abby's character, he at least had some effect in cross-examining Dr. McFarland about his uncle's irrationality:

Judge Davis: What did he say that was irrational?
Dr. McFarland: He spoke about his wife.
Davis: And you think it was irrational to talk about his wife? What did he say?
McF: He was very demonstrative.

Davis: And you call that irrational?

McF: He talked very earnest, very excited, and very loud.

Davis: And the loud tone made you think it was irrational?

McF: Yes, sir.

Davis: He didn't say any words that seemed irrational?

McF: No, sir; but it was his manner that seemed irrational.

Davis: The manner was all?

McF: Yes, sir.

Davis: Anything else in his manner beside the loud tone?

McF: No, sir; not that I could recall.

Judge Davis thus showed he knew how to reduce a claim of "irrationality," which rang of "insanity," to mere excitability. But, for some reason, he did nothing similar with other witnesses. More than forty persons, medical and nonmedical, had testified to McFarland's odd behavior during the period before the shooting, his obsessiveness, his frantic manner, his nervousness. All these witnesses were beginning to have a powerful cumulative effect. And the prosecution was doing nothing to stop it. Graham knew, nonetheless, that he had to buttress the insanity claim with expert medical testimony. But first he wanted to bring out the details of Albert and Abby's love affair.

The Lovers Together

New York Herald

APRIL 19, 1870

THE McFARLAND TRIAL

The Intimacy Between Richardson and Mrs. McFarland

The women had the witness stand almost entirely to themselves today. Mrs. Mason, who had been the landlady of both Mr. and Mrs. McFarland and Mr. Richardson, underwent a long and extensive cross-examination by both sides. The usual morbid curiosity to hear stories with a taint of creamy lasciviousness in them lay at the bottom of the anxiety to catch every word which this witnesses uttered.

Mrs. Mary Mason

Being first duly sworn, sayeth:

As I have said, I operated a boarding house at No. 72, where Mr. and Mrs. McFarland stayed, and Mr. Richardson also had a room. I was at home in the house all the time, so I know what occurred there.

Mr. McFarland and his wife came at the end of 1866. Mrs. Calhoun came first and recommended them. She said Mr. McFarland was a thoroughly educated gentleman, but a little down the hill at the moment. But she expected he would soon get a position under her husband at the Assessor's Office. I let them the back parlor and extension on the first floor. They lived there with their son, Percy. I furnished the rooms, the table and the crockery, etc. They did their own cooking, in my kitchen. They were paying twelve dollars per week. The rent was paid regularly. They had no servant, but their washing was sent out. Mrs. McFarland and my girl took care of the rooms.

Around a month after she came, Mrs. McFarland brought Mr. Richardson to me. She told me she had a friend, a gentleman, who lived across the way, that he was obliged to leave there and he would like to get my rooms.

Mr. Richardson then came, in the evening of the same day, I think, and spoke to me about a room. Mrs. McFarland came with us, to help show the room. I objected to renting it then, because he was going to use it for business as well and work. But the next morning Mrs. McFarland spoke to me and urged me to put a drugget over my carpet to preserve it from injury, and to then let it to Richardson. I let him have the room upon her urgent request.

Mr. Richardson had the front room and closets. The room he occupied was divided from the parlor, where Mrs. McFarland and her family stayed, by folding doors. Those doors were not fastened after Richardson took the room. There was only a bolt to the doors.

Mr. Richardson used the room as an office by day. He was writing a book, and had three who worked with him, the errand boy, a stenographer and an artist. But he also slept there almost every night. There was a bed in the room. He was at home there a good deal.

Mr. McFarland treated his wife very kindly. He waited on her a good deal. I would see him hold her curls. I never saw him in liquor. I never knew him to be under the influence of liquor. He did not go out in the evenings. He would get home about four o'clock, and would remain teaching little Percy. I heard them reciting Shakespeare one or twice, and I saw him teaching the boy from a map. This was in the evening, after Mrs. McFarland had gone to the theater. Percy did not go to school. He was home during the day, but sometimes I saw him go out with Mr. Richardson's errand boy.

I saw Mr. Richardson and Mrs. McFarland going in and out a great deal together. They were often out in the day time when Mr. McFarland was away. They would stay out for hours together. Frequently when she was out on her own and returned, she would knock at his door and he would answer it. He would then come out and they would speak for some minutes in the hall in a low tone.

I can recall three occasions when I saw them together in a room. Once I went to Mr. Richardson to borrow an inkstand. He was sitting there in a rocking chair and she was sitting opposite him in another chair. Their chairs were about a yard or two apart. In about three quarters of an hour I went in again and saw them in the same position. Mr. Richardson made an uncourteous remark to me about the crockery; they both seemed embarrassed and Mr. Richardson went out of the room. The third occasion was when a relative of Mr. McFarland— a young lady—called. I showed her to Mrs. McFarland's room and Mr. Richardson was there.

On the morning of February 21st, when Mrs. McFarland left her husband, Mr. Richardson breakfasted with her in her room. That was after Mr. McFarland went out, about nine o'clock. She went out herself, alone, a short while later, heading toward Thompson st. She did not tell me where she was going. I had no idea she meant to abscond. I knew of no trouble between them.

MRS. MARIA BENEDICT

Being first duly sworn, sayeth:

I operate a boarding house at number 61 Amity st. Mr. Richardson had a room at my house, the front room on the north side. He was there 6 weeks, at the end of 1866 to the early part of 1867. During that time Mrs. McFarland called and asked if she could get rooms. She looked at the front room on the south side. She did not take the room. Mr. Richardson went away two weeks later. He left voluntarily. He never complained as to his room in my house. I know of no cause of his leaving.

MISS KATE STEVENSON

Being first duly sworn, sayeth:

I am a domestic in the dwelling of Mrs. Mary Mason, in Amity street, no. 72. I recollect that Mrs. McFarland often lunched in her room, and Mr. Richardson lunched with her, between twelve and one o'clock. I once saw him and her leave the house and return together. I have seen in Mrs. McFarland's room a large picture of Richardson. I did not think anything about it, but one day when I was in her room the same picture lay on the bed. Her son, Percy took it up and asked me if I knew it. I said yes, it was Richardson. Then Mrs. McFarland snatched it up and locked it in her large trunk.

WILLIAM D. NORRIS

Being first duly sworn, sayeth:

I am sixteen years old. I work as a waiter and servant to Mr. Samuel Sinclair.

You ask if I saw Mr. Richardson and Mrs. McFarland together. I did so a good many times, very often. It was my business to attend the door bell at Mr. Sinclair's house. When Mrs. McFarland came there to stay, after she left her husband, I let Mr. Richardson in ever so many times. He always inquired for Mrs. McFarland when I let him in. I know a boy by the name of Joseph, who was at this time employed by Richardson. He brought letters to Mr. Sinclair's house for Mrs. McFarland. I think he brought five or six letters during that time. Mrs. McFarland gave me an answer to give to Joseph for every letter he brought her from Mr. Richardson.

While she was at the house, Mrs. McFarland and Mr. Richardson used to go out very often together, and they quite often came to the house together. Sometimes they came late at night. It was after ten, near eleven o'clock; they were coming from the theater.

Then when Mr. Richardson was wounded, he came to Mr. Sinclair's to stay until he got better. They put him in the back room upstairs. Mrs. McFarland also came back to stay in the house then. She was in the middle room upstairs. It was all open to Mr. Richardson's room; there are no doors or shutters; when you are in one room, you are in the other. All the time that he lay in bed wounded she stayed with him.

You ask what I saw her doing in and about Mr. Richardson's room all that time. I saw her making up the bed, dusting and putting things in order, to make it look well and decent. I saw them eat together off the same plates, saw her carry up his meals and sit by his bedside holding the tray in her lap. I saw her hold water for him near the middle of the bed.

You ask if I have seen Mr. Richardson take "liberties" with Mrs. McFarland. Yes, I have. I've seen them shake hands together many times.

The last response provoked great merriment in the courtroom. Even Mr. Graham chuckled.

Mr. Norris (continuing)
I also once saw him kiss her, right in front of Mrs. Sinclair and me. And I saw Mrs. McFarland throw her arms round Mr. Richardson's neck and kiss him while he lay sick and wounded.

In a way, Graham's case seemed to be weakening as it failed to satisfy the heightened expectations that he and the press had encouraged. The *Sun* had quoted Mrs. Mason, the landlady, as saying "Mrs. McFarland wanted me to let her sleep in Mr. Richardson's bed." But the most Graham had shown was that Abby sought to rent Albert's room when he was away. The *Sun* had also reported that Albert and Abby "slept in the same room at Mr. Sinclair's house before the divorce." But that proximity had now been shown to have been a matter of nursing an invalid. Graham brought in an official of the Mutual Life Insurance Company, who told of Albert buying a three thousand dollar policy on his own life, payable to Abby, in January 1868. He produced several witnesses who were supposed to have seen Richardson visiting Abby at Mrs. Gilbert's house in New Jersey or picking her up after the theater. With each witness the audience waited for a dramatic, revealing description of the lovers *in flagrante delicto*, or, at least *in flagrante* something or other. It never came.

XXiii

The Philosophy of Insanity

New York Times

APRIL 25, 1870

THE McFARLAND TRIAL

What Is Congestion of the Brain?

How Its Presence Is Positively Determined

The McFarland case entered upon its thirteenth day. The Court-room was well-filled, and the ladies were present in considerable numbers. Among all the classes of spectators the interest felt was as great as on any day since the trial began, for it was generally understood that the defense would bring their part of the case to a close, and that some very important and highly interesting medical testimony would be presented.

The *Herald* was puzzled by the testimony of the defense's first medical expert, Dr. Reuben Vance, telling its readers: "By the time an adjournment for the day was taken the whole atmosphere of the court room became oppressive with the philosophy of insanity, and everybody looked dubiously at his neighbor, as though he were a present or prospective victim of cerebral congestion. The twelve jurymen were utterly bewildered, and hardly knew whether it was safe for them to be trusted in company together."

But McFarland's lawyers did not necessarily care that the jury might be getting bewildered. The point was not to convince them by the reasoning of the experts, but rather by their reputations. If learned and distinguished expert medical men believed McFarland was insane, the jury was supposed to think, how can we poor simpletons have the temerity to disagree?

As if to underscore that point, Graham next rolled out his biggest cannon, the renowned Dr. William Hammond. Hammond was then a professor of neuro-surgery. But he had gained notoriety as surgeon-general in 1862–63, when he stood up to the all-powerful secretary of war, Edwin Stanton, and was eventually court-martialed. As Hammond put it, "I would not quietly submit to the insolence which Stanton constantly exhibited toward his subordinates." Dr. Hammond was a dominating presence, a man utterly convinced of his own genius and his superiority to mere mortals.

DR. WILLIAM A. HAMMOND

Being first duly sworn, sayeth:

I am a graduate of the University of the City of New-York, and have been a practicing physician in the city for twenty-one years. I have devoted the last five years of my professional life exclusively to the study of the mind and have written several works on cerebral diseases.

On the sixth of March, 1870, three months after the homicide, I visited Daniel McFarland in the City Prison at the request of his counsel and saw him for the first time. I examined him at length on that day and several times thereafter to determine both his physical and mental states.

The evidence of cerebral congestion was profound. I found his face and head abnormally hot and a throbbing of the carotid and temporal arteries. His eyes were suffused, intolerant of light, and the pupils were unequal in size. The ophthalmoscopic examination revealed congestion of the retinal and optic disks, with partial atrophy of the latter. His pulse was rapid, 108 and irregular. There was a different degree of sensibility on the two sides of his body as shown by the esthesiometer. The foregoing symptoms were objective. The subjective symptoms were wakefulness, flashes of light before the eyes, noises in the ears, and pain and a sensation of fullness in the head.

On March 29, I showed him photographs of his wife, and asked him some questions about them. At the sight of them he was much moved, tears came into his eyes, his voice trembled, his speech became incoherent and rambling; his articulation indistinct, and his muscular twitching was increased. His pulse rose to 142, and I was for a time apprehensive of serious consequences. After a time however, he began to weep, and I succeeded in bringing him to something like calmness. But during the whole of my interview, which lasted over an hour, he remained excited, and was at times incomprehensible in his language.

The class of insanity which is relevant here—known as transitory mania, temporary insanity, and morbid impulse—is extremely temporary in its character. In cases of temporary insanity an individual suddenly loses control of his will. The immediate causes of this temporary insanity are:

(a) A condition of cerebral exhaustion, in which, owing to excessive wear and tear of the brain, new substance is not formed with sufficient rapidity to take the place of that used. This comes from excessive use of the brain and loss of sleep. When the blood-vessels of the brain are overloaded, sleep is impossible.

(b) The circulation through the brain of blood which is not normal in quality. This may come from drugs or poisons, or from the influence of certain emotions, which renders the blood unfit for use of the brain. Similarly, excessive passion has also been known so to alter the constitution of the mother's milk as to render it a deadly poison to the infant at her breast.

(c) Cerebral congestion. This comes from overuse of the brain. The blood vessels thus become over-distended, and lose thereby their ability to contract. Even after the exciting cause is removed they continue dilated. It can also be produced by an overdistended stomach. I know of such a case. A gentlemen ate hurriedly a hearty meal, and a short time afterward became furiously maniacal. It can also be produced by drugs.

As a general matter, I might add, persons with weak minds are eccentric and easily influenced by emotions such as vanity and pride. They stand on the verge of insanity with a decided predisposition to mental disease, needing only a sufficient exciting cause.

The defense of temporary insanity is often abused. There is a difference between it and "heat of passion." Heat of passion results from an emotion which, for the moment, controls the will, the intellect not being called into action. Acts of temporary insanity appear similar but *the act which marks the height of the paroxysm is always preceded by symptoms of mental aberration, while acts done in the heat of passion are not thus foreshadowed.* Also, effects of passion soon subside, but with temporary insanity *the evidences of disease are still present, and remain in him for days, weeks, or even month and years.* The major symptom is generally cerebral congestion.

In Mr. McFarland's case, I can observe many phenomena that he could not feign. Even as I sit here and look at him across the courtroom, I can see the beating of his carotid and temporal arteries in an unnatural way, indicating a rush of blood to the head. And on April 20, only a few days ago, I tested him using the Dynamograph machine. This machine, which is on the table there, measures the power of a man over his will. It operates by moving a roll of paper beneath a pen. The subject is given the pen to hold. He is instructed to keep it centered on a point so that a straight line is traced on the roll. When I examined Mr. McFarland, I endeavored to make him think it was to his advantage to keep the pen still. Any man in this room, except Mr. McFarland, surely could keep the mark straight. Mr. McFarland could not, showing that he could not control his will.

In conclusion, from the full and decided evidence there can be no doubt in regard to the mental condition of Daniel McFarland during a long period previous to the homicide, and that for about two weeks prior thereto his state was such as to render him entirely irresponsible for his acts. While at the very height of his state of mental aberration, he accidentally met the man most nearly connected with the origin of all his difficulties; the one to whom the wreck of his hopes was to be attributed, the one who had injured him more than all the rest of the world combined. Without an instant's reflection, indeed, in his condition, without the possibility of reflection, he perpetrated the act for which he is tried for his life.

The antecedents of the accused and the concomitant circumstances of the culminating catastrophe leave no doubt that he was affected with mental derangement; that the act itself was done during an attack of temporary insanity, and that immediately subsequent thereto he was not entirely restored to reason.

The prosecution might have challenged Dr. Hammond on a key point. The doctor said that McFarland "accidentally" met Richardson when he shot him, and acted "without an instant's reflection." But all the eyewitnesses to the shooting said that McFarland came in and waited for his victim to appear. Even the defense's own witnesses, such as Mr. Billings, testified McFarland had sought out Albert that evening. The assassination was plotted, not impulsive.

D.A. Garvin and Judge Davis, however, failed to pursue this point. Nor did they pursue the implications of McFarland's drug use, since any causative effects of legally prescribed drugs would only aid his defense. The cross-examination simply enabled Hammond to rehash his testimony. He was too formidable a figure for the prosecution to attack or undermine.

Graham rested the case for the defense.

Victim's Defense

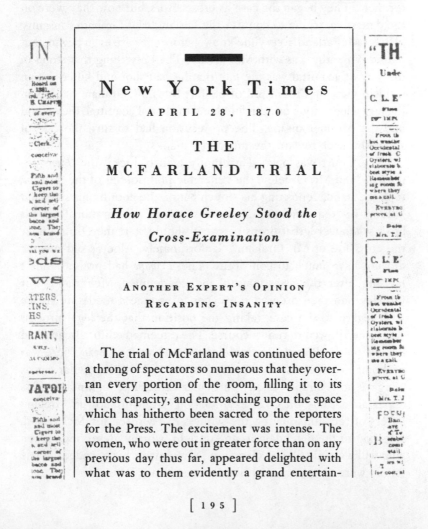

New York Times

APRIL 28, 1870

THE MCFARLAND TRIAL

How Horace Greeley Stood the Cross-Examination

ANOTHER EXPERT'S OPINION REGARDING INSANITY

The trial of McFarland was continued before a throng of spectators so numerous that they overran every portion of the room, filling it to its utmost capacity, and encroaching upon the space which has hitherto been sacred to the reporters for the Press. The excitement was intense. The women, who were out in greater force than on any previous day thus far, appeared delighted with what was to them evidently a grand entertainment, instead of a solemn trial for murder, and particularly so while Horace Greeley and Samuel Sinclair were testifying.

As they turned to their rebuttal, District Attorney Garvin and his privately subsidized colleague Judge Davis had their work cut out for them. They began the case as prosecutors, but now they were on the defensive, trying to counter the onslaught of Graham's insanity plea for McFarland. Everyone knew, before the case even began, that public sympathy was with McFarland. The only thing that stood in the way of acquittal was the fact that he had shot and killed a man in plain view of a room full of people. But now Graham had given the jury a legal hook on which to hang the hat of acquittal; they could find the prisoner insane. The prosecution had to turn the tide of sympathy back toward the murdered man.

"The Court was opened promptly at 11 o'clock," the *Times* reported, "and Mr. Greeley, the venerable philosopher of the *Tribune*, took the stand, depositing his slouch hat on the floor by his side, and holding his red bandanna ready to wipe the perspiration from his brow whenever 'great drops of sweat' should start therefrom under the cross-fire of Mr. Graham." Unfortunately, Albert's old mentor did not have much to contribute. The *Tribune* had praised Albert lavishly after the assassination and condemned McFarland. But Greeley had then ordered the paper to assume a moderate stance with regard to the case, taking the position that the legal process should be allowed to run its course. The esteemed editor already had his eye on the Presidency, which he would seek in 1872. There was no point in unnecessarily allying himself with an unpopular cause. He gave no testimony of any particular value. The high point of his appearance came on cross-examination. Graham showed Greeley letters of recommendation the witness had written for McFarland, referring to the defendant as an "upright, worthy, deserving citizen who will worthily fill any clerkship." Greeley dryly conceded, "those letters were as true as such letters usually are."

Samuel Sinclair, publisher of the *Tribune*, and the man who had provided refuge for Abby when she fled and a bed for Albert when he was wounded, had more to offer. He told of an incident in 1864 when Abby had to send for him, as a friend of McFarland, to help quiet her spouse. McFarland was drunk. Although he had been in a fight and his face was bleeding, he wanted to go back out. Sinclair had a struggle getting him to stay in bed.

The *Tribune* publisher also described in detail the "family council" at his house on February 24, 1867, just after Abby left her husband. This was the meeting at which Abby confronted Daniel and confirmed the finality of their separation.

SAMUEL SINCLAIR

Being first duly sworn, sayeth:

As I recall it, Mrs. McFarland led the conversation that evening. She advised her husband, "Mac, (for that is the name by which she called him familiarly) I often told you that if I came to the conclusion to leave you, that conclusion would be irrevocable." He admitted, "Yes, you did," and he also admitted that "at times, when I have been intemperate, I have not treated you as I should have done." But he complained of her coldness to him in letters when she was away. Her reply was, "Mac, I have told you that long since your conduct had destroyed all the love that was for you in my heart, so how could I put it in my letters." She repeated she had come to the deliberate conclusion that under no possible circumstances could she ever live with him again.

McFarland told her she was making a great mistake in coming to such a decision; that it would not only affect him, but herself and the children; and that she would live to regret it. He said, however, that if such was her decision, he could only bow in submission to it.

Sinclair had some influence with McFarland, because he had often been helpful in getting jobs for the hapless entrepreneur when his business ventures collapsed. As the family council broke up, McFarland again asked Sinclair's help in assuring that his current job in the appraiser's office would not be jeopardized by his marital difficulties. Sinclair agreed to do what he could, and he even wrote a letter of recommendation to Chief Justice Chase of the Supreme Court proposing McFarland, "one of the few radical anti-slavery Irishman," for a patronage appointment as a register of bankruptcy.

But, Sinclair testified, his relations with McFarland became strained after he learned, in March 1868, that McFarland had refused to put Percy in school, and that he had berated his wife in front of Percy when she came to New York to visit her son. "I told him I thought it was outrageous; that he had no right to prejudice the mind of his son against his mother."

Sinclair's testimony was hardly spectacular, but in its quiet way it began to shed some new light on the relationship between Abby and Daniel, and on McFarland's character. The next witness, Mark "Brick" Pomeroy, editor of the *New York Democrat*, told of McFarland's efforts to sell him, for one hundred dollars, copies of Abby's personal correspondence. These were letters that McFarland had either intercepted or stolen from his wife. Pomeroy was a sworn enemy of Greeley and the *Tribune*, which had tried to get him arrested during the war because of his Southern sympathies. McFarland tempted him with the notion that the letters, which included correspondence with the wife of the *Tribune* publisher (Mrs. Sinclair) and with one of its correspondents (Mrs. Calhoun), would be embarrassing to that paper. But even Pomeroy refused to stoop this low.

Judge Davis's case seemed to be gathering strength as he played Graham's game, introducing irrelevant character assassination rather than real evidence. But then the prosecution tried to establish McFarland's sanity by introducing a magazine article, "My School-Boy Days in New York City Forty Years Ago," that the defendant published in the *American Educational Monthly* in March 1869, ostensibly showing his mental coherence at the time. Schooling, he wrote "was nothing but blows! blows! blows! Terrible flogging was really believed to be an indispensable requisite for making a good boy out of what was esteemed a bad one, and a scholar out of a dunce. For more serious infractions, such as playing 'hooky,' the 'Iron Bar' came into play. When this engine of torture—an inch wide bar set a foot off the floor—was used, the offending boy was made to mount upon it with his bare feet. He was allowed no means of balancing himself but the dexterity of keeping his equilibrium by the support of his feet alone. If he fell off, or let one foot touch the platform, the master sitting within striking distance would lash him with a savage stroke of the 'Cat.' " This article painted such a dismal portrait of McFarland's boyhood that it won him new sympathy with the jury.

Davis also called on Oliver Johnson, the husband of Mary Ann Johnson, Abby's colleague in Shelburne for the summer of 1866, to testify as to Abby's honorable behavior in leaving her husband. But, on cross-examination, Graham produced a letter that Johnson, a man twice her age, sent Abby, enclosing a book of sermons. The sermons, he wrote, "have been the means of comforting a great many sinners, of whom you are chief among ten thousand, and one altogether lovely, and of such is the Kingdom of Heaven." No one knew what he meant by this, but the jury's surmise could not have been favorable.

As an expert on insanity, to rebut the illustrious Dr. Hammond, the prosecution summoned Dr. Gonzalez Echeverria, professor of mental and nervous diseases at the University Medical College and physician in chief at the Paralytic and Epileptic Hospital. Although his credentials were respectable, Dr. Echeverria's testimony was worthless. He had never examined McFarland personally, nor had he heard the trial testimony, not even Dr. Hammond's. Instead he formed his opinion solely on the basis of newspaper reports. "I have read the *Herald, World, Tribune, Sun,* and sometimes the *Times,"* he averred proudly, "and I believe these provide sufficient information for me to formulate an opinion in the case." He thought McFarland was not insane, only a disgruntled husband.

Garvin and Davis were in deep trouble and they knew it.

•*EXCITING SCENE IN COURT*

PERSONAL RENCONTRE

BETWEEN MR. GRAHAM AND

JUDGE DAVIS •

New York Times

APRIL 29, 1870

Just after the adjournment of the McFarland trial, a lively passage occurred between the two leading counsel on either side. As the courtroom was emptying, Judge Davis made a remark to Recorder Hackett with regard to Mr. Graham's conduct of the defense, saying that the latter had stated something in one of his bitter speeches that he could not prove. Mr. Graham, who stood near talking to the prisoner, overheard him, and rushing up to Judge Davis, shouted, "Do you mean to say that anything that I have said is false?" Shaking his clenched fist in Judge Davis' face, Mr. Graham continued, "You ——— country pettifogger, you are not fit to associate with gentlemen; you ———, I could undress you and spank you like a child. You have insulted every witness I brought on the stand and you've been paid money to hang this man!" Officers then came between the parties and they were separated, and this ended the matter.

The expletives which Mr. Graham used were not very choice. The crowd became highly excited, and one man proposed three cheers for John Graham, which were loudly given. When Mr. Graham went out he was cheered by hundreds who had assembled on the staircase.

Mrs. Calhoun

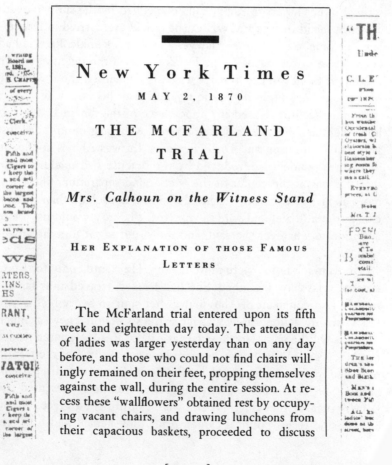

New York Times

MAY 2, 1870

THE MCFARLAND TRIAL

Mrs. Calhoun on the Witness Stand

HER EXPLANATION OF THOSE FAMOUS LETTERS

The McFarland trial entered upon its fifth week and eighteenth day today. The attendance of ladies was larger yesterday than on any day before, and those who could not find chairs willingly remained on their feet, propping themselves against the wall, during the entire session. At recess these "wallflowers" obtained rest by occupying vacant chairs, and drawing luncheons from their capacious baskets, proceeded to discuss them with their more fortunate companions. One coterie had a complete "set out" upon one of the tables, and refreshed the inner woman in a truly "sister"-matic manner.

Soon after the reassembling of the Court, after recess, a sensation was created by the entrance of Mrs. Runkle, *nee* Gilbert, afterward Mrs. Calhoun.

Lu Calhoun's first marriage, and the housekeeping bliss she described in her letters to Abby, had been ended by the sudden death of her husband that past May. But she quickly remarried in December, this time to the *Tribune*'s lawyer, Cornelius Runkle. Runkle had been active in recruiting Judge Davis to aid in the defense, and in raising the money to pay him. He was very concerned about what the trial disclosures might do to the reputation of his new wife.

The prosecutors hoped the appearance of the famed L. G. Calhoun would enable the prosecution to recover the ground it had lost with Oliver Johnson and Dr. Echeverria. Lu was Abby's confidant. The correspondence introduced by the defense had made it plain that she was at the center of the McFarland separation. She knew more about what went on in the McFarland household than anyone except the husband and wife themselves. The jury would pay close attention to whatever she said, and she could say it to a fare-thee-well.

Mr. Runkle's hopes were more modest. He wanted only for Lu to emerge relatively unscathed. She had been portrayed thus far not merely as a confidant of Abby but as her spur to every bolder and less womanly action. Lu was, as far as the spectators knew, as much the cause of the whole sordid affair as Albert. Runkle wanted justice for Albert and Abby, but even more he wanted some of the tarnish removed from his wife's name. Judge Davis understood this, perhaps better than he understood anything else. Runkle represented the powers that were paying him and whose future good graces would be valuable to his political career. And Abby herself had told him that it was more important to clear the names of her friends than to get a conviction.

Lu was dressed demurely, but fashionably, for her appearance as witness. She wore a black silk dress and velvet jacket trimmed with black lace and a Mary Stuart lace collar. Her outfit was complimented by a straw hat, appropriate to the warm season, trimmed with brown velvet and ostrich feathers, and brown gloves to match. As the clerk called "Mrs. Lucia Runkle," a hundred voices in the audience murmured "Mrs. Calhoun." The object of all this attention moved briskly forward and took her seat with great composure. At first she was a little nervous and spoke so rapidly and quietly she could not be understood ten feet away. But as the testimony continued she grew in confidence. Her responses to Graham on cross examination were quick and assured.

NEW YORK CITY.—AN INCIDENT DURING THE McFARLAND TRIAL, HELD IN THE NEW COURT-HOUSE—MRS. CALHOUN-RUNKLE ON THE STAND LISTENING TO THE READING OF A LETTER BY COUNSEL FOR DEFENSE, WRITTEN BY ALBERT D. RICHARDSON TO MRS. McFARLAND.

MRS. CALHOUN TESTIFIES.

Mrs. Calhoun

Being first duly sworn, sayeth:

I first met Mr. and Mrs. McFarland in January 1866, at an evening party at the home of a friend. We formed a friendship and I saw her very often. Usually she came to my house, at 77 Clinton place.

That spring, in April, I attended a reading of hers at Steinway Hall that was gotten up by her friends. I was most impressed, and I encouraged her by correspondence over the summer to embark upon a stage career. I enabled her to meet Mr. Stuart, of the Winter Garden, and her opportunity to go on the stage was arranged for that winter.

One afternoon during this period I was at her rooms at 72 Amity st. It was in January of 1867. She was alone with her children. I had a manuscript with me and was reading it to her, when Mr. McFarland came in. He had been drinking. The room was stifling, hot and small, and the air became very unpleasant when he entered. I spoke to him civilly, but he answered me so rudely I could not stay any longer. I gathered up my manuscript and said "Good afternoon" to Mrs. McFarland. But before I could leave he turned to her and said violently, "You damned gossip, you shall not have your friends here in my absence. You have received a letter from some lover (alluding to the manuscript I had); you have been reading the letter, and this woman has brought it."

I went out, but I feared for her and did not want to leave, so I went upstairs and waited on the landing. I heard loud and violent talking from their rooms. When the turbulence subsided, I knocked on her door, and asked her to go home with me, but she would not.

I cannot tell you in more detail what happened that day, or what transpired between her and her husband on other private occasions, but she described it all to me in letters which she wrote to me on January 2, 1867 and on February 21, 1867.

Graham would have none of this. He had introduced Lu's letters because he wanted the jury to hear how members of the intellectual

"*Tribune* set" had led Abby down an unwifely path. But he had no interest in having them hear how Abby herself justified her actions or how she portrayed her marriage to Lu. Davis argued valiantly, but he met a legal stone wall. "The rule is invariable," proclaimed Recorder Hackett, "which forbids a wife or husband to testify against the other. This evidence is in the form of a written declaration, which was written to Mrs. Calhoun, in which Mr. McFarland's wife makes a statement. That statement cannot be received, nor can any other letter or statement from Mrs. McFarland, no matter how relevant."

It was a devastating blow for Judge Davis's case. McFarland's view of the world, of his wife and of her relationship with Albert, had been laid before the jury in the utmost detail. But when the prosecution attempted to look at the same events through Abby's eyes, the door was slammed shut on a legal technicality. She was the wife of the defendant, or at least had been his wife at the time of the critical events, and nothing she said could be used against him.

Mrs. Calhoun was left to defend herself without Abby or Abby's letters.

Mrs. Calhoun (continuing)

I will explain why I wrote as I did, what were my motivations, without referring to Mrs. McFarland's letters.

I knew Mr. Richardson well. He was a good friend. During the period from May 1866 (when Mr. Calhoun and I purchased our house at 77 Clinton st.) until May 1867, he lived at our house, as a boarder, for much of the time. I also knew Mrs. McFarland well. She, too, is a very good friend, as I have indicated.

But my only motivations in all my relations with the McFarland family were to enable Mrs. McFarland to earn a livelihood for herself and her children. Insofar as I aided her efforts to go on the stage, I know that Mr. McFarland was delighted.

When Abby got ready for her roles, she did not have any proper wardrobe. Her own wardrobe was very scanty. Mr. McFarland came to my house and asked me to go with them to Mrs. Sinclair's to see if she was willing to lend a dress. Mrs. Sinclair obliged. Mr. McFarland approved of it—it was a black and red satin of very rich material. He said she looked very well. But he made some suggestions, saying it needed more flowing drapery, and some alterations were made. He spoke with interest and enthusiasm of her talents, saying she had more genius for the stage than any living woman. He said she lacked confidence and had faults, but that those would be overcome by practice. He said he would train her himself, that he was the best teacher for her. On another occasion I saw her at her rooms on Macdougal st. and Mr. McFarland was there. When going on the stage was mentioned, he appeared perfectly willing. She said she was afraid she would not be well enough; he said, "you must be well or you will forfeit your engagement."

Her first role was that of the "Player Queen" in Hamlet. There was not much in that role; if they left all in there would have been about a dozen lines. But he knew her career had to commence there. Her next role, as Lady Capulet, had perhaps sixty lines more. She also played Nerissa in the Merchant of Venice, and other characters who had more dialogue and presence. I would say they were twenty-times more important. She assumed these roles very shortly, before the first of January. I thought that she was well embarked on a new career.

I do not think, as you suggest, Mr. Graham, that Mr. McFarland merely acquiesced in his wife's career because he could not control her, or because he was so infatuated with her that he could not oppose her. He was fond of her, it is true, but nothing more than that. I never heard her boast, as you suggest, that he was wrapped up in her, or that she controlled him by threatening to leave if he got drunk three times.

Mr. Graham

Mrs. Calhoun, do you know that, in his infamous intercepted letter, Richardson boasted that when he was after a woman he could not be bullied by public sentiment? Did you know he ended that letter, "Good night, my love, my own, my wife," when she had only just left her husband and had no idea she could get a divorce? Did you know he addressed sentiments like, "I have not been waiting for you darling all these long years to wear haircloth and serve seven years now. I want you always. A hundred times a day my arms seem to stretch out toward you," or "I never seek my pillow without wanting to fold you to my heart for a goodnight kiss and blessing;" that he addressed sentiments like this to the wife of another man? Did you ever know of his writing that letter?

MRS. CALHOUN (CONTINUING)

No, I have never read that letter. But I think it is susceptible of different constructions. I think it matters that, although they were still married, Mrs. McFarland was not living with her husband, that she was separated from him. I think that makes a moral difference.

MR. GRAHAM

Say what you will, Mrs. Calhoun, you cannot wipe out your pen with your tongue.

Lu's husband and friends thought it detestable that Graham should be able to malign her reputation in this public forum and that she should not be able to respond more fully. "But for august advice, I think her husband would have done somebody harm," Junius wrote Gay. "However, Mrs. Calhoun-Runkle has not been hurt by the abuse heaped on her. She is literally besieged with sympathizers and hardly has time to take her meals." Even the *Herald,* which was no friend of hers, reported that she "left a very general impression of being smart, determined and clear-headed" and that "few, after listening to her straightforward replies, were disposed to attach much weight to the clap-trap" said about her by the defense. The *Herald* also reported that Lu, who was thirty-two, looked twenty-eight years old. When she was asked about her age thereafter, she conveniently deducted a few years.

But none of this had much effect in rebutting the insanity defense. The prosecution was down to its last batch of rebuttal witnesses, Abby's other friends and family.

New York Herald

MAY 4, 1870

THE MCFARLAND TRIAL

Free Love Finds an Advocate at Last in Mrs. Sinclair

The morning part of the trial today was confined to the examination of another lady whose name has figured largely in the great current sensation of the day—Mrs. Samuel Sinclair. She might be about thirty-four years of age, and is tall, tolerably good looking and intelligent. She was dressed in a style of careless elegance, and wore an easy, placid expression of face, indicating an acquaintance with fashionable and refined society.

MRS. CHARLOTTE A. SINCLAIR

Being first duly sworn, sayeth:

I formed the acquaintance of Mrs. McFarland in the Winter of 1861–62, I think. I met her and her husband at Mr. Cleveland's, in Cottage place. I saw her frequently during that winter, and heard her giving readings several times. All the time I knew her, Mrs. McFarland's circumstances were very poor, and she was obliged to give these readings to help support the family. She read nearly every week. The readings were given as entertainments at Mrs. Cleveland's ordinary reception nights. Her reading was very much admired. A great many of my friends went there purposely to hear her.

The income from these readings was not enough to alleviate her poverty. When they were living in Forty-sixth street, I took her $50 at one time, and $50 at another. I told her I was deputized to give it to her from friends. She returned it in a noble letter, saying she felt she could not receive it, and that she must go to her father for a loan. Part of the money I returned to the donors; some who gave it said no, they would not take it, and that I must use it for the benefit of the family. I used it to purchase necessary clothing for her and the children. Another time, in the Spring of 1866, I found Mrs. McFarland and her family in a miserable house which I scarcely dared enter. She was sick in bed, unable to take care of her two children, with no one to assist her, her husband away. I took her home with me and kept her there until he returned. Again, in the Fall of 1866 when she was living in McDougal street, she was sick most of the time. She was there with her little children and Mr. McFarland, but without assistance. I carried her food from my table for a week or two at least. I asked her why she did not have a physician, and she said she could not afford it. I sent my own physician to her at my expense.

These conditions persisted over the years that I knew her. Coming to the Winter of 1866–67, I went to Washington with Mrs. Calhoun for several weeks in February and March. That is when I wrote her the letter that has previously been read in evidence. I would like to tell why I wrote as I did.

Graham was on his feet as soon as Mrs. Sinclair uttered the word *letter*, but Davis for once beat him to it. "Don't say anything about letters," he warned his witness, "they are rabid on the subject of letters." The audience broke into laughter.

But Graham would not be stilled, as he took the chance to remind the jury, "That is the letter in which she says 'I must suggest one thing, and that is, to get Percy away from his father as soon as possible,' is it not? If we had thought it necessary to open the boy's mouth he could have told some things particularly startling. But on account of his tender age, we could not consent, under the obligations of our oaths, to permit him to be a witness."

The tender boy was of course sitting right there in the courtroom, next to his father, with a front row seat for this drama portraying one of his parents as wanton and the other as insane.

Mrs. Sinclair (continuing)

May I say only that I wrote to Mrs. McFarland in response to a letter I had received from her. I understand that the Court will not permit me to discuss the contents of that letter. However, I had no knowledge of Mrs. McFarland intending to leave her husband before I received the letter. All that I had done for her and her family was out of concern for their extreme poverty. I never intended to drive her from her husband.

I never knew of or suspected any relations between Mrs. McFarland and Mr. Richardson until the time of the first shooting. Prior to that I had never seen them together except casually. I had never seen them speak except as one person speaks to another. When she told me that Mr. Richardson had become interested in her, I was amazed, and I advised her to be prudent. However, I did not see anything wrong in it. Believing him to be a good man and a pure man, I thought it was right that she should marry him.

Lizzie Sage

Being first duly sworn, sayeth:

I visited with my sister in Brooklyn, in 1858, to help her when she was having her first child. I was eighteen years old at the time. I stayed there five months at their cottage. It was on the corner of Clark and Willow streets.

I remember the first time I saw Mr. McFarland intoxicated. It was on a Saturday in November that he offered to take me over to a play. I was to spend the forenoon at Barnum's Museum looking at the curiosities, until the matinee commenced. He started with me about half-past nine—our breakfast hour was nine; I went there, and he came as he promised and took me to the play.

I had been there about half an hour, when he told me he had

business, and must go out, and would soon come back. He went out and returned in about three quarters of an hour, I think, and I smelt liquor from his breath. He stayed about fifteen minutes, and again went out, and told me he would be back soon. I didn't see anything of him until the matinee was through. I went out, and at the vestibule of the door I met him very much intoxicated, I should judge, by the manner in which he walked, and spoke, and looked. His breath smelt very strongly.

I started with him, and got a few steps, when he staggered so I had to help him along. We went along the street and then he said he had to go into an office. When he came out I told him his conduct was not at all satisfactory. He came up and took my hands and kissed them, and the only two words I distinctly heard were "love," and "dearest." I was as much staggered as he was; and it was some little time before I recovered myself and made him take me home.

On another occasion while I was staying there, Mr. McFarland came home very much intoxicated and vomited liquor on the floor, which Abby and I had to clean up.

JUNIUS HENRI BROWNE

Being first duly sworn, sayeth:

I reside in the City of New York. I knew Richardson for fifteen or sixteen years. I was with him in the South—two years in the field and two years in prison. We were taken prisoners at the same time and escaped at the same time. I was one of his most intimate friends—absolutely one of the most intimate. I am engaged to Lillian Gilbert, who is a good friend of Mrs. McFarland, and the sister of Mrs. Calhoun.

I saw Richardson and McFarland together on two occasions. The first was at 72 Amity st. I should judge it was about two days after the separation. I went down that night with Richardson to the city, and stayed in his room with him. In the morning after we got up there was knock at the door. Richardson opened it, for he was dressed first, and I saw McFarland standing there. That was the first time I saw him, though I thought I remembered seeing his face round abo Printing House square and the *Tribune* office.

They went together into the hall and had a conversation. I don't know what it was about; I could not hear. But there were no harsh words; I could have heard if there were. Then Richardson returned into his room, and we finished dressing and went away.

The other time was the last day of November, 1867. This was some time after the first shooting. Richardson and I were sitting in the gentleman's parlor corner of Barclay street, and McFarland came in. Mr. Richardson's face was toward the door. McFarland walked toward him in an excited and threatening manner. Richardson saw him and met his eye with a calm eye. McFarland then turned away his gaze and went to a window. He stood there a little while and stared out. Then he turned round and went out without looking at us.

Judge Davis also wanted to use Junius to introduce some of his correspondence with Albert, letters in which Albert discussed McFarland's attacks and in which Albert forswore any attempt at retaliation. Unfortunately, Davis forgot to tell Junius to bring the letters, and the opportunity was lost. Now Junius was exposed to a nasty cross-examination by Graham.

Graham: Mr. Browne, how long have you spelled your name in the way you spell it now—with an "e"?

Junius: Ever since I was born.

G: Isn't your proper name plain Henry Brown?

J: My name is Junius Henri Browne.

G: Do you mean to say that Junius is the name your father gave you?

J: Yes.

G: When did he give it to you?

J: When I was born; I don't remember any of the particulars.

G: Mr. Browne, do you believe in a Supreme Being?

J: I do.

G: Do you believe in a state of rewards and punishments after death?

J: Not according to the Calvinistic idea. I believe in a spiritual system of compensations, of rewards and punishments for good and evil; but I don't believe in hell fire and brimstone.

G: Suppose a man violates an oath; what compensation does he get?

J: I suppose he would be indicted for perjury.

G: But how do you suppose he is punished otherwise?

J: Well, I think there would be a loss of self-respect, and that would be one of the greatest punishments.

G: Do you believe there is any other punishment for violating an oath, in this world or the next?

J: Do you wish me to unfold my theological theory? I am not very well versed in the affairs of the next world; perhaps you are.

G: Do you believe in the Bible?

J: Yes, I believe in it.

G: Do you believe it is a Divine production?

J: Yes, I believe parts of it have a divine character.

G: What parts?

J: You had better give me a week, and I will prepare an essay for your special benefit.

The prosecution also got in the last word on this theological question. After Graham had finished his cross-examination, Judge Davis asked the witness, "Mr. Browne, counsel has asked you your views on the future punishment of a person who violates an oath. What do you think will be the future punishment of a person who commits assault and battery?" There was no time for an answer before Mr. Graham, who saw where this question was leading, jumped up and objected, to the great amusement of the audience.

The prosecution's rebuttal case had ended. It may have given Junius some satisfaction that he had enabled them to close on a high note. Graham had, of course, been right about his last name. Junius *had* added the "e" for a little style when he was a young reporter in Cincinnati. But he had coolly bluffed Graham on this point.

Abby's friends had been keeping her up-to-date on the trial proceedings. But she told them she was trying to give it as little attention as she could. She wanted to move forward and she had a large family to consider. Although Albert's children remained with his family

Massachusetts through the trial, the plan was for them to come to live with their new mother as soon as it was over.

In the meantime, Abby was staying in Albert's house in New Jersey with her mother and her five-year-old son. She no longer called the boy Danny. The thought of going through life with McFarland's name always before her, and the thought of her child burdened with the reputation of his father, was more than she could bear. So the boy now was not "Daniel McFarland, Jr.," but rather "William Sage," the name of Abby's father. Abby's mother supported her in this name change. When asked about it, she said, "The child likes to be called 'Willie,' and if he wants to repudiate his father, we certainly have no objection."

Summations

New York Times

MAY 6, 1870

THE
McFARLAND TRIAL

Mr. Graham's Argument

AN UNPRECEDENTED FORENSIC DISPLAY

The first step in the ending of the great McFarland–Richardson trial was taken today, when Mr. John Graham commenced his argument to the jury. Few other great trials have occupied as much time, and in none has the interest felt been as intense as in this. Richardson was known all over the country through the columns of the *Tribune,* and when he fell by the hand of McFarland there was a universal desire to learn the circumstances. If there had been a possibility of the cessation of interest, it would have been awakened by the Astor House marriage—the "unholy alliance," as counsel has frequently characterized it.

The address today of Mr. Graham has attracted to the Court-room a larger audience than has ever before been packed within its walls. Judges of other Courts forsook, for the nonce, their benches, and adjourning, hastened to the trial chamber wherein Mr. Graham was announced to speak. The Bench and the Bar, almost without exception, made a grand holiday in order that they might listen to the eloquent words which were expected to flow from the lips of the "greatest criminal counsel of the present age."

Mr. Graham commenced his address at 11:10 and continued throughout the day, with only a brief recess for lunch.

MR. GRAHAM

May it please the Court and the gentlemen of the jury. How consoling must be this day to this afflicted, sorrowing, and heartbroken man! He is at last where he has no cause to dread to be, before a jury of his peers—the highest social privilege guaranteed him by the laws of his country. To you, my fellow men, through me, his humble and undeserving advocate, he turns, as to the arbiters of his worldly hopes and earthly destiny. His story can be briefly told. "He loved not wisely, but too well."

For the purpose of enabling you to judge how strong a feeling is aroused by the compromise of a husband's honor, I desire to call your attention to the marriage relation as exhibited in Scripture, Proverbs, Sixth Chapter.

Who committeth adultery with a woman lacketh understanding; he that doeth it destroyeth his own soul.

A wound and dishonor shall he get; and his reproach shall not be wiped away.

For jealousy is the rage of man; *therefore he will not spare in the day of vengeance.*

Where jealousy—what the scripture calls jealousy, which is what we call insanity for the purposes of this trial—takes possession of a man's breast, he will not "spare in the day of vengeance"; that is, he cannot spare; for the Deity did not make man strong enough to stand a provocation like that.

Graham went on in this style for hours. Finally he came to his legal propositions. Deadly vengeance by aggrieved husbands had acquired some recent notoriety in high circles, and two cases were a rod and staff to comfort McFarland. One was the *Sickles* case in 1859, on which Graham himself had served as cocounsel with James T. Brady. More recent, and closer to home, was the *Cole* case. In 1867, only two years before Daniel McFarland acted, George W. Cole, another former Civil War general and the brother of Senator Cornelius Cole of California, had put a bullet through the head of his wife's lover in an Albany hotel lobby. The victim was a member of the New York State Assembly. Albert, ironically, had discussed the Cole case with Senator Cole, who had been his companion on a train to Chicago only two months before McFarland's attack. Albert had sat uneasily as the senator defended his brother and lectured on the fate due a home breaker. "The killing was eminently for the protection of the family," Senator Cole explained.

Cole had also been defended by the renowned Brady (without Graham), and he, too, had been acquitted of murder on grounds of temporary insanity. Graham led the jury through a detailed description of the *Sickles* and *Cole* precedents, and gloried in the wisdom of those decisions.

MR. GRAHAM

Oh, how just that retribution! How well would those libertines do to consider, when they plan these moral demolitions, that before they reach the goal of their ambition, they may be intercepted in their pursuits as these men were.

Who would not exclaim to these unhappy husbands, "Hasten, hasten, hasten, to save the mother of your child, although she be lost as a wife! Rescue her from the horrid adulterer, and may the Lord who watches over the home and family guide the bullet and direct the stroke."

And what is Mrs. Calhoun's role in this? Her first letter is dated 24th of January, 1866, to "My dear Mrs. McFarland," (after a while it is "My Darling," and she is ready to eat her up pretty soon), "I could wish myself with you in the smallest farm house that ever took root in the cleft of the hills." Why this inordinate love of a person she had scarcely known six months? This was to impress a weak and probably unsuspecting woman at the time with the idea of her disinterested love for her. Then on the 1st September, 1866: "My Dearest Child, Do you know what is my panacea for all my woes? Mr. Richardson." Why should she compliment this man to another woman? This is for the jury to explain.

Everyone in the court room understood that Graham was alluding to the free-love innuendoes that had been lurking about the case from the beginning. There was a story making the rounds of gossip that purported to be the tale of the veiled lady who had caused so much courtroom conjecture. She was the woman who attended every day, but behind a veil of such density that no one could ascertain her features. When it became clear that she was not Abby, it was speculated she was Mrs. Calhoun.

Those hypotheses were eventually displaced by a sensationalist fiction, published as the so-called *Confession of the Veiled Lady*, about an innocent young girl who is seduced by a clique of free lovers, known as the Forty Firm Friends, who control the city's leading newspapers. Adding fuel to the fire, the current issues of *Frank Leslie's Illustrated Newspaper* contained, along with full coverage of the

THE VEILED LADY;

OR,

THE MYSTERIOUS WITNESS IN THE McFARLAND TRIAL.

athing Exposure of certain Parties in High Life.

McFarland trial, a three-part series on the Oneida Community of Free Lovers—depicting it as a den of Fourierism, where there were no families, only men and women who did as they pleased with each other. Another newspaper stated in its coverage of the trial that Mr. Sinclair's house was "the rendezvous of many literary ladies and gentlemen whose names are quite familiar and whose topics of conversation embraced among other things the relations of the sexes and the principle of psychological affinities." This report said Richardson was introduced to Mrs. McFarland one evening at this house, and that she was "sufficiently educated and metaphysically inclined to understand and take an interest in these novel themes of controversy, and Mr. Richardson, who had a similar tendency of thought, naturally began to take some concern in his new and attractive acquaintance." According to this report, Richardson was not "an apostle of free love doctrines or Fourierite vagaries, but he relished the discussion of socialistic theories and was finally led to take an advanced view of sexual relations by stronger minds than his own."

Graham did not come out and say such things in his arguments. Allusion sufficed. On and on he went, for two full days—all of Friday, May 6th, and all of Monday, May 9th, as well. Observers were unsparing in praise of his performance. It was a spellbinding piece of theater, and it did seem to captivate the jury. D.A. Garvin, who summed up for the prosecution, had no reputation for similar oratorical gifts.

District Attorney Garvin

If your Honor please, Gentlemen of the Jury: Did it occur to you, as you sat here and heard accusations heaped upon them, that it might be a fact in this case, whether proved or unproved, that Albert D. Richardson and Mrs. McFarland were entirely innocent of those charges? Here is a man who, when this Union was rocked from center to circumference by a civil war that shook the civilized world, was in the Federal army, endeavoring to put down an unholy rebellion, which struck at all the best interest which are garnered up in the Government of our country. He is a man who suffered two long years of imprisonment in Salisbury Prison, in the hands of the

Rebels. And yet this man, without any proof against him, without any fact, except such facts as occurred in the presence of numerous witnesses who have been brought here, is charged with deeds for which this prisoner took the law into his own hands and sent him to his long account, without preparation, without question, without trial.

Gentlemen, I put it to you as sensible men, I put it to you as men of experience. Would Albert Richardson have sought to marry Mrs. McFarland, would he have aided her in getting a divorce to marry him, if he had seduced her? Does a man seek to marry his mistress except upon compulsion? Why, if she prostituted herself to him, she may have done the same thing to hundreds of others—and does he want to take her to his bosom, to rear his children, and bring them up, and travel with him on the line of life down to the grave? Does he want to take to his embraces as a wife a woman who has before submitted to him and who may have submitted to the embraces of others?

You as common-sense men are to determine these questions as they arise in your minds. Look over this whole case and see what the probabilities are, and see what the position was in which they stood toward each other. I am not here to defend adulterers! I am not here for the purpose of tearing up the sacred interest of society. I am not here for the purpose of breaking up happy homes!

If you do not vindicate the law of the land in this case, you will see the crowning of your work all over this great Empire State, one murder after another, until the public mind shall be brought to a state or condition in which the laws cannot be enforced, property and life protected and the citizens of this great commonwealth made sure and safe.

After the lawyers had finished their grand speeches, the judge issued his instructions to the jury. On the key point, Recorder Hackett told them that if they entertained "a reasonable doubt as to the perfect sanity of the defendant" when he killed Richardson, they were bound to acquit. Whose sanity is not doubtful at the momer he commits such a barbarous and heinous act? Still, there was r possibility of a compromise verdict. In the *Cole* case, where the adultery was unquestioned, it had taken two trials and many days of jury deliberation to get an acquittal. Albert's sympathizers hoped the McFarland case, with the adultery claim unsubstantiated, might give the jury even more difficulty.

XXVii

The Verdict

AN AUTHENTIC REPORT OF
THE MCFARLAND TRIAL
May 10, 1870
By a Practical Law Reporter

The judge retired from the court room, as did the prosecutors, but counsel for the defense and the audience did not. They seemed to know that the jury would not be long with their business. Graham leaned wearily on his hand, his elbow resting on the long desk-like table before him. His associate, Mr. Gerry, was nervously moving about in front of the desk, trying his best to appear cool, and even claimed to be; but his face was white and eyes seemed starting from their spheres. The audience stood conversing eagerly and excitedly.

The man whose life depended upon the deliberations of that fearful period alone looked thoroughly unmoved. Percy climbed on his knee and stroked his face with his little, plump hand, but soon left him to play with a poor hunchbacked boy who sat among the empty chairs of the absent jury-men. Moved by pity at the torture of suspense which must be scorching the brain above McFarland's face, this reporter went to him and engaged him in conversation. The power of McFarland's self-control was wonderful. He spoke of his visit to Paris, his attendance on the lectures at the Sorbonne, of Leverrier, Girardin, and Chevalier, of the facilities afforded students in Paris, of the emotional character of the students, their intense patriotism, of the big libraries. He indulged in speaking a li French, which he did well, laughed at an anecdote of Clapp's.

him by the writer, and all this time the hundreds around him were feverishly surmising how many minutes more lay between him and the possibly fatal fiat of a verdict of murder.

About fifteen minutes before the re-entrance of the jury, Gerry's restlessness calmed a little, and he took his seat beside Graham, who had scarcely moved. Graham's hand would occasionally be thrown behind him, on McFarland's knee, as if to feel that his client was still there.

At 4:20 the gas was lighted, and the process of illuminating the room was watched closely, as if the person performing it was shedding some light upon the dark subject. Mr. Graham's anxiety was at this time intense, as was evident from his nervous manner. Meanwhile, "heaven's artillery" added solemnity to the scene. The storm which had been lowering all day burst forth into a thunder-shower of unusual violence for this season of the year, and flash after flash of lightning shot through the sky, followed by peals of the grandest thunder.

Amid this disturbance of the elements without, came presently a scene within which will not soon be forgotten by those who witnessed it. After one hour and fifty-five minutes had past, amid surmises that if the jury did not return before six o'clock, they would return for further instructions from the Court, and just as Percy and his crippled play-fellow were bursting out in boyish laughter at some prank of the latter, the voice of the crier was heard, "Hats off in Court, gentlemen; take your seats."

"Make a passage there for the jury! Clear the aisle!" shouted the constable of the Court, and in came the twelve men, in single file, the foreman leading. The silence was now as deep as that which fills an empty cathedral in the watches of the night. Little Percy now clung to his father closer than he had ever done before, and furtively glanced toward the jury, as if his youthful mind could divine the secret which yet reposed in their breasts. Gerry's face was as pale as the leaf of a white camellia, and down the broad cheeks of the burly Graham tears coursed in rapid succession. No face unmoved, un-hanged, but McFarland's; even the judge's lips twitched, and his ?ers moved restlessly. One by one the jurymen took their seats; as the last head was lowered, the Clerk of the Court, with paper in his hand, rose. As he did so, a rustle of paper proceeded from the reporters' table; they were getting ready to write. McFarland was directed to stand up, and did so, supported by his chair.

"Gentlemen of the jury, please answer to your names." Each name was called and answered. "Have you agreed upon your verdict?"

"We have," answered the foreman. A murmur rose from the crowd so faint as to be more *felt* than heard.

"How say you, gentlemen, do you find the prisoner at the bar guilty or not guilty?"

Another pause of a second in time that seemed a year in duration, and the foreman clearly and loudly answered, "Not guilty."

The second syllable of the second word was not heard a yard beyond the speaker. It was drowned in a shout—not a cheer, not a hurrah—a simple emission of voice, in which though it burst from over 300 persons, there was not a discordant note. It was one long clear sound, that seemed to proceed from one throat. It shook the windows, and seemed to vibrate back from the very walls.

The judge took up his mallet as if about to strike for silence, but quietly laid it down. Then rose cheer upon cheer, hats were waved, and ladies springing from their chairs waved their handkerchiefs, and joined their high notes to the deeper cheers of the men. Little Percy leaped upon a chair, and, waving his handkerchief, joined in the popular demonstration.

Gerry waited until the crowd, partially exhausted, allowed a lull in their shouting. "May it please your Honor, I move the discharge of my client."

"Three cheers for Gerry, three cheers for Graham." Up rose cheer after cheer, and in their unstillable midst, the discharge was inaudibly ordered, and the Court adjourned.

Quick as a regiment of Ariels, the ladies crowded around McFarland, some shaking hands with him, some kissing him. They surrounded Percy, too, and hugged and kissed him. The men came further forward to where Graham, who had at last risen, was now standing, and shook him by the hand. He seemed much moved, far more than at any time during the trial, but still occasionally the left hand would be thrown wanderingly out as if seeking something always resting on McFarland.

In the midst of this turmoil, the jury filed out, shaking hands with Graham and Gerry as they passed them, and receiving the thanks of both. Even then, McFarland, save in the politeness which so many congratulations evoked, seemed the least moved of all, and to the last Percy sought his poor little play-fellow, as if to have his romp out ere he left a scene of whose mighty meaning not the dimmest conception seemed to have glimmered into his young mind.

•EDITORIAL: THE ACQUITTAL OF MCFARLAND•

New York Times

MAY 11, 1870

It is stated that the jury stood ten for acquittal and two for conviction of one of the grades of manslaughter, when they first entered the jury-room. The matter was discussed, and finally the two jurors yielded. The jury saw, it may be presumed, that McFarland's provocation was very great, and that it was of a nature to unsettle the foundations of his reason. They had the evidence of medical witnesses, whose character and motives are beyond suspicion, to the effect that they found in the prisoner every symptom of insanity. Even without reference to the connection between Richardson and Mrs. McFarland, the jury could scarcely have brought in any other verdict then the one they did.

Justice

New York Times

MAY 12, 1870

MCFARLAND

The Excitement by No Means Abated

MRS. MCFARLAND'S AFFIDAVIT

Though the McFarland trial ended two days ago, the excitement in relation to the action has not in the least abated, and the public mind is still interested with every detail respecting this important case. The hero of the hour, Mr. McFarland, came down town early in the morning, visited several of his friends and then retired to his temporary home at his brother's house, where he remained throughout the day, enjoying the society of little Percy, and receiving the visits and congratulations of his friends.

With respect to Mr. McFarland's demeanor, it

> may be observed that he appears precisely as he was during the trial. He greeted a reporter from the *Times* with cordiality yesterday, and easily divined the object of his visit. His allusions to Mrs. McFarland-Richardson were marked with great delicacy of expression and he refused to comment upon the issues, contenting himself to rely on the trial as his complete vindication. He is, perhaps, as sane as any man can be who has been afflicted with congestion of the brain as long as he has.

To Albert's friends, the result of the trial was a disgrace. "A mad howl," Junius called it. "Graham ought to have his ears cut off," he wrote Gay. "Both with tongue and pen I denounce him everywhere and at all times. Since our friend's murder, I have been in a perpetual state of bitterness and rage with the capacity for a hundred tragedies in me." As it turned out, they would have been better off to have forgone the trial altogether. McFarland walked out from the courtroom a free man. The jury had found only that he was insane *when* he killed Albert. It had not made any finding about his current and continuing sanity. Hence the only effect of the verdict was to relieve him of punishment. All the trial did was make McFarland a hero, and make Abby's future even more difficult.

Dr. Hammond, whose testimony had been instrumental in gaining McFarland's acquittal, was giving lectures saying that he was liable to further attacks of mania. "Indeed," *The Nation* observed, "there is no reason why he should not have as many mania as he has enemies, until, at last, he can proudly say that he has not a foe above ground." A petition was circulated in Brooklyn, asking the governor to shut McFarland up. But the state's chief executive had no authority to do anything of the sort, assuming he wanted to.

Dan Frohman had perhaps more difficulty than anyone in coming to terms with the result in the case. The image in his young mind of McFarland pointing the gun and pulling the trigger was so powerful it overwhelmed all the testimony he heard. He had been forewarned, but he was nonetheless stunned by the verdict. For Dan the sense of Albert's loss was only slowly sinking in. So long as the trial continued, it was as though he and Albert were still together, fighting for his rights. Albert, his hero, was invincible, and no John Graham or Dr. Hammond could triumph over him.

Now he was worried about Abby's safety. Since McFarland had been vindicated, might he not turn his anger on her? But it was unlikely. McFarland blamed everything on Albert; he could never believe that she, a woman, could have acted on her own. Now that his villain was vanquished and he had emerged a public hero, McFarland had achieved his lifelong dream. What his real estate speculations and his gas illuminating patent could not accomplish, his killing of Albert Richardson had. Daniel McFarland had finally achieved success through bold action, and he was famous.

Abby had other priorities. She had long ago written off the trial as a forum for justice. The version of the events that she had carefully been setting down all during the proceedings was now ready. She published it, in the form of a sworn affidavit, in the *Tribune* on May 11, the day after the trial ended. It was a powerful and detailed description of her years with McFarland and her struggle for freedom, and it had some effect. Readers, such as George Templeton Strong, the diarist, saw the case in a new light. "The homicidal McFarland is acquitted, of course. The trial disgraces everyone concerned in it. The counsel and court stink harmonious in the nostrils of mankind, but I fear they are good enough for this community. There was a long narrative in this morning's *Tribune* from Mrs. McFarland—well written, temperate, and seemingly candid. It reads like a fair statement, and puts the case in a new light. The Indiana divorce was wrong and bad, of course, but this poor woman was, according to her own story (which fits with the evidence), so tormented, bullied, badgered, insulted, beaten, and generally outraged by her drunken, half-crazy husband that she may be pardoned, or at least but gently censured for any proceeding by which she could be freed from him under color of the law."

ABBY, FROM HER AFFIDAVIT

You have heard my true story. I said when I began that I would tell the whole and I have. I think the same thing might have happened to any man or woman who lives, without bringing to them either remorse or shame.

I believe now, as I have believed for years, that Mr. McFarland was a man born to do a murder. The fact that he was always uttering threats of bloodshed does not so much convince me of this as the fact of his temperament, which had become one of uncontrollable violence. I believe he feared this himself. Often during our early married life, when I told him in his reasonable moments that he would kill me in some of his fits of passion, he asserted with vehemence that he "should never harm a hair of my head." Towards the last of my life with him, however, he said in answer to my expressed fears, "I shall never harm you, if I *know* you," which convinced me that he did not feel sure of himself. I believe that if I had stayed with him, sooner or later I should have been the victim of his blind fury.

I write this without malice or hard feeling against him. Mr. McFarland married me a girl in years, a child in experience. In every way he abused his claim in me, he turned my love to bitterness, he took all the bloom and sweetness from my life. When I went away, and he found I had begun, perhaps, to feel a hope of happiness, his wounded vanity and desire for revenge turned his naturally mad temper into blackest madness. He swore to my friends, by all the fiends, that he "would rob me of my reputation, my children, all I held dear." He has done so, and I pity him from my soul.

There are those who say that my marriage to Albert Richardson was the act that led to Mr. McFarland's acquittal by setting the public against Mr. Richardson. If so, it does not matter. As I have said, I wished Mr. McFarland no ill, and I believe that he was, and is, insane. I believe he would have been acquitted in any event, justice being so lax in New York, malignity so strong and the sympathy for crime so increased for a criminal who commits a capital offense. Indeed it seems as if we need only commit murder to have the public sympathy. Perhaps it is a protest against capital punish-

IN THE VEILED LADY.

THERE IS NO RELIABLE PORTRAIT
OF ABBY. THESE ARE THE IMAGES
PRESENTED TO THE PUBLIC IN 1870—
A DEMURE ABBY, A COY ABBY, AND
A FORMIDABLE, ALMOST MASCULINE
ABBY. THE ABBY WHO WOULD LATER
BE DESCRIBED AS "ONE OF THE MOST
BEAUTIFUL WOMEN OF HER TIME,"
AND "A WOMAN OF EXTRAORDINARY
BEAUTY," MANAGED, DESPITE HER
ACTIVE CAREER, TO AVOID PUBLIC
PHOTOGRAPHERS ALL HER LIFE.

IN FRANK LESLIE'S
ILLUSTRATED NEWSPAPER.

ment and may end in its abolition. If so it will leave its good fruits.

There is but one word more to say, and I will say it briefly. It is well known that I was on trial before a New-York Court as much as Daniel McFarland, and for a crime more heinous and more bitterly punished in a woman than murder committed by a man. And it is clearly seen by all who see dispassionately that wherever a loop-hole was opened for any truth about my conduct or Mr. Richardson's it was immediately stopped. I have tasted to its dregs the cup of justice which, in the nineteenth century men born of women mete out to one whose worst crime was the mistake of marrying a man who was half madman from natural inheritance, half brute from natural proclivity. Of the justice I have received let those who have read my story be witness.

Abby Sage Richardson

Abby S. Richardson, being duly sworn, deposes and says that the above statement is true according to her knowledge and belief. Sworn to before me, this 9th day of May, 1870,

Wm. Barker
Notary Public

BOOK THREE

AFTER

XXIX

The Extended Family

The excitement was now over. The morality play known as *The McFarland Case* had finished its run. The newspapers and the public could go on to other matters. But the principal players in the case—except for Albert—had to live out their lives in the shadow of this great event. The ultimate justice lay in their futures.

Abby's immediate concern was the fate of her elder son, Percy, who remained with his certifiably unstable father. If she brought legal proceedings to recover custody, she would reopen all the issues of the trial regarding her behavior and fitness as a mother, and, given the tide of public sympathy for McFarland, there would be little chance of success. Her only option seemed to be to bide her time, and depend on her many friends who also knew McFarland to keep a close watch on the situation. Even her women friends supported this course. They all doubted her mental well-being could tolerate another trial right then and they knew she had enough other problems to concern her.

The thirty-two-year-old widow had to make a life for herself and her other son. And she had to fulfill her promise, made to Albert in his final hours, to become the mother of his children. It was not an easy task. As *The Nation* foresaw, Abby's new family "consisted of two sets of children, the father of one having murdered the father of the other—she herself being the cause of the crime—and each being to the other a perpetual reminder of a sorrow and shame for which the world has no balm. The heathen Furies may have, before n created households like this, to furnish illustrations of the blindness and cruelty of Fate; but we are sure that nothing of the kind was ever before set up under the benediction of the Christian church."

But, true to her word, Abby established the new household. "A year ago," she wrote a friend just after Albert's death, "I fancied I would now be the center of a happy home circle and the wife of the man who was to me the very best and noblest of men. Today I have four little children here and am doing my best to make them happy—I suppose that is why I did not die, as I feel I ought to have done." The oldest, Leander, now fourteen, was an adolescent testing his limits. Maude, age eleven, was resentful of this woman who was imposing herself in the role of mother. Eight-year-old Albert, Jr., had never been quite "right," and the traumatic events of the preceding months had aggravated his condition. Abby's own child—now named Willie, which the little fellow garbled into Lillo— age six, was the sort who was always getting into something. It seemed that *The Nation* had, if anything, understated the problem.

Finances were also an issue. Albert was not a wealthy man, despite his success as an author. Sales of *Beyond the Mississippi* approached 150,000 copies, *The Secret Service* was almost as popular, and his life of Grant was selling well. These books were credited with helping establish the reputation and financial stability of the American Publishing Company, which went on to become Mark Twain's publisher. But, as usual, the publisher earned more from this success than the author. Albert had even been forced to borrow twenty thousand dollars from them, as an advance against his next book, and most of that seems to have been spent before his death on travel and living expenses.

Albert's possessions said something of the kind of man he was. His house at Woodside, near Newark, was fully furnished, including several bedrooms for his children and a housekeeper. There were four bedroom sets, three lounges, three rockers, many tables, and odd chairs. But the most valuable pieces of furniture, aside from a black-walnut bedroom set, were his bookcases. And his one most valuable asset, worth more than any of the furniture, was his library of books. He also had two watches, which at that time, were among the most impressive of mechanical marvels. Albert had written a glowing account in *Harper's* of the production line at the Elgin watch factory and ever after had a weakness for time-pieces. None of this helped to pay for the board and bed of his survivors, however.

Albert had tried to invest. He had bought land when he was in Kansas and Colorado, succumbing to the almost universal passion for land speculation. But all his properties, including his house in New Jersey, were hardly worth more than their mortgages. There was only one investment that mattered, stock of the *Tribune*. The proceeds from sale of his shares provided enough to pay off Albert's debts and funeral expenses (including five dollars that they kindly paid to the Astor House for Dan Frohman's expenses while keeping vigil there) and furnish a nest egg for his family. Abby received about ten thousand dollars (in addition to the three thousand she had collected on the life insurance policy Albert had bought for her). The remaining twenty-two thousand dollars was put in a trust for his three children, Leander, Maude, and Albert, Jr., under the control of Albert's brother Charles. This was a fair sum when a large, new house like Albert's in Woodside sold for nine thousand dollars.

The new family lived at first in the Woodside house. They stayed there almost a year. Abby sought her salvation in work. She gave readings all over—in Montreal, at the state fair in New Hampshire, wherever she could. From each location she wrote journalistic letters and sought to sell them to the papers. She completed a brief, but moving, biography of Albert. It was published along with a selection of his essays and articles (including his final essay advocating better treatment for Chinese immigrants in California), in a volume titled *Garnered Sheaves from the Writings of Albert Deane Richardson*.

But New Jersey, a little too far from New York for Abby to have convenient access to her friends, yet too close to avoid the continuing ripples of scandal, was not a comfortable location for the new widow. Abby's dream was to put the past behind her and follow through on the plans that she and Albert had made for a move to Chicago. She had begun a correspondence with Sidney Gay and his wife almost immediately after Albert's death. In the summer of 187 she decided to act.

Abby to *Elizabeth Neall Gay (Mrs. Sidney H.)*

CHARLESTOWN, MASS., AUG. 8TH, 1871 •

My dear friend,

Your letter bears a date three weeks back and I meant to write you very soon after it. I am coming back to Chicago to stay very soon now. Your hospitality on my brief exploration in June has borne fruit. On Thursday the 10th I start for New York, and unless affairs there detain me, I shall be in Chicago by the 20th. If not that day certainly very near it.

I suppose then that place at which Mr. Richardson boarded is open to me. The only thing about that which was objectionable was the price ($15 for Lillo and myself) which Miss Howells said she thought rather too much. Still it will not be for very long and they seem kindly people—and <u>very best of all</u> it is not very far from your house—so I can visit with you when I like. Do you think they expect me to write them when I shall be there? Because I have actually forgotten the address. That is stupid of me, is it not?

So far this is all about business, and it seems selfish of me to spend so much time on myself and my plans. Now I must tell you that I think about you very often and hope you are not too lonely. I look upon you as one of my oases in Chicago. It is really something of a trial to leave the East to one who was born here and I take deep roots. So whenever I dread migrating to Chicago I think of you and how busy and bright you seem, and I feel quite consoled. I also like this Roberta whom we saw at the Unitarian book rooms. She seems to me very kind and good.

If we only look at it in one way how very full of grief and sorrow life is, full of nothing but parting. You say you were glad not to find me with a hardness and bitterness. I had a great deal of both in me before I knew Albert—a growing hardness and bitterness which I feel quite sure now, would have overflowed my life and made me see it all at its worst if he had not stepped in just there. But, once knowing and loving him—so sweet and human and tender, with such a cheerful philosophy of life that it was contagious—all hardness melted away and bitter became sweet. So hard as the parting was from him, as intolerable as his absence sometimes is, to bear, I would not exchange the lessons his life taught even for the happiness of being always with him. I see all things in so much clearer and better light ever since I knew him. It is really like being born again. I say this to you because I know you love him and I want to make you understand something of what he did for me. I never, (since the first blackness of my desolation) have felt altogether without comfort. Because grief is better than despair and before I knew Albert I was in the very bitterness of despair. Now I feel Albert's presence in everything (I don't mean in the way of the modern psychiatrists but in a better way, which you will understand). The influence of his life permeates all my life and this is the key to all that is best in what I am and do and all the cheerfulness and sweetness which I ever hope to attain.

I don't often write so much as this to anyone but I like to have you understand me although it is impossible to explain myself altogether and I hate to seem egotistical and write too much about myself.

I wish you would write me a little line next week to tell me if those people, whose names I forget, are expecting me, and if I can come about the 20th without further confirmation.

Tell your little Marnie that both Lillo and Maude are eager to make her acquaintance. Lillo will come with me and Maude after I get home ready. Just now Lillo has been emulating some aerobatic performings at the circus, and has a bumped head and cut knee. He informed me coolly that he had only 36 black and blue spots—he had counted them. He practices the most heart-rending gymnastics and I am powerless to prevent him. But I hope soon he can be got to a nice school and there he will work off some of his wonderful vitality.

Have you seen my pen floating about your house? I think I left it behind me in Chicago. I have searched my trunk for it. It is not valuable, but Albert gave it me several years ago.

Now good night. My love to Mr. Gay and Marnie and <u>much love</u> for yourself.

Yours—*Abby S. R.*

By September 1871, a new household was established in Chicago—Abby, Lillo, Maude, and also Leander, who hesitated but then decided to accompany his sister. Nine-year-old Albert did not join them however. He was placed that fall in Dr. Brown's school for the Education of Feeble-Minded Youth, at Barre, Massachusetts. Abby and the children's trustee, Charles, were fortunate to have found such an institution, and to have been able to afford it, for Dr. Brown was a pioneer in his belief that such children could be educated and improved, not merely held, in institutions. Some of his charges, who included epileptic and palsied children, profited greatly from such a regime. Albert, Jr., however, was to remain in institutions and protective custody for the rest of his life.

Even without the burden of this boy, the Chicago household did not have an easy time of it. Only two weeks after Maude and Leander arrived, the great fire ravaged Chicago, destroying virtually all of that then wooden city and leaving almost 150,000 people homeless. The fire compounded Abby's adjustment to her new home in other ways. Sidney Gay was discharged from the *Chicago Tribune,* as the paper was forced by the fire to take drastic economy measures, and her one sure source of friends moved back to New York.

Most people in her situation—a lone woman with three children, no job and no friends—would have turned back, returned to New York or Boston where circumstances and established relations were much stronger. But, showing a strength of character and determination that few had seen in her, she did not quit. Life with McFarland had taught her one thing, how to survive. She was there and she was going to make the best of it.

Abby to *Whitelaw Reid, Editor, New York Tribune*

75 24TH ST., CHICAGO
10 P.M. OCT. 10, 1871 •

My dear Mr. Reid,

I send you a hastily written account of our great fire whose horrors no pen can possibly describe adequately, thinking you may like it for the Tribune. If you use it, please pay me for it as much as you justly can, for we who live in Chicago are all more or less impoverished and need money.

Will you let me know its fate, and believe me yours very respectfully,

Abby Sage Richardson

The *Tribune* printed the account and paid Abby twelve dollars. She published other articles in the press. She found an occasional position as an amanuensis for Miss Bross, daughter of the former Illinois lieutenant governor who had traveled through the West with Albert in 1865. She began again to give the lectures and readings that had sustained her in New York during the worst of times. Albert's friends tried to be helpful. Whitelaw Reid, Gay's successor at the *Tribune,* arranged for some favorable notices, which Abby was not too shy to solicit. Albert's old Colorado contacts arranged for appearances there.

• *MRS. RICHARDSON READS* •

Colorado Transcript

GOLDEN, COLORADO

OCTOBER 23, 1872

Well, we'll not start off by saying that Abby Sage Richardson was greeted by a full house on Friday evening of last week, for such was not the case. However, we have seen larger audiences in Golden on far less worthy occasions, and on occasions, too, where the consideration returned was not even worthy of comparison with the literary treat that Madame Richardson afforded her listeners. The stage appearance of this lady is a model of good taste, and could proceed only from a mind at once beautiful in its conceptions and highly cultivated in that which renders life somewhat more than a succession of eating and sleeping, varied, perhaps by an occasional change of clothing, or by a more frequent exchange of gossip. In the line of readings, we had not looked for so brilliant a performance from Madame Richardson, and were, therefore, agreeably surprised. She has a handsome face, a fine figure, and a clear melodious voice, which shows thorough elocutionary training. Suffice it to say that her renditions of Longfellow's musical words was entirely worthy of America's first poet, while her reading of the "Minister's Housekeeper," by Harriet Beecher Stowe, was accurate as to character and quite amusing in effect.

Dan Frohman accompanied Abby on this Colorado trip. Albert had introduced them that first day in the Astor House, as he lay dying. Dan always remembered the moment. "I knew that I had found a friend. I became as another son to her." He had even considered moving to Chicago when she did, until a new job in New York editing a small paper kept him in the East. He welcomed the chance to see the great West with Abby, but he was also concerned about her health. These trips were wearing on her. In one week, she read in Central City, in Denver twice, in Golden, and in Greeley, all the while suffering from a severe cold aggravated by the fatigue of the journey.

The audiences were respectable in number, and uniformly enthusiastic about her performance. Some people came out of morbid curiosity more than cultural interest, but they went away with a respect for her. That may have been part of the appeal for her, too, the idea of showing people that she was an elegant, refined woman, of presenting herself personally as a refutation of the nastier rumors that flowed from the trial. With ticket prices of fifty to seventy-five cents, the tour probably did more for her reputation than her pocket book. It is doubtful she cleared very much after paying her expenses. She had to supplement the fees in any way she could. In the midst of the lecturing, she also arranged a trip to the mines and to Clear Creek Canyon so that she could prepare an article on them for the *New York Independent*. Abby and Dan went on this trip with several other journalists and, according to local press reports, were given a spectacular tour, including "a dash up the canyon on the narrow gauge railway and a visit to the picnic park being laid out at Beaver Creek."

LEANDER PEASE RICHARDSON, IN 1890.

Home life in Chicago was no less hectic. Maude was not happy away from her aunts and grand-parents, the only family she had known, and she told Abby so. She was sent to an exclusive day school where the tuition was a rather expensive twelve dollars per month, paid fortunately by her trust. Leander, despite his father's emphasis on education, did not want to remain in school. In 1872, at sixteen, he began working on the *Chicago Inter Ocean*, and by the following year, 1873, he was on his own. For a while he wandered, traveling to Buffalo, Memphis, and other cities, helped financially by a small allowance from the trust. But then he settled down in New York. Abby helped him find a place to live, with Dan Frohman's father, and a job working for the *New York Tribune*.

Besides tending to her family responsibilities and her lecturing, Abby managed to complete another book in 1872, *Stories from Old English Poetry*. This was a collection of romantic tales, as told by her based on stories of Chaucer, Spencer, Shakespeare, and others, al with small biographies of the poets. She followed this with a cc tion of *Songs from the Old Dramatists* in 1873. The books apparently sold respectably, in both America and England, and met with enough approval that H. O. Houghton, her publishers, encouraged her to proceed with a project that she and Albert had often discussed, a grand history of the United States.

Albert had wanted to write, as Abby recalled it, "not merely a record of wars, and state politics, but a picture of society and social changes—of the employments of a growing people—of the way they lived, and talked, and what manner of men and women they were—of the growth and history of all the great inventions which have helped or wrought upon our national prosperity and growth. For years he had filled one volume after another with scraps cut from newspapers, books, pamphlets, everything met with in his immense field of reading, which could add anything to his stores of information about this country. His books, desks, drawers, and even his pockets constantly overflowed with scraps containing facts about early settlements, ancient houses, anecdotes and descriptions of distinguished men—anything which swelled the material for such a history as he wished to write." She picked up where he had left off and worked feverishly, with the publishers constantly reminding her how important it was to finish in time for a publication coinciding with the coming national centennial in 1876.

In the summer of 1873, the family traveled back to New England for the dedication of a monument at Albert's grave in Franklin, Massachusetts, on Decoration Day, May 30. There was a moving service at which Junius delivered a eulogy, and a fifteen-foot high shaft of Portland freestone was unveiled. It bore the simple inscription,

> *THOUSANDS GIVE THEE THANKS WHO NEVER KNEW THY FACE,*
> *SO, THEN, FAREWELL, KIND HEART AND TRUE.*

This memorial still stands, tall and proud, in the old cemetery on Green Street.

Maude remained in Franklin for the summer, staying with her t Clarissa, and then enrolled in Miss Porter's boarding school. uition and board were as expensive as that of her unfortunate brother at Dr. Brown's, and on top of that she had expenses for vacations, for dresses imported from Europe, and other such things of which young Albert never conceived. Yet she was not pleased, changing schools four times in the three years from 1873 to 1876.

For a brief time, in 1874, the public was reminded of Abby's deathbed marriage, when Rev. Henry Ward Beecher was charged with seducing the wife of his trusted assistant and parishioner, Theodore Tilton. But Beecher's minor blunder in performing Abby's marriage was soon forgotten as the sordid Tilton case went on for almost six months and produced three thousand pages of testimony that was widely published in pamphlets. Though Beecher's guilt was clear, he somehow managed to prevail with a divided jury by presenting himself as the victim of ordinary human weakness. Tilton, on the other hand, was forced into self-exile in France, his marriage and career destroyed.

But Abby had long since moved beyond concern about the McFarland case. She continued to work on her history of the United States. Taking good advantage of her relative peace and quiet, she managed to complete the book in time for the centennial. It was a formidable volume, over six hundred pages long with many engravings, and the publishers included an appendix describing the Philadelphia Centennial exhibit so that it could be used as guide. The book continued for many years to be a popular history, with new editions published every few years until 1903. It was adopted, in one of those charming coincidences of history, as a text at Dr. Brown's school in Barre.

Then tragedy drew Abby back into Maude's life. The girl had taken ill over the summer of 1876. By the fall, she was too sick to return to school. At first her family in Massachusetts, where she was then staying, hoped it was only influenza, and that she would recover. But Dr. Weak, a specialist in New York, confirmed their worst fears. It was October 16, Maude's seventeenth birthday, when he gave them the news. Maude had consumption.

Abby proposed the cure that Albert had always advocated. When he was sick with lung fever after his imprisonment, he traveled west convinced that the fresh air of open spaces, away from the miasmat atmosphere of the cities, was the answer. It had worked for him.

why not his daughter? Abby enrolled William, now age twelve, at The Gunnery, in Washington, Connecticut, a boarding school favored by liberals of the time. She then picked Maude up in New York, and the two went off to Colorado for treatment.

The entries in Maude's trust account tell the story of her life with Abby over the next eight months:

1876 Oct.	Dr. Weak's bill and medicine	10.17
	Telegram to Denver	2.50
	Guardian & ward's fare to Chicago	26.00
	" " Pullman car exp.	10.00
	Board at Dr. Taylor's	21.00
	Medicine	10.00
	Attendant	3.00
	Medicine, fruit, etc.	7.50
	Outlay by Mrs. C.A. Richardson —Shawl	17.00
	Flannel night gowns	13.00
	Cloak	14.00
	Cotton night gowns & hose	8.00
	Wrapper	5.95
	Photographs	4.00
	Medicine, fares, telegrams, etc.	8.39
	L.R. bill on acct. Maude at Chicago	81.20
Nov.	Abby's bill for fares to Colorado	91.80
Dec.	Mrs. E.H. Byer's board bill, Colorado, 1 month	115.00
	Board, week ending 17th	27.00
	Board to 24th	27.00
	Board to 31st	27.00
1877 Jan.	Board to 7th	27.00
Feb.	Board to Feb. 1st	97.00
	Doctor's bill	7.00
	Abby's board for Feb.	29.62
Mar.	Board to March 1st	111.54
	Hats	4.10
	Washing, druggist & medicine	14.25
Apr.	Board to Apr. 1st	69.14
	Abby's board for March	23.60
	Board, exp. for March	88.13

May	Household expenses, May 1/15	27.50
	Board at Beek house to May 22	25.75
	Care of ward in Colorado	100.00
June	Board May 22 to Jun 5	62.75
	Photographs	3.00
	Doctor's bill	34.50
	Doctor Reed's bill	40.00
	Carriages	39.50
	Coffin	35.00
	Sexton, pall bearers, etc.	16.00
	Horse hire	10.50
	Telegrams	6.36
	Seamstress	5.00
	Sundries on acct. sickness and burial	17.00
	Freight on box from Colorado	18.71
		1,442.46

Balance of this account transferred to C. A. Richardson as Guardian for Leander P. Richardson & Albert D. Richardson, brothers of said Maude, deceased.

XXX

Daniel McFarland

The reputation of McFarland's lawyer, John Graham, soared after the trial. In 1873, he was retained to defend the infamous Tammany Hall leader Boss Tweed against criminal charges of corruption. Though the aggressive lawyer's powers of invective had not slackened, Tweed was found guilty on 204 counts, perhaps because the judge in the case was Graham's old adversary, Noah Davis, who had gone on to become a federal prosecutor and then was elected judge again. After sentencing the fallen politician to twelve years in jail, Davis summoned John Graham before the bench, and levied a $250 personal contempt-of-court fine on him for abrasive court-room tactics. Graham continued nonetheless in active and successful practice until 1894, when he died from complications following surgery, with Daniel Sickles, his first temporarily insane client, keeping vigil at his side.

As for McFarland himself, he lived on for a time, in his way.

• *RICHARDSON'S MURDERER SPENDS A NIGHT IN A ST. LOUIS CALABOOSE* •

St. Louis Globe-Democrat

FEBRUARY 21, 1876

About 1 o'clock yesterday morning, Daniel McFarland, the murderer of Albert D. Richardson, the well-known New York *Tribune* correspondent, was arrested near the Southern Hotel while in a beastly state of intoxication, and locked up in the Chestnut St. Police station. McFarland, it seems, was making a great deal of noise about the hotel, telling every one he met that he was the man who had killed Richardson. At the station he repeated his statement and kept constantly uttering it until he sank into a senseless state of drunkenness. He was released when sober, and, in reply to the Sergeant's questions, stated that he was the veritable Daniel McFarland, and was here in the city on business. He is a fine-looking man, apparently about fifty years of age, and wore side-whiskers. He seemed greatly surprised when he found he had been arrested, and looked very sorrowful at the condition of his broadcloth suit, after wallowing over night in cell No. 3 at the Chestnut Street Police Station.

• RICHARDSON MURDERER

CONFRONTS WIFE •

Chicago Tribune
SOUTH BEND, INDIANA
NOV. 28, 1878

Mrs. Abby Sage Richardson was here in South Bend last evening to give a lecture arranged by the former Vice President Colfax and his wife.

Since the announcement in the *Tribune* some months past that McFarland had been discovered here while on a drunken spree, and that he had been living here *incognito*, he has considerably straightened up, and has delivered a few lectures in this vicinity. Although his friends had tried to dissuade him from doing so, McFarland insisted on attending his former wife's performance, saying "I will go; I'll show her I am no common gutter drunkard."

He and his friends had planned for him to enter just after the lecture commenced, but he went too early. Majestic as it was possible for one of so small a stature, he marched up the center aisle, walked to the front row of seats, and seated himself a moment before Mrs. Richardson appeared on the stage. While he was passing to his seat a whispered hum of "That's McFarland," and a general stretching of necks took place. During the lecture McFarland evidently tried to attract the attention of his divorced spouse by moving unnaturally in his seat, but she had command of nerve sufficient to give the audience no token of acknowledging him.

She is represented as saying to a friend, after the lecture, that she did not recognize him. So ended an anticipated scene.

• *THE SLAYER OF ALBERT D.*
RICHARDSON IS NEW RESIDENT •

Leadville Daily Chronicle
LEADVILLE, COLORADO
MAY 5, 1879

Last evening the famed Daniel McFarland arrived in Leadville. He looks older by thirty years then on the day that Richardson stole his wife and children years ago, but he has lost but little of his gentlemanly bearing and classical air. To a *Chronicle* reporter who called at his lodgings this morning McFarland said:

"I came to Leadville to get rich. Yes, I look older, but I am not broken down. There is plenty of hard work in me yet.

"I have been pretty well over the world since the encounter with Richardson. I came to Leadville directly from South Bend, Indiana, where I have been sojourning the past year.

"I have never regretted the killing of Richardson. My little boy Percy, whom Richardson and my wife stole, I recovered after great difficulty and large expense. He is now in the University of Michigan.

"To converse about the encounter with Richardson is not painful to me. The destruction of my home came near breaking me down, it is true, but I have rallied from it to a great measure. My life has been threatened by the friends of Richardson, but I have never entertained fear from that source.

"I think some of commencing the practice of law in Leadville, but am undecided."

• *ONLY WAITING*

A ONCE WEALTHY NEW YORK CAPITALIST DYING IN A LEADVILLE HOSPITAL •

Leadville Daily Democrat
LEADVILLE, COLORADO
APRIL 20, 1880

Among the invalids who assemble regularly every morning in the little chapel at St. Vincent's hospital to send thanks on high for earthly blessings is a man who once occupied the highest position in wealth and influence at the national metropolis. He owned long rows of costly dwellings and business blocks and in his presence governors, judges, senators and even the president of the United States uncovered their heads. Daniel McFarland once wielded an influence in national politics, but he shot Albert D. Richardson, and now he sits dozing in the large ward at the Sisters' hospital in this city, a pensioner upon the county, and quite unknown and forgotten, He was pointed out to a reporter yesterday, who picked his way among the cots to the one where the mighty fallen sat, and said:

"Mr. McFarland?"

"Hi!—so—me? What?"

"This is Mr. Daniel McFarland, I believe?"

"Oh, my name. Yes, yes. Daniel McFarland. That is it."

"You once lived in New York, Mr. McFarland?"

"Yes, sir, I recollect it. I did once live in New York."

"If my memory serves me correctly, you were once very wealthy in that city."

"I was in quite comfortable circumstances at one time,
"

"An editor, I believe; an associate on the Tribune with Horace Greeley?"

"Not exactly that; although I have been often credited by the papers with occupying an editorial position on the New York Tribune, but it is a mistake. Mr. Greeley was a warm, personal friend of mine, and for several years I was in the habit of writing more or less for his paper, but not as a salaried editor. I was above writing for pay at that time. My income was ample from other sources."

"You must have been intimately acquainted with many of the great men of a quarter of a century past."

"Yes, sir, I was on quite intimate terms with William H. Seward, Daniel Webster, Stephen A. Douglas, Abraham Lincoln and well, I knew them all and have often entertained them at my house in New York."

"You look quite feeble."

"My health is not good."

"Do you hear often from your wealthy New York friends."

"I hear from no one."

"Are you comfortable here?"

"A pauper on the county could not expect more."

"You are penniless?"

"Penniless and friendless, dying among strangers in a county alms house in the wilds of the Rocky mountains."

"But you may re—"

"No, I never wish to leave this place. I am tired of this life, and am only waiting a summons to another."

As with everything else, McFarland exaggerated the likelihood of his forthcoming death. He was out of the hospital two days later, and back living in a cheap boarding house, the companion of laborers and miners, not plutocrats. That was the last anyone heard of Daniel McFarland. After a decade of drifting on the sea of troubles he had caused, he finally sank from view. Rumor had it that he died somewhere in the West shortly thereafter.

XXXi

The Final Years

After Leander went off on his own, in 1873, and Maude died, in 1876, Abby had only her small family to worry about. She found she could live in reasonable security with the income from her lecturing and writing.

All her books, even *Percy's Year of Rhymes* published ten years earlier, remained in print. Her collections of old stories and songs continued to generate income and provide a basis for her tours. To expand her lecture repertoire, she developed a series on the history of classical English literature, from Chaucer to Byron, Shelley, Keats and Scott. Done as a series of fifty-nine "talks," with biographical discussions, samples of work and explanations, it was an absorbing presentation. Abby published the series in 1881 as *Familiar Talks on English Literature*, which was reprinted in ten editions.

By the 1880s, Dan Frohman had moved from journalism to a career in the theater. In 1885 he took over the lease of the failing Lyceum Theater and turned it into a popular repertory house that was remembered with affection by theater lovers years afterward. With his brother Charles, he went on to develop the commercial side of the theater so well they were accused of monopolizing it with a theatrical trust. He became known as the "dean" of American theatrical producers, honored not only for his greatness as a manager but also for his role in founding and developing the Actors' Fund to help impoverished performers and his work with Jewish charitable causes.

He did not forget Abby, who had returned to New York. The

Frohman brothers were famed for exploiting the wealth of material being produced for the British and French stage. Remembering her "brilliant mind" and her "wide knowledge of French and English dramatic literature," Dan began to draw on Abby's talents in preparing these works for his productions. Among others, she translated and adapted Victorien Sardou's *Americans Abroad*, which was a great success, running nearly through the season. She also adapted Mark Twain's *The Prince and the Pauper*, for the stage. Samuel Clemens himself introduced the first performance, saying it was the realization of one of his fondest dreams. Later he prepared his own stage version, but Dan thought Abby's was superior and continued to use it.

Abby's life and work had become satisfying and fulfilling. Percy eventually returned to her and adopted the surname Sage, as his brother had earlier, thus casting his lot with hers. With Dan Frohman's encouragement, Percy became a theatrical agent and manager, and for a while had his own touring company. He remained close to his mother, but not so close as William (Lillo) who lived with her until he was thirty-six. William became a banker and stockbroker, but

WILLIAM SAGE, IN 1900.

eventually found his metier as a writer of romantic novels. He managed to combine both careers for much of his life. Both sons married late in life, and though neither graced Abby with grandchildren, they were devoted to her and she to them.

Leander followed his father's wandering ways for some time. He soon left the *Tribune*, where Abby had helped him locate, to travel in the West. He sent back reports from the Black Hills that rivaled A.D.R's best, including graphic descriptions of Custer's last stand, and spent time with Wild Bill Hickok, who, story has it, once cut the ear off a man and gave it to Leander. After a stint as managing edito of the *Rocky Mountain News* in Denver (much like his father twenty years earlier), he returned to the East and became a European correspondent for the Boston *Herald.*

By the 1880s, however, Leander felt the influence of Abby and Dan Frohman and settled into the world of the theater, working as a critic and playwright. He was the drama critic for the *Times* and the *Morning Telegraph,* and, for several years was part-owner and editor of the *Dramatic News.* Several of his plays were produced on Broadway.

In 1892, Abby bought a house on the emerging Upper West Side of Manhattan (at 256 West 100th Street) where she lived with William. Her position in the New York literary and theatrical community was now firmly established, and her home was known for distinguished social occasions, with guests such as Mary Mapes Dodge, William Dean Howells, and Edmund Stedman. Abby's old friends Junius and Lilly, who now lived on Fifty-seventh Street, frequently stopped by with their three sons. Junius had left the country for a while after the trial, but had eventually returned and married Lilly. He had settled into a reasonably contented existence as a writer and man about town in New York. Abby sometimes saw Lu Calhoun Runkle, now widowed again, who had become an ardent feminist and a popular speaker for the women's suffrage campaign. But Abby, for understandable reasons, always held back from involvement in controversial causes.

Her greatest theatrical successes came from her collaborations with Grace Livingston Furniss just before the turn of the century. The two women first met in 1898, as Miss Furniss tells it: "I had a few things published and had written a few plays, which had not found a producer. I showed one to David Belasco and Daniel Frohman, who thought that it might amount to something with proper revision. I told them I agreed, but I had no idea how to go about it. Mr. Frohman said, 'Go up and see Abby Sage Richardson. She is an old dramatic critic, and knows all that is to be known of technique.'

"I followed his advice and took my imperfect play to her. When she read it, she saw right off what needed to be changed. In Mrs. Richardson I found what I lacked. She taught me coldbloodedness toward my work. I learned to be merciless to it."

JAMES K. HACKETT AND BERTHA GALLAND
in the *Pride of Jennico*, adapted by Abby Sage Richardson

The two coauthored three plays in 1898–99 that were produced by Dan Frohman without great success. But the next year, they triumphed with the *Pride of Jennico*, which they adapted from the popular Agnes and Egerton Castle novel. Dan had commissioned their work after rejecting the Castles' own adaptation as "manifestly unsuitable." Grace and Abby's *Pride of Jennico* was a "prodigious success." With James K. Hackett (the son of Recorder Hackett) in the starring role, it opened in March 1900 to reviews that praised it as a "steadily entertaining romantic comedy of forty-shock power." It finished the season and reopened the following fall for an additional run. Later, in 1914, when Dan expanded his producing activities into the new medium of the movies, he would select this as one of his first epics, filming it on location in Cuba.

In the fall of 1900, flush with the success of the *Pride of Jennico,* Abby and her son William went off to Italy, where they planned to spend the year dramatizing his recently successful novel *Robert Tournay: A Romance of the French Revolution.* The journey, with its echoes of the Italian sojourns of her beloved Shelley, Byron, and Browning, was a life-long dream.

It was not to be fully realized. She visited Milan, Florence, and Venice and celebrated her sixty-third birthday in Italy. But shortly after arriving in Rome, Abby contracted pneumonia and, after a brief illness, died there on December 5.

New York mourned this "rare conversationalist" and "woman of extraordinary beauty," whose youth had been marked by "one of the great tragedies of the century." So far as the tragedy was recalled, Abby was praised for her "great courage and constancy" in escaping from a worthless husband. Even the once virulent *Sun* now reported that she left McFarland because he was an "eccentric" who rarely supported her, and that she became involved with Albert only "after" her separation. Time had set the story right from her viewpoint. After years of unhappiness she had found almost everything. Maybe she did not need what was missing. As her collaborator, Grace Furniss, suggested, "There is only one reason, in our time when women can make homes for themselves, why a woman should marry, and that is love. If she doesn't love she shouldn't marry."

Abby never loved again, or perhaps one should say, she never stopped loving. A dozen years after Albert's death she published a book of *Old Love Letters,* full of wisdom on the meaning of love from an array of writers ranging from Pliny and Socrates to Aaron Burr, Balzac and George Eliot. It was dedicated, in a quiet allusion that no one missed, "To my lost friend." And in her final listing in the New York City Directory, for 1900, after a lifetime of achievement, she did not refer to herself as a playwright or author or lecturer. She remained, to her death, simply "Richardson, Abby Sage, widow of Albert."

General Notes

1. *The Assassination and the Trial*—Press coverage of the Richardson–McFarland case was remarkably comprehensive, if not always accurate or consistent. During the period Albert languished at the Astor House and again during the time of the trial, most papers carried both lengthy news stories and supplemental features such as excerpts from McFarland's habeas corpus action and reports on Abby's divorce hearing in Indiana. Several also included what purported to be verbatim transcripts of testimony, including the full text of Graham's summation that ran to forty thousand words (half the length of this entire book). This extensive coverage was collected and published immediately after the trial in several "instant" books. These sources are catalogued as *Trial Sources* in the Bibliography and will be cited collectively as such. I have freely consolidated and edited these sources, no one of which is complete, to get a single coherent and complete narrative. All descriptions of key events are derived from these materials, and all voices of persons testifying at the trial are distilled and condensed from the same, modified as necessary to convert the question-and-answer format to a straightforward account.

2. *Newspaper Items*—All items referenced in the text to a newspaper or newspapers are derived from the source there noted. However, I have, of necessity, extracted from and condensed all such items, while attempting to maintain the actual language and tone, and have usually adjusted the date to show when an event happened rather than when the story appeared in the newspaper. I have also occasionally blended stories (as noted in text and Chapter Notes).

3. *Albert Deane Richardson*—The primary biographical sources for Albert are Abby's lengthy sketch in *Garnered Sheaves,* his autobiographical descriptions in *Beyond the Mississippi* and *Secret Service,* and his correspondence. Additional sources are noted under his name in the Bibliography.

4. *Abby Sage Richardson*—The primary biographical sources for Abby are her Affidavit and her correspondence. Additional sources are noted under her name in the Bibliography.

5. *Correspondence*—Most letters have been condensed and excerpted and in a few instances closely dated letters written by the same person to the same correspondent have been consolidated. All are used by courtesy of the owners as follows: Letters of Albert, Abby, Lu Calhoun, Junius Henri Browne, and Charles Richardson to Sidney Gay are from the Sidney Howard Gay Papers, Rare Book and Manuscript Library, Columbia University *[Gay Collection].* Letters of Albert and Abby to Whitelaw Reid are from the Reid Family Papers, Manuscript Division, Library of Congress *[Reid Papers].* Letters of Albert to Charles and Jennie Richardson are from the Richardson Family Papers, Massachusetts Historical Society *[Richardson Papers].* Abby's letters to Daniel McFarland are from *Veiled Lady,* pp. 81-94, except as noted below.

Chapter Notes

The following notes give sources of quoted material not otherwise fully cited in the text or covered by the General Notes.

Prologue: At the Tribune Counting Room (pp. 1-5)

Dan Frohman's voice is from his memoir, *Daniel Frohman Presents,* pp. 11–21. See also his testimony at trial and newspaper reports for November 25-26, 1869. For Daniel McFarland's statement, see *RM Tragedy,* p. 23, as well as newspapers noted in text.

Chapter I (pp. 9-12)

Albert's quotes are from *Garnered Sheaves,* p. 26, 31–32. For his marriage date see Marriage Record for Louisa Pease and A. D. Richardson, Probate Court for Hamilton County, Ohio. *Garnered Sheaves* puts the marriage date six months earlier, in "April, 1855," no doubt to make the date of Leander's birth more acceptable. Albert always refers to his wife by the affectionate name "Lou" in his letters to Charles and Jennie Richardson.

Chapter II (pp. 10-17)

Abby's story of finding Shakespeare miniatures is from the introduction to her *Stories from Old English Poetry.*

Chapter III (pp. 18-25)

The quotes and dispatches of A.D.R. all are from *Beyond the Mississippi,* pp. 155, 256–59, and 313–24. The quote about him caring for a sick woman and family is from *Garnered Sheaves,* p. 49–50. See also *Beyond the Mississippi,* p. 324–25.

Chapter IV (pp. 26-36)

Abby's letter of November 21, 1859, is from *DM Trial,* p. 170–71, combined with material from a letter of Nov. 22, 1859, in *Veiled Lady,* p. 86–87.

Daniel's letter to Abby is from the *Herald,* May 5, 1870, p. 4.

Chapter V (pp. 37-50)

Junius's description of his first meeting with Albert is from *Garnered Sheaves,* p. 27–28. His comments on war correspondents are from *Four Years,* p. 7–22. The quotes and dispatches of A.D.R. are from *Secret Service,* p. 195, 211, 337–346. Junius's description of the battery-running expedition is from *Four Years,* p. 79–80, 231–32, and *Garnered Sheaves,* p. 55–57.

Chapter VI (pp. 51-59)

The quote from Schuyler Colfax appears in his affidavit submitted in Abby's divorce case, and reprinted in the *Times,* May 12, 1870, p. 2.

Chapter VII (pp. 60-73)

The telegrams regarding the imprisonment of Albert and Junius are from *Official Records*, Series II, Vols. 5–6. The quotes and dispatches of A.D.R. are from *Secret Service*, pp. 402, 403, 411–24, 428–35, 508–509. Albert's letter to R. T. Colburn (dated June 4, 1864) is in *Gay Collection*. Charles Richardson's description of Mary Louise's death is in a letter of March 4, 1864 from Charles to Sidney Gay, in *Gay Collection*, supplemented with information in *Garnered Sheaves*, p. 59. Junius's description of Salisbury Prison is from *Four Years*, pp. 322 et. seq. Dan Ellis's quote is from his *Thrilling Adventures*, p. 352–53.

Chapter VIII (p. 74-89)

Lu Calhoun's letters to Abby are from *DM Trial*, pp. 65–68. The Winter Garden was renamed as such in 1859 by a new owner who cut its seating by half and filled the place with live and artificial tropical plants, according to Henderson, p. 107–08.

Chapter IX (p. 90-99)

Colfax's career came to an abrupt end in the early 1870s as a result of the Credit Mobilier scandal, involving bribes and favors in the construction of the Union Pacific Railway. Though not found guilty of any wrongdoing, he had taken some favors that were difficult to justify.

Albert's comments on his trip by Overland stage are in a letter to Sidney Gay, May 28, 1865. The quote from Samuel Bowles is in his *Across the Continent*, p. 48. Albert's letter to Governor Bross (dated November 13, 1866) is #34, Box 5-R, War 1861–5 Manuscript Department, New-York Historical Society.

Chapter X (p. 100-109)

Abby's letter to Lu Calhoun of January 2, 1867, is incorporated in *ASR Affidavit*.

Chapter XII (p. 113-116)

Albert's letter to Junius (dated December 1, 1867), is in *DM Trial*, p. 239. His letter of March 31, 1867, to Abby is in *ASR Affidavit*.

Chapter XIII (p. 117-126)

Albert's letter to Junius (dated December 1, 1867), is in *DM Trial*, p. 239. Abby's articles on the Indies appeared in the *Tribune* on May 15 (front page) and July 10, 1869, without byline. The quote from Albert about the content of his new paper is from *Garnered Sheaves*, p. 74. The quotes about the divorce proceeding were reprinted in the *Sun*, December 13, 1869, and the *World*, December 4, 1869. Abby's description of her last meeting with Albert is from *Garnered Sheaves*, p. 74–75. Albert's comments on buffalo hunting are from his letters of October 13 and 17, 1869, to Whitelaw Reid. His comments on Reid's social life are in a letter of September 26, 1869.

Chapter XIV (p. 127-133)

The newspaper reports of November 26, 1869, are supplemented with material from *Daniel Frohman Presents*, p. 21. The quoted material in the wedding ceremony is from *RM Tragedy*, p. 25.

Chapter XV (p. 137-144)

The quote from the *Herald* on "Socialistic circles" combines its editorials of December 3 and 4, 1869. The *Herald* story on Mrs. Norton is from December 3, 1869. The quote from President Grant is paraphrased from the *Herald*, December 1, 1869. *The Nation*'s comment appeared on December 9, 1869. (This quote and others from *The Nation* have been condensed from the original.) The *Times* editorial on the divorce law is from April 20, 1870. The quote from Henry Adams is from his *Education*, p. 37–38. The Frothingham discussion of elective affinities is from his sermon preached December 19, 1869.

Chapter XVII (p. 147-156)

Lu Calhoun's comments on Abby are from a letter to Sidney Gay, dated February 1, 1870. Other quotations are from *Trial Sources*.

The defense opening was delivered not by John Graham but by Charles Spencer, a third lawyer on the defense team, who dropped out after a few days.

Chapter XVIII (p. 157-165)

The *World* story on Abby and Albert's trip to Hartford first appeared on December 3, 1869, and was later reprinted elsewhere. Abby's next book, a collection of children's stories titled *Pebbles and Pearls for the Young Folks,* was in fact published by Albert's publisher, the American Publishing Co., in 1868.

Chapter XXII (p. 184-189)

The voice of Kate Stevenson comes from her Affidavit submitted in McFarland's habeas corpus case rather than from the trial. The suggestions in the *Sun* that Albert and Abby slept together appeared on December 4, 1869.

Chapter XXIII (p. 190-194)

Regarding the Hammond–Stanton conflict, see Dr. Hammond's statement and the U.S. Army Judge Advocate General's reply, both cited in the Bibliography.

Chapter XXIV (p. 195-200)

McFarland's article on his school days is cited in the Bibliography.

Chapter XXV (p. 201-214)

Horace Greeley went on to run for President in 1872 against the incumbent General Grant, on a platform that advocated reconciliation. The Greeley candidacy carried only six states, and his wife died during the campaign. Greeley himself, with a broken spirit and a broken heart, died less than two months later.

Lu Calhoun's birth year is listed as 1844 in *Who's Who.* The correct year is 1837, based on Brookfield, Massachusetts, town records.

The letter of January 2, 1867, from Abby that Lu Calhoun and Charlotte Sinclair could not discuss appears in full in Chapter X. For information on Junius's name, see *William's Cincinnati Directory.* The name change occurs in 1861, when Junius is twenty-eight.

Chapter XXVI (p. 215-222)

Senator Cole's quote is from his letter of November 1, 1867 (recipient unnamed), and his train ride with Albert is noted in a letter of September 17 or 18, 1869, to his wife, both in *Cole Papers.*

The report on the "Oneida Community of Free Lovers," by Isaac Reed, is in *Frank Leslie's Illustrated Newspaper* for April 23, 1870. The quoted discussion of sexually advanced goings on at the Sinclair's house is from *Full Particulars,* p. 1.

Chapter XXVII (p. 223-226)

The Report of A Practical Law Reporter appears in *DM Trial,* p. 223–24.

Chapter XXVIII (p. 227-231)

The Nation's comments appeared on May 19, 1870. The portion of Abby's final remarks that deal with capital punishment are from a letter she wrote to Sidney Gay on December 25, 1869, rather than *ASR Affidavit.*

Chapter XXIX (p. 235-247)

The Nation's comments regarding the new Richardson household appeared on May 12, 1870. Abby's comments about her expectation for a "happy home circle" are from her letters of December 17 and December 25, 1869, to Sidney Gay. Information on Albert's estate is based on court records from New York City and Essex County, New Jersey (where he was domiciled at his death).

Information on Albert Deane, Jr., and Maude is derived primarily from the guardian accounts of Charles A. Richardson and from the biennial reports of Dr. Brown's school at Barre. The trust suffered a serious financial setback in the early 1880s when bonds in which Charles had invested became valueless. He contested the matter all the way to the U.S. Supreme Court, without gaining redress. See *Richardson* v. *Traver.* Albert, Jr., was eventually declared legally insane and placed with a relative.

The review of Abby's lecture in the *Colorado Transcript* includes some comments from a review in the *Central City Register,* October 16, 1872. Dan Frohman's quote is from *Daniel Frohman Presents,* pp. 21, 24. The description of Albert's plans for a history of the United States is from *Garnered Sheaves,* pp. 74–75.

The Gunnery, where Abby sent William, was a secular institution founded by Frederick Gunn and his wife, Abigail, former abolitionists and founders of the camping movement. Well-known figures, such as Harriet Beecher Stowe, sent their children there.

Chapter XXXI (p. 254-258)

Charles Frohman died tragically in 1915, one of twelve hundred persons who drowned when the passenger ship Lusitania was torpedoed by German U–boats.

The Grace Furniss quotes are from the interview by Ada Patterson cited in the Bibliography.

Abby's city directory listing varied from year to year. Only once, in 1876, did she list a profession—authoress. Otherwise she was either plain Abby (or Abbie), widow or, as in 1900, widow of Albert. By contrast, in 1900 she listed her profession as author in response to an explicit question from the U.S. Census. She also engaged in a little bit of vanity with the census taker, giving her birth year as 1840 instead of 1837, thereby holding her age to fifty-nine.

SELECTED BIBLIOGRAPHY

[WORKS CITED FROM OR RELIED UPON]

TRIAL SOURCES:

New York City daily newspapers: *The New-York Times, New York Herald, New-York Daily Tribune, The Evening Post, The World, The Sun,* for relevant periods.

New York City weekly journals: *Frank Leslie's Illustrated Newspaper, Harper's Weekly, The Independent, The Nation,* for relevant periods.

Full Particulars of the Assassination of Albert D. Richardson, the libertine, shot by the injured husband, McFarland (1869) *[Full Particulars].*

The Richardson–McFarland Tragedy (Barclay & Co. 1870) *[RM Tragedy].*

Graham, John, *Summing Up to the Jury, Trial of Daniel McFarland* (1870).

The Trial of Daniel McFarland for the Shooting of Albert D. Richardson, the Alleged Seducer of his Wife, by a Practical Law Reporter (American

News Co. 1870). Also compiled by A.R. Cazauran, etc. (W.E. Hilton 1870) *[DM Trial]*.

The Veiled Lady; or The Mysterious Witness in the McFarland Trial (C.W. Alexander 1870) *[Veiled Lady]*.

OTHER MATERIAL ON THE ASSASSINATION AND TRIAL

Hammond, William H., *Papers read before the Medico-Legal Society of New York*, Second Series, Rev. Ed. (1882).

Indictment of Daniel McFarland, December 17, 1869, Records of the New York District Attorney.

"The Lessons of the MacFarland Trial," 2 *Old and New* 476 (1870).

"The People against Daniel McFarland for the murder of A.D. Richardson." Law Points Ruled, *Abbotts Practice Reports*, pp. 57–108, viii N.S. (1870).

"Some Notable Trials: The Case of Daniel McFarland," *New York Times*, December 15, 1895.

Stern, Madeleine B., "Trial by Gotham 1870, The Career of Abby Sage Richardson," *N.Y. History*, July, 1947, pp. 271–87.

Strong, George Templeton, *The Diary of George Templeton Strong*, Vol. 4, *Post–War Years 1865–75* (Nevins & Thomas ed. 1952).

ABBY SAGE RICHARDSON

Blanchard, Charles, *Counties of Morgan, Monroe and Brown, Indiana. Historical and Biographical* (1884).

Best Plays of 1894–1899, Chapman, John & Sherwood, Garrison P. (ed.), (1955).

Best Plays of 1899–1900, Mantle, Burns & Sherwood, Garrison P. (ed.), (1947).

Estate of Abby Sage Richardson, Surrogate's Court for New York County, New York.

Morse, James Herbert, *Diary* in Manuscript Collections of New-York Historical Society.

Obituaries in *New-York Daily Tribune, Dramatic Mirror, The Evening Post, The Sun, Evening Telegram,* and the *Brooklyn Daily Eagle*.

Patterson, Ada, "The Story of a Successful Woman Dramatist," 7 *The Theatre* 301-04 (Nov. 1870).

Richardson, Abby Sage, Affidavit published in the *New York Tribune*, May 11, 1870. Reprinted in *DM Trial* and *RM Tragedy*. *[ASR Affidavit]*.

Richardson, Abby Sage, Letters in Gay, Stedman and Conway Collections, Rare Book and Manuscript Library, Columbia University; Reid Family Papers, Benjamin Holt Ticknor Papers, and Abby Sage Richardson Collection in Miscellaneous Manuscript Collections, Manuscript Division, Library of Congress; The Houghton Library of Harvard University; Paltsits Collection, Manuscript Department, New-York Historical Society; J. S. Bliss Collection, Arents Library of Syracuse University; Historical Society of Philadelphia; and Barnard College Library.

Registry of Deeds, New York, New York.

Sage, Charles H., *The Sage Family, Genealogical Record of the Descendants of David Sage* (1919).

PRINCIPAL WORKS BY ABBY

McFarland, A. S., *Percy's Year of Rhymes* (1867).

————, *Pebbles and Pearls for the Young Folks* (1868).

————, and Abby Sage, *Stories from Shakespeare*, Blackie & Son: London (n.d.)

Garnered Sheaves from the writings of A. D. Richardson, collected by his wife, biography of author added (Richardson, Abby Sage ed. 1871) *[Garnered Sheaves]*.

Richardson, Abby Sage, *Stories from Old English Poetry* (1872).

————, *Songs from the Old Dramatists* (ed. 1873).

————, *The History of Our Country from Its discovery by Columbus to the Celebration of the Centennial Anniversary of Its Declaration of Independence* (1875).

————, *Familiar Talks on English Literature* (1881).

————, *Old Love Letters, or, Letters of Sentiment Written by Persons Eminent in English Literature and History* (1882).

————, *Abelard and Heloise: A Mediaeval Romance*. With selections from the letters of Heloise and Abelard (1884).

————, Articles and stories in *The Riverside Magazine for Young People, The Atlantic Monthly, The American Magazine* (1867–1887).

————, *Donna Quixote: A dramatic idle of the Eighteenth Century* (1890).

————, Playscripts including *Americans Abroad, The Prince and the Pauper, A Colonial Girl* (with G. L. Furniss), *The Pride of Jennico* (with G. L. Furniss).

ALBERT DEAN RICHARDSON

Brown, Louis A., *The Salisbury Prison*, A Case Study of Confederate Military Prisons 1861–65 (Rev. ed. 1992).

Browne, Junius Henri, *Four Years in Secessia* (1865) *[Four Years]*.

————, Letter to Luke Blackmer, 3/4?/1889.

————, "Eulogy for A.D.R.," *New York Tribune*, 5/31/1873, p. 3, col.6.

Barry, Louise ed., "Albert D. Richardson's Letters on the Pikes Peak Gold Region," 12 *Kansas Historical Quarterly* 14–57 (Feb. 1943).

Cunningham, O. Edward, "Strike for Liberty," *Civil War Times Illustrated*, Vol. 14, No. 6, at 31–34 (1975).

Ellis, Daniel, *Thrilling Adventures of Daniel Ellis* (1867).

Estate of Albert Deane Richardson, Surrogate's Court for New York County, New York.

Estate of Albert Deane Richardson, Surrogate's Court for Essex County, New Jersey.

Glazier, Willard W., *The Capture, the Prison Pen, and the Escape* (1869).

Ingalls, John James, Article in 1 *Kansas Magazine* 15–18 (1871).

Kilmer, George L., "Prisons and Escapes," in Johnson, Rossiter, *Campfire and Battlefield* (undated).

Mac Bride, Van Dyk, "A Letter from Salisbury Prison," *Stamps*, Vol. 80, No. 4, at 128–29 (July 26, 1952).

Marriage Record for Louisa Pease and A.D. Richardson, Probate Court for Hamilton County, Ohio.

Richardson, Albert Deane, Letters in *Gay Collection; Reid Papers; Richardson Papers*; Albert Deane Richardson Collection in Miscellaneous Manuscript Collections, Library of Congress; War 1861–65 Collection, Manuscript Department, New-York Historical Society; The Houghton Library of Harvard University; and Historical Society of Philadelphia.

Richardson, Mary Louise Pease, Letter in *Gay Collection*.

Registry of Deeds, Essex County, New Jersey.

Starr, Louis M., *The Civil War's Bohemian Brigade* (1954).

Vinton, John Adams, *The Richardson Memorial* (1876).

Westwood, Howard C., "Adventure in Reporting Civil War News," 42 *J. Miss. Hist.* 316 (1980).

PRINCIPAL WORKS BY ALBERT

Richardson, Albert Deane, *A full and authentic report of the testimony on the trial of Matt. F. Ward* (1854).

————, *The Secret Service, the Field, the Dungeon, and the Escape* (1865) *[Secret Service]*.

————, *Our New States and Territories, Colorado, Utah, Montana, Idaho, Nevada, Oregon, Washington Territory and California* (1866).

————, *Beyond the Mississippi: from the Great River to Great Ocean. Life and Adventure on the Prairies, Mountains, and Pacific Coast* (1867) *[Beyond the Mississippi]*.

————, *A Personal History of Ulysses S. Grant* (1868).

————, "Through to the Pacific: The New Route to the East," *New York Tribune*, May 29; June 5, 22, 25, 26; July 10, 1869.

————, *Ancient and Modern Time Keepers* (1872).

————, Articles in *The Atlantic Monthly, Harper's* (1868–69).

MISCELLANEOUS AND GENERAL

Adams, Henry, *The Education of Henry Adams* (Sentry ed. 1961).

Accounts of Charles A. Richardson, Guardian of Leander P., Maude and Albert D. Richardson, 1869–85, Probate Court for Middlesex County, Massachusetts.

Appleton's Cyclopedia of American Biography (various years).

Blood, Grace Holbrook, *Manchester on the Merrimack*, (1948).

Biennial Reports of a Private Institution for the Education of Feeble-Minded Youth, Barre, Massachusetts (1870 and subsequent).

Bowles, Samuel, *Across the Continent: A Summer's Journey to the Rocky Mountains, The Mormons, and the Pacific States* (1865).

Brooklyn Historical Society, *The Great Divine* (Pamphlet 1986).

Browne, Junius Henri, *The Great Metropolis; A Mirror of New York* (1869).

————, *Sights and Sensations of Europe* (1872).

Cameron, M. W. & Lee, E. C., *Biographical Cyclopaedia of American Women* (1925).

Cole, Cornelius, *Papers*, University of California at Los Angeles (Special Collections) *[Cole Papers]*.

Colorado newspapers: *Rocky Mountain News, Colorado Transcript* (Golden), *Denver Gazette, Rocky Mountain Herald, Western Mountaineer, Denver Tribune, Central City Register, The Daily Chronicle* (Leadville), *Denver Times, Leadville Daily Democrat.*

Dictionary of American Biography (Malone, Dumas, ed. 1935).

Fisher, Ben Van D., *The Runkle Family*, New York (1899).

Frohman, Daniel, *Daniel Frohman Presents* (1935).

Frohman, Daniel, *Memories of a Manager: Reminiscences of the Old Lyceum and of Some Players of the Last Quarter Century* (1911).

Frothingham, O. B., *Elective Infinity: A Sermon*, Preached in Lyric Hall, December 19, 1869.

Frothingham, O. B., *Recollections and Impressions* (1891).

Greeley, Horace, *An Overland Journey, from New York to San Francisco, in the Summer of 1859* (1860).

Hammond, William A., *A Statement of the Causes Which Led to the Dismissal of Surgeon-General William A. Hammond from the Army*, Pamphlet, undated [1864 per catalog].

Henderson, Mary C., *The City and the Theatre* (1973).

Kluger, Richard, *The Paper: The Life and Death of the New York Herald Tribune* (1986).

Lewis, Alfred Henry, *Nation-Famous New York Murders*, New York (1914).

McFarland, Daniel, "My School-Boy Days in New York City Forty Years Ago," *The New York Teacher and American Educ. Monthly*, Vol. VI, March 1869.

Miscellaneous Manuscript Materials: Denver Public Library (Western History Collection), State Historical Society of Colorado, Lake County (Colorado) Library (Colorado Mountain History Collection), Rowan County (North Carolina) Library, Barre (Massachusetts) Historical Society, New Hampshire Historical Society, Tennessee State Library.

National Cyclopedia of American Biography (various years).

New York City Directories (Goulding's and Trow's) 1860–1900.

Richardson v. *Traver,* 112 U.S. 423 (1884).

Sweetser, M. F., *The White Mountains: A Handbook for Travellers* (1876).

U.S. Army, Judge Advocate General, *Reply of the Judge Advocate, John A. Bingham, to the defense of the Accused, before a general court-martial for the trial of Brig. Gen. William A. Hammond, Surgeon General, U.S.A.* (1864).

War of the Rebellion, Official Records of the Union and Confederate Armies, Washington: G.P.O. (various dates) [*Official Records*].

William's Cincinnati Directory (1851 to 1861).

ILLUSTRATION ACKNOWLEDGMENTS

PAGES [xii, 142]—Picture Collection, The Branch Libraries, The New York Public Library.

PAGES [4, 11, 132, 149, 219, 232 (except image from Frank Leslie's), 255]—General Research Division, The New York Public Library, Astor, Lenox and Tilden Foundations.

PAGE [21]—Courtesy, Louis A. Brown, from his *The Salisbury Prison.*

PAGES [49, 66]—*Secret Service,* Courtesy, Columbia University Libraries.

PAGES [16, 171, 203, 232 (image from Frank Leslie's)]—Courtesy, American Antiquarian Society.

PAGE [39]—Private collection of Philip K. Browne.

PAGES [87, 243, 257]—Billy Rose Theater Collection, New York Public Library of the Performing Arts, Astor, Lenox and Tilden Foundations.

PAGE [154]—*Daniel Frohman, at 20 Years of Age,* Museum of the City of New York, The Theater Collection.